IN YOUR OWN BACKYARD

IN YOUR OWN BACKYARD

A GUIDE FOR GREAT PLAINS GARDENING

by

CHUCK MARSON

BARANSKI PUBLISHING CORPORATION

Topeka, Kansas

Copyright © 1983 by Chuck Marson

All rights reserved.

Reproduction or translation of any part of this work beyond that permitted by Sections 107 and 108 of the 1976 United States Copyright Act without permission of the copyright owner is unlawful. Requests for permission or further information should be addressed to Baranski Publishing Corporation, P.O. Box 4527, Topeka, KS, 66604.

Cover photo by: Phil Parker
Typesetting & Design by: Graphic Arts Inc.
Chapter Heading Illustrations - Cynthia Clasgens

ISBN 0-941974-01-4

This work is dedicated to my wife Eleanor,
whose love and support have made this book possible.

FOREWORD

Windswept...harsh...variable...hot and dry...all these words and many more have been used to describe the Great Plains of the United States. The hardy pioneers that trudged across the Plains on their westward journey found the Plains to be a challenge for their survival. But for those of us that live in the Great Plains area, there is beauty in this broad, expensive country that gives us great pride and enjoyment.

Gardening in the Plains can be a challenge, but gardeners that recognize the unique environmental conditions of the Plains and adjust their gardening practices accordingly will find great pride and enjoyment for their efforts. Certainly, Plains gardeners are the most proud and hardy individuals I have ever met.

Chuck Marson, like most of us, has developed a sense of awe and respect for the Great Plains. He appreciates the great natural beauty here, the unique gardening challenges, and the solid horticultural practices necessary to garden in the Plains.

This book is based on a lifetime of experiences. Chuck Marson not only talks and writes about gardening, but he practices his gardening skills as he has done for many years. Most important, however, is the fact that Chuck talks to and listens to people. You will find in the pages of this book you will hold a conversation with Chuck Marson. He has many suggestions, based on his lifetime experiences, that will be useful to you as you develop a sense of accomplishment and pride in your Great Plains garden.

Charles W. Marr
Professor of Horticulture
Kansas State University

ACKNOWLEDGEMENTS

I am indebted to the fine personnel of the Kansas Extension Service for many helps, including the use of some of the sketches from their bulletins. I am especially grateful to Dr. Chuck Marr for the foreword and for reviewing my efforts and giving some practical advice. Many thanks to my patient wife, Eleanor, for pushing and encouraging me. Without her help I could not have made it. Thanks to Cynthia Clasgens, my cohost on the TV show, for her fine and whimsical art work and for believing in me. I am very grateful to all the readers of my column and viewers of my TV show for encouraging me.

I have appreciated the many fine bulletins of information put out by the All American Rose Selections, the National Garden Bureau, and Bedding Plants, Inc. Thanks to them for the use of some of their sketches and pictures. Also the various seed companies that are so generous with helpful information and illustrations. Also the sample seeds that I have tried. Thanks to George Stanley for the use of his greenhouse at Stanley's Flowers here in Topeka. I am happy that Dennis Baranski had enough faith in me to publish this effort. I am grateful to the many people that had faith in me.

Charles E. Marson
Topeka, Kansas

INTRODUCTION

It has long been a thought of mine to compile information about gardening on the Great Plains. I have gardened in the area for over 20 years and written about the experiences as long. Judging from the thousands of letters I receive each year because of my television program and *Kansas Farmer* column, it is apparent that many people do have problems. To my knowledge no one has ever written a complete book tailored directly for this locale. All the garden books I have seen are written by Easterners, Far Westerners or Europeans. We have problems with which they are not familiar as they are not found in other areas. The problems are not insurmountable, but they require some effort and planning. This book is an effort to help solve some of the problems. It is not a panacea for all ills but a help to the average gardener who has a desire to work with nature.

Which brings to mind the story of the preacher that saw a beautiful garden in a vacant lot. An elderly gentleman was gardening diligently. "What wonders the Lord has wrought," observed the preacher. The old gentleman straightened his aching back and said "You should have seen it when the Lord had it alone." The same might be said about most of us that garden.

We appreciate the many advantages the Lord has given us and realize we have to work to make use of them. I hope this effort will help you take advantage of these blessings and have a better and profitable gardening experience. I am grateful to many wise and talented gardeners that have helped me in my research for this book. Special thanks go to the Extension Service for many aids.

TABLE OF CONTENTS

1. Basic Facts About the Great Plains 7
2. Soils and Fertilizers 15
3. Lawns and Ground Covers 23
4. Landscape Ideas 37
5. Shade and Ornamental Trees 45
6. Flowering Shrubs and Evergreens 55
7. Flower Gardens 67
8. Vegetable Gardens 101
9. Home Grown Fruits 121
10. Wildflowers 133
11. Insect and Disease Control 145

1
Basic Facts About The Great Plains

The Great Plains area poses some problems for the uninformed gardener. They can be faced and solved with the proper approach.

First consideration must be given to the weather. Most the garden books include areas in the Plains states with Plant Zones that run east and west across the country. It is true that certain plants can be grown in individual plant zones, but a plant adapted to Zone 6 in Indiana or the East Coast would have problems in the same zone in Kansas or Oklahoma. Better information comes from observation and practical experience. Depicts the Plant Zones as laid out by the USDA

Most experts divide the Mid-Plains at the 100th Meridian, but the 98th Meridian seems a more accurate division. This is a line running through Niobrara, Nebraska, down through Hastings to Beloit and Hutchinson in Kansas and then through Enid to Lawton Oklahoma. The elevation varies from 800 to 1000 feet above sea level in the eastern section to over 4000 feet in the western section. The east gets from 30 to 40 inches of rainfall per year, while the western area gets from 16 to 20 inches in good years. Generally speaking, the eastern section has clay-loam soils that are fairly neutral while the west is quite alkaline with more sandy and prairie type soils.

The most important factor in the weather in our area is the wind. It seems sometimes the wind will never quit blowing, and windbreaks play an important role. The wind blows very consistently from the southwest in summer and from the northwest in winter. These winds are very

PLATE I

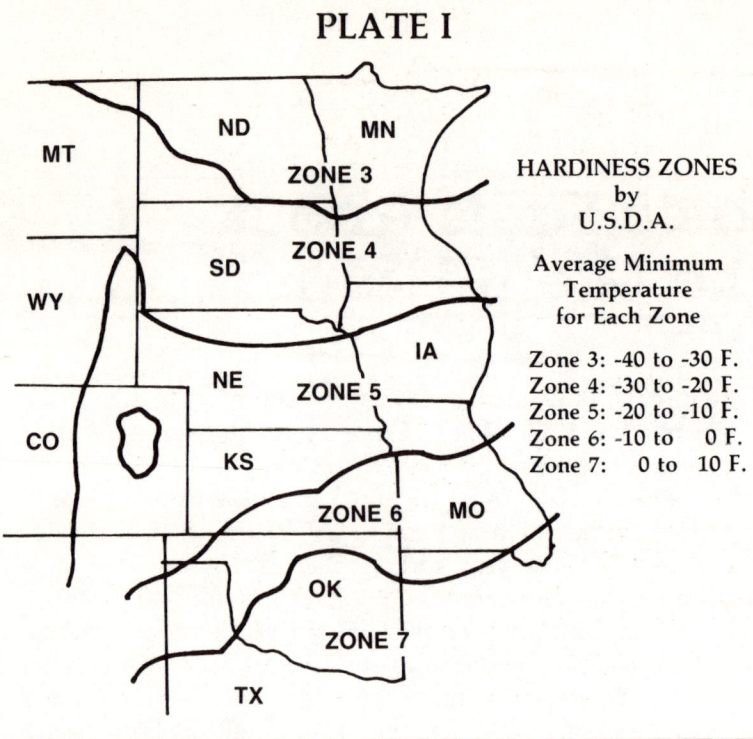

dessicating and must be considered when planting. There are many plants that will do fine if given protection from the wind but will fail miserably if they have none. More detail will be given on individual plants as we go along.

The amount and timing of the rainfall has to be given careful consideration. There are large variations as we move from east to west. Eastern Kansas averages 30 to 40 inches of rainfall per year. Western Kansas averages 17 to 20 inches. In southeastern Oklahoma rainfall averages 35 to 40 inches and northwestern Oklahoma averages only 20 inches. Approximately the same effects are true in Nebraska from east to west.

A look at the various areas provides a better chance to judge conditions for our own neighborhood. Northern Oklahoma lies mostly in Zone 6 and the southeastern one half in Zone 7. Most of the state except for the far west receives good rainfall. Soil conditions are variable with the eastern one half more acid and short of phosphate. The

PLATE II

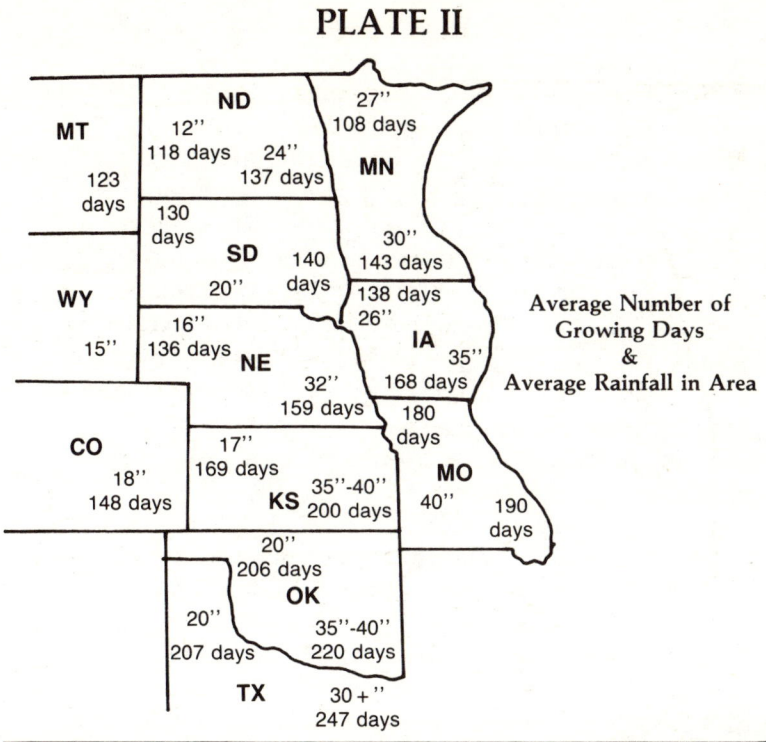

west tends to be more alkaline and most soils are deficient in organic matter. The incorporation of organic material is vital to good gardening. A very wide variety of ornamentals are grown commercially in the south and east. Vegetables do very well, as do many fruits. Of all the Great Plains states, Oklahoma has the widest variety of plants that do well.

Kansas is divided diagonally across the state with the north and west areas in Zone 5 and the south and east in Zone 6. The altitude rise from east to west makes a two week difference in planting time and length of growing season. Climatic conditions are variable especially in rainfall. From 35 to 40 inches of rainfall per year in the east to 16 to 17 inches in the west. Wind velocities pose a problem, but good use of windbreaks and extra irrigation make it possible to have good gardens and landscape plantings. The alkalinity of most of the western area make it important to control.

Nebraska lies largely in Zone 5 excepting the northern one third, which is in Zone 4. It is a state of many rivers running east to the Missouri. It rises from east to west toward the Rockies with an elevation of less than 1000 feet above sea level in the southeast to over 4000 feet on the western edge. This makes a shorter growing season by between two and three weeks in the west with more severe winter weather. High average wind velocities combined with high temperatures and low humidity in summer forces the transpiration rates high. Windbreaks are necessary for any vegetables, flowers and most landscape materials. Nebraska has a program for planting windbreaks that is enviable. Most vegetables, flowers and landscape materials common to the Midwest can be grown with proper protection. Irrigation is essential but fortunately in available almost everywhere.

South Dakota lies primarily in Zone 4, and the changes in plant growth follow the change in latitude: Rocky Mountain types thrive in the west; the Great Plains types that grow in the central region and Northern Plains and in the east. All horticulture proves somewhat difficult due to the cold and open winters and the drought periods brought by the drying southwest winds during the growing season. Windbreaks are a great asset, and a source of irrigation is practically essential. With protection and irrigation most vegetables, flowers and ornamental materials can be sucessfully grown. Three fourths of the annual rainfall comes during the growing season. Not an easy state in which to grow things but one that can produce with some help.

North Dakota is mostly in Zone 3 except for the southeast corner that is in Zone 4. Comparatively cool summers and longer days contribute to quality crops in horticulture. Heavy rainfall in May and June give plants a good start. Midsummer irrigation is very important due to high transpiration rates. Most vegetables and flowers can be grown merely by attending to planting dates. Perennials, trees and shrubs should be chosen for winter hardiness.

The bordering fringes of eastern Montana, western Minnesota, eastern Wyoming, eastern Colorado, western Iowa and western Missouri compare closely with the adjoining areas. The areas to the west are shorter on rain, with shorter growing seasons caused by the altitude and nearby mountains. Areas to the east have better rainfall conditions and on the whole are better for horticultural crops.

Serious consideration should be given to micro-climates or little climates which occur on every homesite. The house itself gives complete shade during some part of the day. In those areas where the amout of light is low, the temperature will be lower too. Variations in moisture and soil have an influence on plants. You can alter this with good management. When a house is built the soil around the house is altered by excavation, and excess soil is spread over the old surface. This is one reason why it can be difficult getting plants started near a building. The best way to help this is by the addition of organic material into the soil by tillage.

Cold air is heavier than warm air and will slide down a slope and settle in low areas. In these areas flora should be planted later in the spring. Additionally, these same spots will receive earlier frosts than the higher ground. The sunny side of the wall, usually the south, gives off a great deal of heat from reflection and should be taken into consideration.

The moveable shade of a tree will, for instance, keep crab grass from germinating because the soil temperature in the shaded area will remain cooler. This is different from the dead shade of a building. It is difficult, if not impossible, to grow Zoysia or Bermuda grass in the moving shade areas. Roses like full sun for at least one half of the day, so they won't do well if there is too much shade. There are plants that do enjoy partial shade, and they will be pointed out in the plant lists.

Another factor frequently ignored is drainage. Very few plants like "wet feet". Heavy clay which abounds in the Plains area will drown plants by cutting of the supply of oxygen when in a saturated shape. To check for heavy clay or gumbo soil follow this plan. First, a hole 12 to 18 inches deep as you would dig when planting, then fill it with water. If the water has not drained away in four to six hours, supplement the drainage. To supplement the soil, dig twice as deep as is necessary to plant, then add coarse gravel to the desired planting depth. Another method is to drill a dry well in the bottom of the planting hole with a post hole digger and fill it with coarse gravel. These holes allows excess water to dissipate.

In some sandy and silty soils the water will drain away too quickly. The solution for this is to mix in lots of organic material. Adding 30 to 40 % of organic material to a depth of two or three feet will do the job. Organic material retains enough moisture to keep plants in good shape. Peat moss, compost, rotted manure, ground corn cobs and chopped up straw all work well. Tilling in green manure will also help.

If all this has discouraged you, cheer up. The answers to most of your problems are in this book. Common sense plus these tips will make it possible for you to create a fine lawn, garden, and landscape. The objective of the following pages is to point out some problems you may encounter and give you an easy means to a better environment.

2
Soils and Fertilizers

The heart of soil improvement is organic material. In both clay and sandy soils this holds true. Organic material will loosen up clay soil, improving drainage while adding water holding capacity. It tightens up and adds to the water holding ability of sandy soils. Organic material contains millions of living organisms that help break down the material and add tilth and food to the soils. We term good-textured soil loam. Loam is made up of minerals, silt and clay particles. One would think that the addition of sand alone could improve clay, but it has the opposite effect. Sand mixed with clay seems to form almost a cement. Organic material must be added also. Crop residues, lawn clippings, sawdust, compost, peat moss and rotted manure all make great organic additions. They break down relatively slowly and add needed tilth to the soil. Cover crops such a rye can also be tilled into the soil with good results. There are two things to remember about working clay: (1) never work it when it is wet as it will clod up and give you trouble all season; and (2) never over-work it so that it fluffs up. This breaks down the structure and it will turn into a sticky gumbo with the first rain. Organic material tilled into either clay or sand will do much to improve the garden.

Good drainage is vital to plant development. Of course there are some exceptions, but very few plants do well with wet feet. The circulation of air in the root zone is just as essential as water and food. The roots must have oxygen and the soil must be able to allow the carbon-dioxide escape. If the soil is too wet it will literally drown the plants. If you have a wet and soggy soil it will definitely pay to improve the drainage. This can usually be done by working the soil deeply and adding organic material. In severe cases, tile drainage may be in order. Clay tile laid down a couple of feet with a good outlet for the water will allow you to work the ground days earlier in the spring. It will also drain off excess water any time. Tile seems to help in dry spells as the clay tile will draw water from below by osmosis and get water up to the root zone of most plants. Have you ever noticed that plants seem greener and more vigorous in dry weather when near a tile line? This is because they get water more uniformly. Another method which I have used successfully is to have raised beds. Railroad ties laid on the ground around the garden area and then filled with good rich soil will make a big difference. That raised beds take more watering in dry weather represents the only drawback. Take a good look at your garden area and see if it needs more drainage. Improving the drainage will be money and effort well spent.

The use of mulch is one of the very best natural ways to retain moisture, keep down weeds, hold down temperatures and, when incorporated into the soil, add good organic material. Nature through the dying and falling of foliage makes a natural mulch. Go to any prairie or wood lot and see the good job that natural mulches do. There are many materials that make good mulch and here in the Plains we usually have plenty of good straw and prairie hay. Use them 4 to 6 inches thick. The only fault with them is that they may contain some weed seeds and you must be careful of fire. Very good luck can be obtained with grass clippings. Be careful to spread them thinly in successive layers as they dry. If spread too thickly they heat up and can cause fungi to grow. Another mulch readily available is newspapers. Spread them between rows, 4 or 5 thicknesses deep and throw a little dirt on them to keep them from blowing. Flowers and vegetables will produce much better when mulched. In the fall till the paper into the soil. It makes a good addition to the organic material. The ink on the newspapers is alkaline so don't use them around acid loving plants. Other mulches that can be used are peat moss, stone mulch, plastic, shredded bark and wood chips. Some of these will be available in your area. One of the finest mulches I have ever used was ground corn cobs. They look good and add to the appearance of a garden.

Apply two or three inches thick. They may be hard to find, but if you are on a farm or have a farmer friend it is simple to run some cobs through the grinder. Leaves do not make a good mulch as they pack down too much unless ground up. Better add them to the compost pile so they will get broken down. Aluminum foil makes a good mulch for squash and other cucurbits. The reflected light drives away the squash bugs and aphids. Try it.

Make a compost pile. It is simple and the results will delight you. Pick an unobtrusive spot in the yard and make a bin with snow fence or concrete blocks. Good air circulation is very necessary so lay the blocks with spaces between them. Debris from the yard, leafy garbage, leaves, grass clippings and other similar materials are fine. It is best not to put any animal refuse in as it will atract dogs and rats. Place about a six inch layer of the material on the ground in the bottom of your pit. We prefer a pit without a bottom as contact with the soil aids in the proccess. The bacteria and enzymes will work up into the material from the soil. You can also buy a compost enhancer from your garden center. On the six inch layer of the material scatter a pint or two of 5-10-5 or 10-10-10 fertilizer. Some people add about an inch of soil on top, but that is a matter of choice. I have done it with and also without the added soil and have had good results both ways. Make the pile low in the center so it will catch the rain. If rain is scarce you must water the pile to keep it moist. Build up the pile in successive layers. Coarse plants should be chopped up. Stirring the pile every six weeks or so hastens the process but is not essential.

After about five months of warm weather you will have some fine compost. As the material decays it heats up, and this heat will kill most of the weed seeds, insect eggs and disease organisms. Peony tops with botrytis blight, cabbage roots with black rot or corn stalks with borers or smut should be disposed of by burning. If the compost pile stands for a year or more, even these diseases should be eliminated. If you use compost in a potting mixture, run it through a half inch mesh screen to remove the coarser material. In the flower or vegetable garden this is not necessary. Compost does not have a great deal of nutritional value so should be used with plant food for best results. The greatest value is the improvement in the texture of the soil.

The pH factor of soil is important because plants do much better with the proper amounts of acid or alkaline. The pH factor is the measure of the sweetness (alkalinity) or the sourness (acidity) of the soil. A pH factor of 7.0 is neutral. Higher figures denote higher alkalinity and lower figures higher acidity. A simple test kit can be purchased from any garden store and is easy to use. The common garden crops do well with a slightly higher acid soil. High acidity soils may require some lime to neturalize the acid condition. Here in the Great Plains this is found only occasionally. Most of the area has a normally alkaline soil. Lime is therefore rarely needed. Limestone rock is near the surface over most of the area to keep the soil about right. Most garden plants do best between 5.5 and 7.0. Anything under 5.5 should have lime added for general use. Fifty pounds of lime per 1000 square feet is a good general rule if needed. On the other hand if your soil tests over 7.0 it would be adviseable to add some acid by using sulphur, ammonium nitrate, or aluminum sulphate. Sulphur costs less but works slower. Use sulphur at one or two pounds per 100 square feet. Aluminum sulphate or ammonium nitrate should be applied at about one-half pound per square yard. Work these into the soil and water down the area. The main reason for being concerned with pH is that fertilizer works much better with the correct pH. Chlorosis causes the familiar yellowing of oak leaves. Getting the soil to the proper pH will correct this. Iron chelates may have to be used for especially bad situations. The minor elements that are released by the proper pH are important to plant growth. Boron, zinc, manganese, iron, copper, magnesium, sulphur, calcium and molybdenum are all important to plant growth. They are needed in very small amounts and are generally present in the soil. The right pH factor and good watering practices will take care of them. A good soil test can determine if some need to be added.

Should manures or chemical fertilizers be used? This is always a much discussed question. A plant cannot distinguish if the nitrogen it is absorbing is from natural fertilizer or from a chemical. Any food has to take a form that the plant can absorb, and it winds up that way chemically regardless of the source. I am a great believer in a balance of both methods. The addition of organic material adds a great deal to the tilth of the soil. This is a priority for good garden production. The food elements in organic material are released slowly and are really beneficial. The chemical fertilizers take a form that the plant can readily absorb. If a cheap manure is available, by all means use it plentifully with the addition of a small amount of chemical fertilizer to help break down the organics and give the plants a bigger boost. Be sure to use well-rotted manure as fresh manure can burn if used directly on the plants. Spread the manure over the surface and let it lay for a time before plowing or tilling it into the soil. The greatest drawback to farm manures is the possibility of spreading weed seeds and disease organisms. If you can compost through a good heating process, such problems can be overcome. All animal manures are useable. Be sure sheep and chicken manure has aged enough that it won't burn. Most all manures are short of phosphate so include about 30 pounds of good superphosphate per 1000 square feet. Nitrogen is the element that gives the good green color to plants, promotes leaf and stem growth, and helps break down organic materials into a more useable form. Phosphate promotes root development, gives plants a good start, speeds up maturity, and stimulates blooming and therefore fruit production. Potash increases vigor and disease resistance and makes good strong roots and stems. The proper balance of elements is most important. If you have a question about the fertility of your soil, have a soil test made by your county agent. The test is not expensive and can be a extremely helpful. For general use a 5-10-5 or similar formula will do a good job in the garden. Apply about 30 pounds per 1000 square feet—that will be sufficient for most of the season. Some crops that need more food may require a side dressing. Tomatoes, snap beans, and root crops all respond to extra food.

    To sum this all up, a good balance of both manure and compost plus chemical fertilizers will do the best job. You can make a good soil out any you may encounter by adding organic material and improving drainage. Never work clay ground when it is wet. You will lose more than you can possible gain. Work the ground deeply, incorporating the organic material down six or eight inches. Do not over work the ground to a powdery consistency; leave it granular with a texture that has small particles rather than dust. There is no reason for organic gardeners being afraid of chemical fertilizers. They are more help than a hindrance and have no effect on the taste of the products. And by all means, use mulch. Any kind, but use it. You will reap benefits that will delight you. Study your ground. If you will help it, you can have bumper crops.

3
Lawns and Ground Covers

Grasses are among the finest parts of our environment. They provide the background for the landscape picture. Children at play enjoy them as well as adults playing golf, tennis and other sports. They line our highways with beauty. They tie down the soil to prevent erosion. They absorb carbon dioxide and freshen the air with oxygen. They supply food for animals, Grasses are truly one of our finest assets.

GRASS SELECTION

Selection of turf grasses depends largely on climatic conditions. Cool-season grasses grown best in the north and warm-season grasses in the south. Here on the plains there exists a diversity of conditions and an over-lapping of the warm and cool areas. The growing of a good lawn is not as difficult as some imagine if approached in the right way.

For eastern Kansas, Nebraska and farther north, Kentucky bluegrass still makes the prettiest lawn but does require some extra effort. Kentucky 31 fescue does very well in bright, sunny exposed spots. There are now some new varieties on the market that are as fine as Kentucky bluegrass. They have the vigor and drought resistance of the larger leaf fescue. Some of the named varieties are Olympic, Rebel, Mustang, Falcon and Houndog. From Topeka and Kansas City on to the south zoysia makes a fine hot weather grass. The one drawback to zoysia is that the length of the season depends on the frost dates. It does not green up until after the last frost and turns brown with

PLATE I

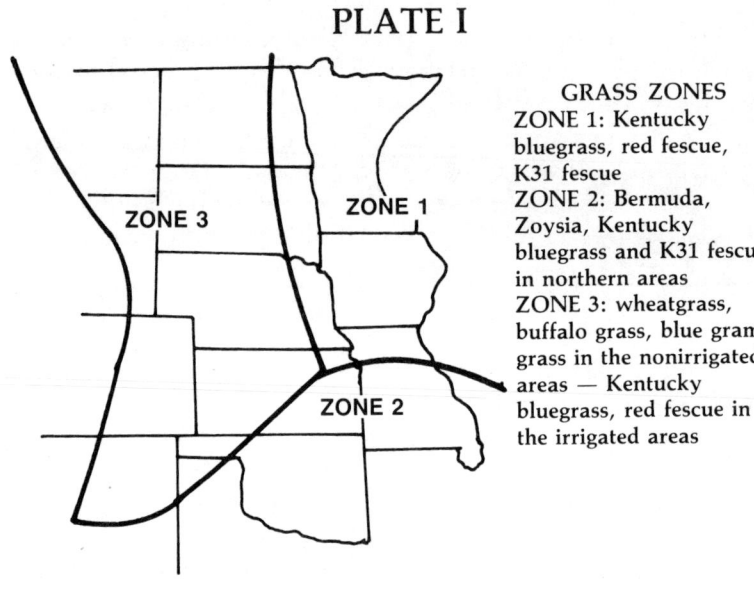

GRASS ZONES
ZONE 1: Kentucky bluegrass, red fescue, K31 fescue
ZONE 2: Bermuda, Zoysia, Kentucky bluegrass and K31 fescue in northern areas
ZONE 3: wheatgrass, buffalo grass, blue grama grass in the nonirrigated areas — Kentucky bluegrass, red fescue in the irrigated areas

the first frost in autumn. Bermuda grass has somewhat the same characteristics, but it does spread badly into flower beds and vegetable gardens where it becomes an obnoxious weed. In western Kansas and Nebraska, eastern Colorado and up into the Dakotas, crested wheat grass, blue grama, and buffalo grass do very nicely in unirrigated areas. Irrigated areas will grow good Kentucky bluegrass, red fescue and in sunny areas Kentucky 31 fescue. The cool nights and high altitudes of the north do hurt the growth of the K31. The chart of page (33) shows the seeding rates and the best times for seeding or plugging.

SOIL PREPARATION

Soil preparation for a new lawn is most important. So many times a builder will spread out poor soil from excavation over good top soil. If the top soil is removed and replaced you are very fortunate. Take this up with your builder.

For a new lawn, remove all the debris from the soil. Old boards, concrete, plaster and other debris gets buried around a building site. Be sure to remove all of this. It is important to add organic material into the top six inches. Spread it on the surface with some starter fertilizer and till it all into the upper six inches of soil. Spreading it deeper won't hurt. Be sure the drainage is good and directed away from the house. This is the time to establish the proper grades. Once grass is growing it is impossible to correct the grade without tearing things up. Slope away from the house and fill in any low spots that show up by pulling some soil from any high spots. Double check the grading and be sure it is correct before you put down any seed. The best seed bed for grass seed is firm and not fluffy. If a footprint sinks into the soil over ½ inch, it is too fluffy. Firm it up with a lightweight roller. Rake after that to loosen up the top ¼ inch to a texture that is slightly granulated but not real fine. The granular surface makes a lodging place for the seed and will not pack down with rain or watering. The picture on page (34) shows the preferred texture.

    I feel that planting should be done by seeding at one-half rate in one direction and then at right angles with the other half. This assures good distribution. Drag the seed in lightly with the back of a rake or by dragging an old ladder section, a piece of chain link fence or even an old bed spring over the surface. This insures a light cover of soil over and around the seed. It also helps take out minor irregularities. A light straw mulch is very effective in getting good germination. Cover very lightly—one bale to 1000 square feet. The soil should be visible through the straw. The oats or wheat that does start to grow will die out with mowing. The straw will deteriorate and help build the soil. I like to roll the lawn with an empty water roller to set the seed and the straw into the soil. Do not use a heavy roller as this will pack the soil too much.

    Now for the most important step. Water lightly and often. It is not necessary to soak the ground but the surface must be kept damp so the seed will germinate. It is important to keep this light watering up until the grass is one and one-half to two inches tall. After the first mowing you can resume a regular watering program. Set the mower at a two inch height and mow off each additional half-inch of growth. This helps tillering and thickens the stand.

    Sodding with nursery grown sod is the easiest way to

start a lawn. The initial cost is higher, but you can have an instant lawn. Not all kinds of grass can be obtained as sod, so check with your local garden center for advice and help. The soil must be prepared for sod the same as for seed. Sod usually comes in strips 18 inches wide by six feet long. It comes in rolls, and the method of application is to unroll at the spot where it is wanted. Stagger the joints. Plant the long way across down grades. On steep slopes it may be necessary to pin down the strips with wooden pegs. Before laying sod, wet the soil surface throughly. This keeps the moisture in the sod and makes a much better job. Lay the joints together tightly. After laying, roll the sod with a heavy roller. This presses the roots down into the soil. Then immediately start sprinklers going. Soak the sod heavily and keep the new sod soaked for from 10 days to two weeks. The sod should be rooted down tightly by then. Keep foot traffic off the new sod during this period. After about two weeks let it dry out enough to get on it with a mower. Mow at not less than two inches and during very hot weather set the mower up to three inches. After a month or so, it will help to fertilize with a good lawn fertilizer in addition to the fertilizer used in the grading process. This will give you an instant, weed-free lawn, and

PLATE II

Some Common Mowing Patterns

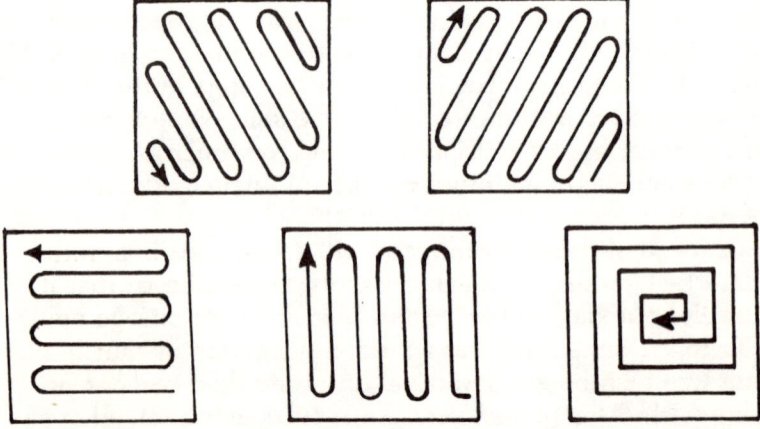

with regular care a good lawn for many years. The initial cost is higher, but not much more than starting from seed where you must fight weeds. Obtain some comparative figures before making a decision.

Grass mowing heights for the Great Plains must be quite high. The reasoning behind this is that with the dessicating conditions prevalent, taller grass will withstand our summer conditions better. A three-inch mowing height will make a difference of about 10 degrees in the soil temperatures. Keeping soil temperature at a lower level inhibits the growth of weed seed and allows the grass to manufacture more food for itself. All plants make food through the action of the light on the foliage (photosynthesis) so the more foliage present, within limits, the more food available. I suggest minimum mowing heights as follows:

Kentucky Bluegrass - fine fescue .... 2½ to 3 inches
Kentucky 31 fescue .... 3 inches
Zoysia .... 1½ inches
Bermudagrass .... 1 inch
Buffalograss - Blue grama .... 1½ inches

Lawn fertilizer should be applied at least three times each season. An application on cool season grasses in early June will carry it through the summer. Another shot in September followed by one in November or earlier if the grass is still green will carry through the winter and into early spring. The reasoning behind this is that the grass will store food in its roots to get off to a fast start in the spring. Late application is not lost but will be there for spring. Root development continues most of the winter except in extreme cold, and the fertilizer will stimulate the root growth.

I think that it pays to buy a regular lawn fertilizer rather than a farm type. the lawn fertilizers are treated so that it is virtually impossible to burn a lawn by over-dosage or spillage. Most of them have a slow release factor that lengthen the time it is effective. Most fertilizer companies make a good well-balanced lawn food that has lots of nitrogen. I suggest a spring application on Kentucky blue grass and K 31 fescue of a crabgrass inhibitor. Always follow the directions on the bag carefully.

Zoysia and Bermuda grass need a high nitrogen feeding in early May. They can take a farm type nitrogen fertilizer if you water it in immediately. The effects, however, do not last as long as the regular lawn products. Do not feed either one after the middle of August. It will stimulate late growth that will be very susceptible to frost and freeze damage. Buffalo grass and blue grama in the Western Plains do not need to be fertilized. In fact, fertilizer could possibly hurt them. Crested wheat grass will need some nitrogen.

In summation, fertilize on a regular basis for best results. I will not go into the pounds per thousand feet for each element as I feel that is is confusing to the average gardener. Be sure to follow the directions on the bag. The manufacturers spend a lot of money testing their products and these directions are the result. They know best, so follow them.

WATERING

There has been a great deal written about watering the lawn. Experimental work has determined that cool season grasses can do quite well with a minimum of 1 inch of water a week. This is true in the cooler humid areas of the country, but in the Great Plains two inches a week is far better, especially during the hot summer months. Here in the Plains it would be unusual to recieve that much moisture from rainfall. Therefore, irrigation of some sort is called for.

Lawn lose water in two different ways. They lose it by direct evaporation from the soil surface and by transpiration. The control of direct evaporation is the development of a good dense turf cover. That is one of the reasons for higher mowing heights in the Plains. Transpiration occurs when the moisture absorbed by the roots is transpired to the foliage and as a vapor through the leaf pores. This is necessary for good growth and for cooling the tissue. When rainfall is inadequate, watering on a regular basis seems the only solution. Regular mowing will help keep the foliage to a proper minimum. Cool season grasses in the Great Plains should be mowed to between two and three inches in hot weather. Make provisions for extra irrigation.

Some of the hot season grasses such as zoysia, bermuda grass, buffalo grass and blue grama can survive on less water than cool season grasses. Their natural habitat is more arid and they have a built-in tolerance for low moisture. It has been observed, however, that these grasses respond to additional moisture during hot dry spells. They will stay greener and much more vigorous if they recieve at least an inch of water every couple of weeks. They tend to go dormant and brown up without the extra water. It does not kill them, but the appearance is poor.

The best way to irrigate a lawn is to apply enough water at one time to penetrate to a depth of six inches. If you do this you can water only every 10 days or so for good results. Watering lightly and often is strictly an no-no. The roots come up to the surface and the grass is made more susceptible to drought damage. Experience indicates it takes an hour or more to get enough water for each section watered. Excessive thatch or a slope can make it more difficult. The speed of application should be slowed down so the water can really penetrate. If it is impossible to irrigate deeply, let the grass go into dormancy and do not tease it along with scanty irrigation, The dormant grass will not look very good, but it will survive and green up with the very first rains.

There are many types of sprinklers on the market, so check them out to find the one that does the best job for you. For a smaller lawn the oscillating type works well. It sprays a fan of parallel jets through holes in a slowly moving cross bar and covers rectangular areas which are typical of most lawns. They have controls to cover a smaller area or to one side only-excellent for most smaller lawns. For larger lawns, a pulsating sprinkler moves slowly either back and forth or in a complete circle. There are controls to regulate the area covered. The jet of water can be controled for the distance to be covered. It allows water to be absorbed before returning to give it more.Sprinkler hoses are fine for odd shaped areas as they can be snaked around corners and into odd spots. A sprinkler hose is a two or three conduit hose with pin holes releasing water in a very fine spray. The ultimate is an underground sprinkler system. There are self applied kits available on the market, but if you go into this type of irrigation it would be better to have a professional lay it out and install it. Pop-up heads are the best for this type of system. Most of them can be controlled in segments for best coverage.

In any case, the best results will come from a system or sprinkler that provides a slow uniform spray so the water can penetrate. Clay soil requires a fine spray for penetration. Sandy soils can take water much faster but it will also lose it faster. Study your soil and use the type of irrigation that fits best.

PLATE III

Recommended Cutting Height For Turfgrasses in Kansas

SPECIES	SPRING	SUMMER	FALL
Bermudagrass	1 - 1½"	1 - 1½"	1 - 1½"
Bluegrass, common	2"	2½ - 3"	2"
Bluegrass, improved	1½ - 2"	2½ - 3"	1½ - 2"
Buffalograss	1½ - 2"	1½ - 2"	1½ - 2"
Ryegrass	2"	3"	2"
Tall Fescue	2 - 2½"	3 - 3½"	2 - 2½"
Zoysia	1 - 1½"	1 - 1½"	1 - 1½"

A well-fed and watered lawn, mowed at the proper height, will give you the minimum amount of trouble. Some fungus infections will attack, but good feeding practices, good watering, and mowing at the height recommended will do much to alleviate problems. It's inadvisable to detail all the various fungi as it can be very confusing. If you suspect a fungus infection take a sample to your favorite garden shop for advice. Apply treatments as directions state. Dethatching every couple of years will also help in the control of fungi and insects. It is impossible to predict insect infestations as they flucuate seasonally, depending on local climate changes and the number of natural enemies. Again, your local nurseryman or garden shop expert can advise you about controls. Weeds can be controlled by proper mowing and the use of herbicides. Use herbicides carefully. Follow the directions on the package. If it says one teaspoon per gallon don't think that two is better. They work best on a minimal dosage. I like to spray most of the broadleaf weeks in the autumn—late October or early November. Spray when the temperatures are warm. This makes a beautiful weed free lawn in the spring. Turf grasses are the most wear tolerant of all living ground covers and if given half a chance will serve you well.

ALTERNATE GROUNDCOVERS

In the broadest sense, the term "groundcover" applies to any vegetation that blankets the soil. In horticulture it means low-growing plants in close proximity, used to dress up areas that would have grass or remain bare. Ground covers such as ivy and many other plants are as useful and decorative as grass and often superior in some areas around the house.

Low growing plants can do a lot of things. They can cover bare spots, stop soil erosion, regulate traffic in the yard and act as a tie for the whole picture. They can be used in spots where no other plant will fit in. They help a great deal on steep banks and in areas of deep shade. One of the best features of ground covers is the low maintenance after they are established. However, establishment does take some time. The soil must be prepared as for a lawn to support the new roots. On uneven ground where the whole area cannot be worked you can dig individual holes. On slopes, dig them over-size and work organic material into the loose soil. On severe slopes it is best to use horizontal growing junipers or cotoneaster.

Space the plants so they will fill in as fast as possible. Small plants can be spaced as close as 4 to 6 inches. Larger ones can be on 12-inch centers plant, junipers and cotoneaster about 4 feet apart. You may have to consider the cost of the plants. If they are too expensive space them farther apart. You will have slower coverage and more weeding to do until they fill in. Ground covers do grow quite slowly so a good mulch will help in the control of the weeds. It will also retain moisture better.

Do not cultivate around the plants as most of them are shallow rooted. Pull the weeds by hand. Water on a regular schedule as this is most important with young plants. Do not water so that the ground is soggy but be sure to get good penetration. An inch of water each week will do the job here in the Plains. Watch the plants during the winter to see if they are heaved by thawing and freezing. If they do heave up, push them back into the soil at once. You may find it advantageous to protect the young plants from the sun in Winter. After the ground freezes lay some burlap or evergreen boughs over the plants so the ground stays frozen. Snow provides excellent winter protection if enough of it falls. On the northern plains snow will probably do the job, but further south secondary protection will be needed.

Some pruning may be necessary to remove any dead wood and to keep the plants in bounds. Some evergreen plants may suffer damage in a cold dry Winter. It pays to water, even in winter, if it gets very dry. Some light shearing will usually take care of light winter damage.

The accompanying sketches show a staggered planting that will fill in sooner. Leave a depression around each plant as shown to trap water. The list is some of the better ground covers for the Great Plains.

CHART A

LAWN GRASS CHART

Variety	Planting Time	lbs. of Seed per 1000 sq. ft.	Number of sq. ft. Sprigs or Plugs per 1000 sq. ft.	Mowing Height	Zones
Bermudagrass	Spring	1 to 1½	5-10	1"	2
Blue Grama	Spring	2 to 2½	—	1" to 2"	4
Buffalo grass	Spring	1½ to 2½	25-30	1" to 2"	4
Crested Wheatgrass	Fall	2 to 3	—	2" to 3"	4
Kentucky Bluegrass	Fall	3 to 4	—	2" to 3"	General
Kentucky 31 Fescue	Fall	8 to 10	—	3"	General
Fine Fescue	Fall	4 to 5	—	2" to 3"	4
Ryegrass	Fall	4 to 5	—	2" to 8"	4
Zoysia	Spring	—	1 plug per 1 ft.	1 to 1½	2

LAWNS AND GROUND COVERS

CHART B
GROUND COVERS

Common Name	Height Inches	Hardiness Zone	Sun	Shade	Comments
Bearberry	6-10	3-4	✓		Slow grower
Bugleweed, (Ajuga)	4-8	4-9	✓	✓	Rapid Grower, tolerates most soils.
Coralberrg	to 36	5-5	✓	✓	Does will in poor soils, need yearly pruning
Cotoneaste, (Ground)	6-10	6	✓		Bright green leaves, showy berries
Creeping Thyme	to 3"	5-6	✓		Tolerates dry soils
Crown Vetch	12-24	3-7	✓		Good for steep banks, spreads widely
Day lily	18-48	3-10	✓		Dry or Boggy soils
Honeysuckle, (Vine)	to 10	5-6	✓	✓	Prune yearly, semi-evergreen
Ivy (bultie)	6-8	5-6	✓	✓	Handsome evergreen cover
Japanese Spurge (Padry Sandra)	to 6	5-6		✓	Good under trees
Janiper (Various)	12-18	3-6	✓		Wide range colors, use type adapted to your area
Lily of-the-Valley	6-10	5-6		✓	Good on north side of house
Moss Pink (Phlox Sabalata)	6	4-6	✓		Colorful in spring
Periwinkle (Vinca minor)	6-8	5-6		✓	Variegated varieties available
Polygonum, dwarf	12-24	5-6	✓		Red foliage in fall
Rose, Memorial, (Widiariana)	6-12	5-16	✓		White flowers
Stonecrop (Sedum)	4	4-6	✓		Does well in dry areas
Wintercreeper (Euonymas)	2-4	5-6	✓	✓	Rapid flat growth
Yarrow	2-3	5-6	✓		Good in dry soil

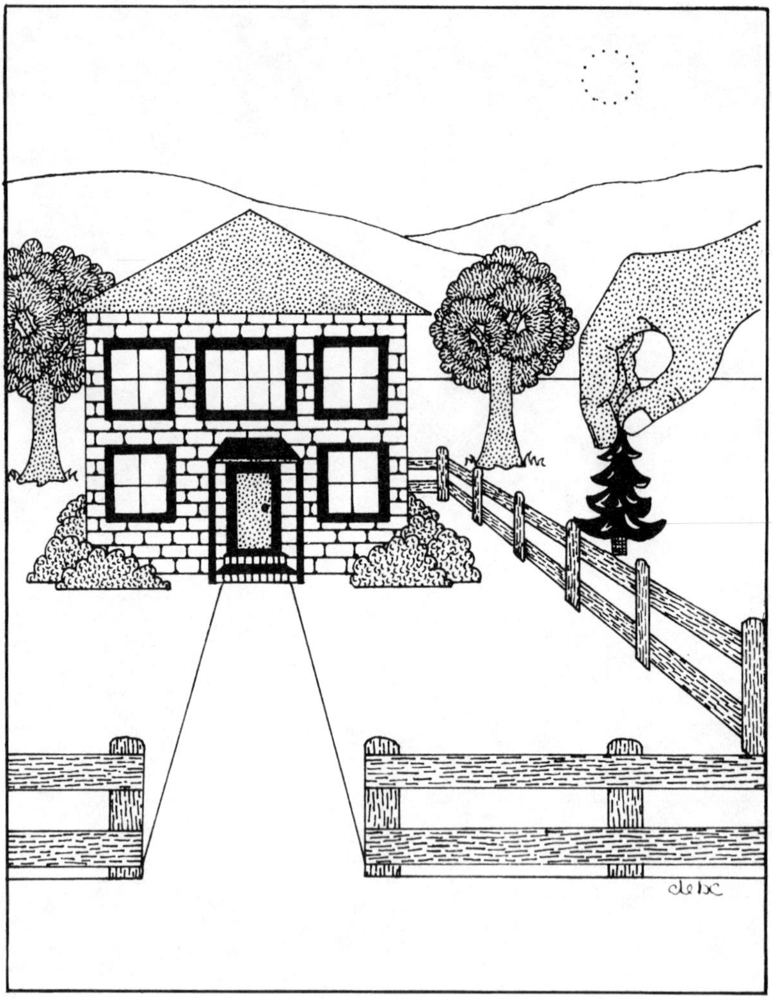

4
Landscape Ideas

The dictionary says landscaping is the improvement or change features or appearance of a park, lawns, gardens and natural surroundings. In other words, it is a way to improve the looks and the liveability of our environment.

The basic purpose of landscaping is to create a pleasant, functional personal habitat. It makes life more beautiful for you and the passerby. Landscapes are varied to conform to the regions and climate, income and personal taste. Following are some basic ideas to help you with your own landscape.

Green plants brought into a city, town, or farmyard have many advantages over wild plants. We can select plants grown for specific values rather than taking a chance on random seedlings. Plants are trained for a certain site so position them to create a favorable environment. We have the knowledge to help the plants achieve the part we want them to play.

Plants make our lives much more pleasant. Sowing randomly generates clutter. Clutter can be overcome by using plants in a smart way by planting in the proper place and planting the right form and shape, color, textures and scent. Some are prettier at particular times of the year. Some look well planted alone and some are better planted in groups or with other plants. Certain trees, shrubs, and plants produce special effects, and these are mentioned in this book.

Many things must be considered in landscape designs, including climate, soils, the use of the area to be planted, and selection of the plants to be used. The first step in planning your landscape is to make a scale drawing of the area to be treated. It does not have to be a professional draughtsman's drawing. Just try to place the buildings, walks, drives, existing plants, and other elements in proper relationship to each other. It is much easier to make changes on paper than it is to dig up a misplaced plant. The ultimate size of plants to be used should be plotted onto your sketch so that placement is correct. Orient your plant with compass directions so that the shade trees are planted where they will give maximum benefit. This is true of all the plants as some may need a protected area and others will like a hot sunny site. In the list of plants you will find some of these details, and if you have a question, ask your local nurseryman.

 I have no desire to get technical on basic ideas, but there are several points that should be covered: privacy, beauty, convenience, and comfort. Although it can have a lot of importance in rural areas, the first point, privacy is most important in an urban area. We all need a spot where we can relax, take off the ties and shoes, and feel a sense of seclusion without confinement. A shady patio with green shrubs separating us from the rest of the world becomes a place to escape. While most of us do not want to be cut off completely from our friends next door, there are times when we like some seclusion. A plan accomplishes this while leaving slots that can be traveled through easily. For instance, it is not necessary to plant shrubs to make a solid hedge. Proper spacing will give privacy without impenetratability. The lists of shrubs give some good ones with proper spacing. However, in a windbreak a good closely planted line of shrubs is effective. This is most important in rural areas but is very helpful anywhere to make micro-climates or little climates.

 "Beauty is in the eye of the beholder" is an old cliche but appropriate as a plant may be beautiful to you while unpleasing your friend. We all have differences in taste but if it pleases you, then use it. Look around you in Nature and in your neighbors plantings. If you see things that are pleasing to your eye then follow through. Some folks see beauty in a deformed rock, a twisted tree or a piece of driftwood, while to others these things have no appeal. I repeat, if it pleases you, use it. You are the one that will have to live with it. If a donkey cart planter and ceramic duck and chickens are your cup of tea, go ahead and use them.

By all means, try to see the plants you are considering in their adult size. A plant that might look fine when small, can mess things up when it attains full growth. Visit your local parks and other yards to find the adult plants. Your local nurseryman can help as he will have many fine pictures and descriptions for your information.

Convenience covers many things. Find out how much maintainance your selections are going to take. If you are a real gung-ho gardener you may not care if a plant takes special treatment and presents a challenge to grow it in your area. On the other hand, if you want good appearance with minimum care, pick your plants with that in mind. Remember, it isn't possible to have a good looking landscape without some effort in maintainance. Anything in life that is worthwhile takes some effort.

Convenience is having water outlets located where you can water easily. Convenience is having your vegetable garden where you can get at it easily. Clothes lines should be placed where they are easy to get at and still sheltered from view. The children's play yard should be at a spot that it is easy to keep an eye on them. Garbage and disposal areas need to have easy access and still be hidden from view of the patio or picture window. Always build a patio to get good shade in the afternoon and to have access

PLATE I

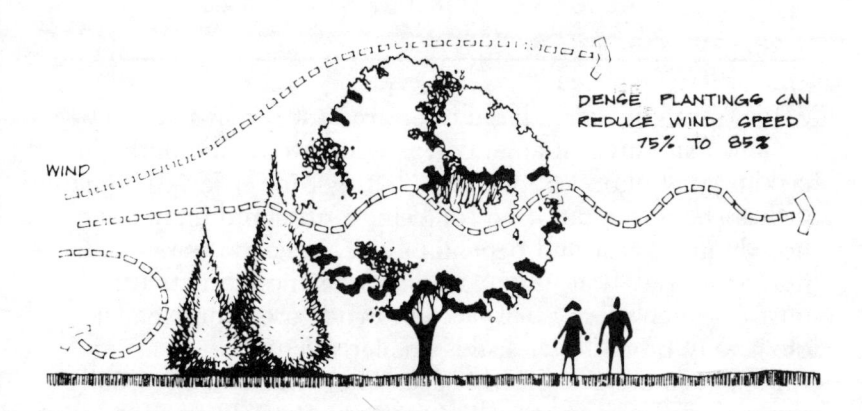

DENSE PLANTINGS CAN REDUCE WIND SPEED 75% TO 85%

WIND

LANDSCAPE IDEAS 39

to the kitchen etc. There are many factors to consider to make the landscape fit your life style. Do plan ahead.

A very basic thought is the use of trees for shade and windbreaks. For maximum benefit, shade trees should be planted west and south of the house. This will give protection from the hot summer sun and if placed properly can save up to 25% in cooling costs. Deciduous trees should be used for this as the foliage will protect in summer and the falling of the leaves in autumn will allow the sun to come through and warm the house in winter. They will not only enhance the appearance of your house but are economically sensible. Shade trees should be planted a minimum of twenty feet from a building and spaced at least forty feet apart. This looks a bit odd when the trees are small but in a very few years you will be glad you spaced them this way.

PLATE II

H = AVERAGE WIND BREAK HEIGHT

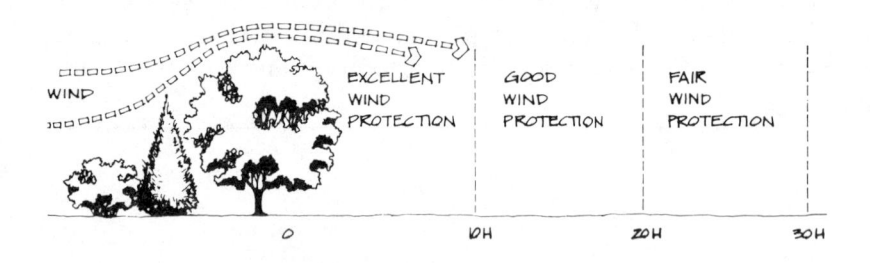

	EXCELLENT WIND PROTECTION	GOOD WIND PROTECTION	FAIR WIND PROTECTION
0	10H	20H	30H

Fast growing, fairly large trees are best for shade. Seedless ash, silver maple, cottonless cottonwood and hackberry are good native trees that get fairly large. Some of these have a reputation for being brittle and dirty but they do grow fast and dependably. They give desired shade in a very short time. They are all large enough that they must be given plenty of space. In urban areas on smaller lots it may be better to use a smaller trees. The ornamentals are fine for this use. They are smaller, usually very colorful and practical in an area of restricted space.

Hawthorns, flowering crabs and golden rain trees all fit in this catergory. They make excellent facers for windbreaks, shade for a patio or play yard, and corner plantings instead of the over-abundant evergreens. Using a hawthorn or small flowering crab underplanted with small shrubs for a corner makes a fine-looking planting. Give your imagination a work-out and dare to be different.

Use plants to screen out undesirable views or to frame a good vista. Use them to give privacy in your outdoor living areas. Use them to separate various elements in your yard such as the children's play yard, the vegetable garden, clothes drying space, or a work area. Make your entrance stand out with eye catching plants. Mark your walkways and drives with plants.

I like to use shrubs and trees that are attractive to birds. Birds are a great help in controling insects as well as pleasant and beautiful to have around. Why not use some of the very attractive dwarf fruit trees for ornamental purposes as well as for fruit. If you like, allow a space for the vegetable garden. A bright sunny, well drained spot is most essential. Even a small garden will pay off with

PLATE III

The patio is an extension of the house outdoors.

delightful fresh vegetables at a great saving. Frame your house with shade trees. Carefully consider the ultimate size of the trees so that they don't overpower a small house with huge trees or demean a large house with little trees. Valuable information appears in the chapter on shrubs and trees to help you make your selections.

With the houses of today it is not essential to have foundation type plantings. There is no high basement wall to cover since modern houses are built closer to the ground. A few well placed plants enhance a house without overpowering it. Use your scale drawing to plan ahead. Cut out cardboard pieces to represent various trees and shrubs (made to scale) and then move them around the plan to get different effects. It will pay big dividends to plan before your plant. Most of the better nurserys have a planning service, and they will be glad to help you. The nursery will have superior plants and will stand behind them even if you plant them yourself.

Make some provision for flower beds. Nothing brightens up the looks of a home as much as bright-colored annuals. They give a sparkle that nothing else matches. They are inexpensive and require little care. They do need **some** care, however, and if you are the type that does not want to do any yard work, be content with lawn, shrubs and trees. A design can be prepared for low maintainance if you plan ahead. A lawn needs care, and shrubs, trees, and evergreens need water, food and a probably yearly trim. Lawns have to be mowed and regular feeding is important. In the Great Plains area, watering during the hot dry summer months is a necessity for a good lawn.

Rock and bark mulches are increasingly being used for the difficult areas to save maintainance work. They help retain moisture and give a neat appearance to these spots. They also assist the control of weed growth. There are some excellent products on the market today that control the growth of weeds. A couple applications each season will accomplish much.

Summing up, you are the one who has to live with your landscape, so plan it to suit your tastes. It makes no difference what your neighbor does or what some book tells you. You are the one who has to look at it all the time and the one that has to care for it. If you like yard work and growing plants, plan for that. If you have children, plan for them. It is more important for youngsters to have a place to play than it is to have an immaculate landscape. Take them into consideration and give them room to play catch and romp around.

　The following chapters will give you more specific details, so I urge you to read on. Make your landscape an expression of your likes and don't worry about all the designers and psuedo-designers. Do your own thing.

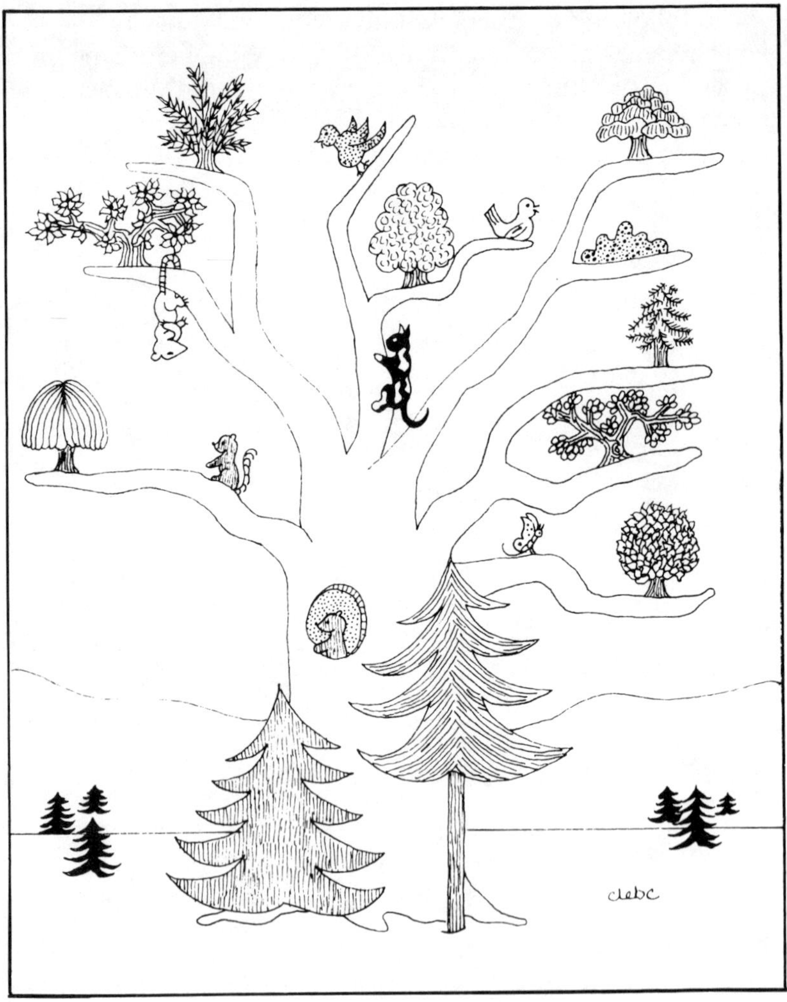
clebc

5
Shade and Ornamental Trees

Shade trees are essential for Great Plains landscapes. Indeed, Arbor Day began on the Nebraska prairie in 1872 to promote the more liberal use of trees. It seemed necessary to grown trees for shade, wind protection, and esthetic values.

Trees are the biggest and longest lived of all plants. Very often when we plant a tree, we will not get the full value. Our children and grandchildren get the benefits. How wonderful it would be if our grandchildren would say, "Grandpa planted that oak and now we are enjoying its protection". This chapter is devoted to shade trees and trees for ornamental purposes. The following section gives advantages and disadvantages of some of the best adapted trees for the Great Plains.

First we have to determine if the tree we want is adapted to our climate and soil conditions. Very often the lack of success in trees is the failure to take these facts into consideration. It would be wise to look around your area and see if the tree you want is growing successfully. Much as we may like to grow an exotic tree, if it is not going to survive with your conditions, it is a foolish attempt.

Secondly, we must consider whether or not it is susceptible to local insects and diseases. Cedar-apple rust is a problem in the Plains because we have so many native cedars. Most of the apple family and hawthorns are inclined to be a victim of this. There are some of the apple family that are resistant so we should be sure to check. Some insects that may be a problem in the Southern Plains will not bother in the north as they cannot survive the cold winters.

Third, some trees are messy and this should be considered. Ash and maples shed a lot of seeds at times that can be a nuisance. Catalpa, although it will grow where many others won't, is messy with falling blossoms, seed pods, and the rather brittle branches. Sycamore, a fine tree, has large leaves that fall over an extended time and loses many twigs and small branches. Locust trees shed seed pods that litter a lawn. However, many of these trees have some redeeming features, and these will be mentioned in the descriptions and uses.

Another factor to take into consideration is the ultimate size of a tree. A large cottonwood can overpower a small house in a small yard but looks fine with a large house with a big yard. Too often we plant large trees to close together or too close to a house or other structures. Most trees will grow broader in a open yard than they will in a forest setting. The trees bought at a nursery at six to eight feet look fine for the first year or two, but as they start to attain their growth they become a problem. They have to be trimmed to keep the branches from the roof or from the power lines. When trimmed this way they lose much of their beauty. Instead of planting the stately sycamore or cottonwood, it would be far better to plant a golden-rain tree, a flowering crab or a smaller-growing "Rosehill" ash. Where we want maximum shade, pick carefully. Some of the larger trees are excellent as long as there is room for them.

Different trees provide different types of shade. Big maples, cottonwoods, and sycamores with their large leaves cast a heavy shade that is cooling on the hottest summer days, but grass may be hard to grow under them. On the other hand, thornless honey locusts with their finer foliage cast a dappled shade where grass and flowers will grow. The seedless and thornless selections are an excellent choice for many sites. The leaves are fine enough that they are no problem when they fall.

Location is very important. Deciduous shade trees are best at the south and west of a house. During the summer when the foliage is on them, they provide the shade that is so good on the Plains. In the winter when we welcome the warming rays of the sun, the foliage is gone and the sun can warm the house. By the same token, large evergreens such as pine and spruce are best on the north where they will protect from the cold winter winds.

It seems as if most people have their favorite trees. The reds and golds of fall attract many people to those trees that have autumn color. Colorful flowers and fruits as in the flowering crab apples and hawthorns are great favorites. Some of the best flowering trees that have such a burst of color in the spring are flowering crabs, hawthorns, goldenrain trees, redbuds, serviceberry or shadbush and Japanese lilac. All of these grow in the Plains and are excellent choices for ornamental uses. Many of them are also good small shade trees. All trees have drawbacks, and you should consider them when you make a choice. Some folks object to falling fruit and blossoms, and these make a mess at times. You must weigh the good things against the bad. The flowering crabs are one of the best of all ornamentals so pick a variety with small or no fruit. Some can drop large quantities of fruit on a patio or lawn. I have a list of desirable trees with their characteristics that will help you make a choice.

Under Great Plains conditions early spring is the best time to plant bare-root trees. Balled and burlaped or container-grown plants may be planted at any time if you will supply plenty of water. You may possibly have to give some extra protection from the hot winds in summer or mulch for the cold weather of winter.

Be sure to get freshly dug plants or container-grown if possible. Trees with one- to one and one-half-inch caliper at chest height and six to eight feet tall are preferred. Trees that are hard to transplant such as hard maple and most oaks are best purchased balled and burlaped or container-grown. Six to eight foot trees of this type are more expensive but are much more dependable.

One very important thing to remember when planting a tree is to dig a large enough hole. Dig the hole at least one foot deeper and two feet wider than required. If the soil is tight heavy clay, run a post hole auger down in the center of the hole for two to three feet and fill it with coarse sand or fine gravel. This will drain excess water away from the root zone. Many plants are lost because in tight soil the water is held in the root zone and will rot the roots.

Before you backfill, add organic material to the fill soil.

Peat moss, compost, or well-rotted manure is good. Do not add granular fertilizer to the top soil. That will come after the plant is established. Using Rapid-gro or Miracle-gro at planting time is a big help. A gallon or so of the mixture, as directed on the package, will be enough for most plantings. New plants need a year or two to get their root systems established. Then chemical fertilizer can be added to the surface.

Plant bare-root trees as soon as possible. It is important to keep the roots wet if there is any delay. I have found that placing the roots in a bucket of water with soil stimulant for a few hours before planting helps give them a good start. Be sure the roots never dry out.

Bare-root material should have the tips of the roots cut back slightly and any broken roots pruned off. The fresh cuts stimulate new root growth. It is normal practice to prune back the tops of bare-root material by about one third. Remove any broken limbs and any that don't fit into the structure that you desire. Pruning is not necessary on container-grown or balled and burlaped plants. On container-grown plants, remove them from the can and loosen up the roots growing on the outside of the ball. Use your fingers, pulling them gently away from the soil so they can get a good start into the new soil. If allowed to grow around the ball it is possible that they could continue to grow around the ball and in the end could strangle it. Balled and burlaped plants can be planted directly with the burlap on them. After planting remove the burlap from the top of the ball and from around the trunk. Take a knife and slash the burlap at a few places. Some burlaps don't disintergrate too well.

With bare-root trees place a mound of soil in the bottom of the hole so that the roots can be spread out to a natural position over the mound. set the tree at the same depth as it grew in the nursery. Fill the hole almost to the top with the prepared fill soil and then settle the soil with water. After the soil has settled, finish the backfill. At the ground level leave a two or three inch deep basin to retain water. A thorough soaking is important at this time to get rid of any air pockets around the roots. No more water will be needed for a week or two. The first year after planting a good supply of water has great importance.

Larger trees need to be supported with guy wires. Run the wire through a piece of hose so it will not cut into a tree. Stakes should be placed as far away from the tree as the first crotch is high and the wires set at the first crotch. I like to put one stake to the southwest and one to the northwest to hold the tree frim against the prevaling winds. The bracing should stay in place for two or three years so the roots become well established. For trees smaller than two inches in diameter, a tall stake can be driven down parallel to the trunk and fastened to the trunk with strips of burlap or other cloth material. Burlap makes a good fastening material as it is strong and will not cut into the bark. A 2"x2" or 3"x3" stake will do and should be long enough to reach the first solid crotch when driven into the ground securely.

A three-foot diameter circle should be cleared of grass and sod around the plant when planting is done. You can leave it as bare soil or cover it with a good mulch of bark, peat, rock or other mulch, This will conserve moisture and hold down the weeds and grass that will compete with your tree for nutrients and moisture. Brick or wood edging around the circle is most attractive and makes mowing easier. The bricks or boards should be set flush with the ground around the circle. Tree wrap is necessary to protect the young trees from sun scald. The smooth bark trees such as hard maples, oaks and honeylocusts are very vulnerable. If we knew for sure which way the tree grew compass-wise and planted it the same way there would be no worry about sunscald. The side to the south in the nursery has been toughened to the rays of the sun, but the north side bark is very tender. You can buy tree wrap at your garden store that is easy to apply. Wrap in a spiral starting at the larger side branches and overlap a half-inch width on each turn. Secure with a cord or string starting at the base and going up in the opposite direction from the wrap. This will also protect the tree from rodent damage. The paper tree wrap will break down in a couple of years and can be removed.

One of my favorite small ornamental trees is the flowering crabapple. It comes in so many sizes, shapes, and colors that their is one for every location. They are very easy to grow and are hardy throughout the Plains. In size they run from six or eight feet tall up to some of the Siberian crabs that grow to 50 feet. There are excellent selections in the 15 to 30 foot sizes. They make good small shade trees for the patio or the porch or even for a small house. Some are broad spreading and others are columnar. Most spread in proportion to their height but Pink Spires and Strathmore grow tall and columnar. They make good corner accent plants. The bloom colors run from the white of the Dolgo and Bob White through many shades of pink to dark red buds of Radiant that open to dark pink. It is my opinion that the flowering crabapple is one of the very best small trees for the area.

   The goldenrain tree is a fine small tree adapted to the area. The blossoms are small and bright yellow that come in early Summer. A rapid grower, it is sturdy and has no disease or insect problems. The seed pods are two-inch balloon-like pods that turn from green to pink to brown. They are attractive as well as the flowers and hang on much of the winter. Washington and cockspur hawthorns are native plants that do well in all the Plains states. They are small trees that grow with dense branches and sharp thorns. The flowers are white and bloom in early spring followed by red fruit that is like by many birds. The foliage of both trees turn a beautiful orange and red in the fall. The cockspur is wide spreading but the Washington grows more upright. Amur maple is a good looking, carefree tree that is very cold resistant. They usually grow with multiple stems and have much character. They bear tiny white blossoms in the early spring that are very fragrant. The masses of bright red winged seeds come in summer and contrast with the dark green leaves. They can be pruned to a single trunk if desired. The foliage turns yellow, orange and scarlet in the fall. It is a desirable and easy to grow small tree.

   The Callery pear is an import from China that has adapted to the Plains in fine style. The selection called Bradford is outstanding. A fast grower with great resistance to disease and insects it is a good choice for an ornament. The Bradford has a columnar form of growth that makes it good for restricted areas. The white flowers appear before the foliage and are followed by small fruit that the birds clear out fast. The foliage turns deep red and scarlet in the fall with a very glossy look. Redbud is a native small tree that I feel is not used enough. It is tough and very attractive. The entire tree is covered with purplish-pink blossoms before the foliage. They are spectacular in early spring. They also have seed pods that linger into the winter. The foliage is heart-shaped and a very glossy dark green that will turn yellow in autumn. It is disease and insect resistant. It transplants best in spring.

The seedless selections of ash make a fine medium-size shade tree. The selection Marshall's Seedless ash is a good choice for all parts of the Plains. It was developed in Nebraska. The foliage is a dark green and turns shades of yellow and purple in the fall. It grows to about 50 feet and is in the green ash family. It is the most popular of the green ashes. The white ash selection "Rosehill" is a medium-size tree. the fall color is a purplish-bronze red that is very attractive. It is seedless and does not grow as tall as other white ashes. It will stay under 50 feet in most cases. Hackberry is a fine native that has great resistance to drought, bad soil, and all kinds of weather. They grow moderately fast and are tough enough to withstand our winds. They grow to a height of 50 feet or more under ideal conditions. They are usually smaller on the Plains. It has a few problems that are not fatal-It is subject to leaf galls that are unsightly but not damaging, and it is good tough tree for exposed locations.

There are some good selections of honeylocust that are well adapted to the Plains. The native locust is very thorny and has many seedpods that make a mess on the lawn. The selections Imperial, Majestic, Shademaster, Moraine, and Skyline are thornless and seedless and make excellent shade trees for the lawn. The shade is dappled and grass will grow under them very well. There are a couple of selections with yellow foliage and one with red leaves. I have found them much harder to grow. The height of the locusts vary from 30 to 35 feet up to 50 or 60 feet on some selections. Check out the ultimate height when selecting a locust. The Kentucky Coffee tree is one that has not been used as much as it should. It is slow-growing with fern-like leaves that make dappled shade. Grass will grow under them. The leaves grow to a length of one and one-half to three feet but contain 40 to 100 small leaflets. The leaflets fall first in autumn and break up in the grass before the leaf stalks come down. They are easy to clear up. The tree bears fat, dark brown seed pods that cling most of the winter. The beans were used in the early days as a substitute for coffee. The tree has a stark look in winter as there are no twigs. The rugged appearance is attractive. One reason it is not used much is because the young transplants look like broomsticks with very few side branches. They develop good limb structure as they grow. Don't let the appearance of the small transplants scare you away. The Kentucky Coffee is native to much of the Plains and is very sturdy and tolerant of most conditions.

There are several of the larger trees that are well adapted to our conditions. Cottonwood, silver maple. many oaks, tulip trees, and sycamores. All have good things going for them, but always there are a few bad things as well. The cottonwood is a native of our western states and is found everywhere. It grows naturally in the watercourses throughout the Plains. It has a broad vase shape and gives good shade. Because of its size it needs a location with a great deal of room. It naturally attains a height of 75 to 100 feet. The seeds are a nuisance and the tree is subject to some disease. There is a male tree available called cottonless cottonwood that does eliminate the seed problem. Silver maple is a very fast growing shade tree every useful where fast shade is needed. It has very beautiful foliage and is widespreading with excellent shape. It will grow from an eight foot transplant to 20 feet in four or five years making it a fine source of fast shade. It does have the drawback of invasive roots and will plug up drainage lines. It is supposedly brittle and subject to damage in ice and windstorms. I have found that it is not as bad as pictured. I planted three six foot seedlings in the country at my son-in-laws home 25 years ago. They are now beautiful trees over 60 feet tall and as broad, shading the house during the hot time of summer. In all that time, through ice and wind storms, there has been little or no damage to them. And they are not sheltered but stand on a hilltop.

The best of the oaks for the Plains are the white oak, red oak, and pin oak. White oaks and bur oaks are close to the same are often confused. they both grow slowly and become huge and imposing when adult. When you plant them you are planting for your grandchildren. They are beautiful, long-living and a wonderful memorial to you. Red oak is a faster growing oak that attain 75 feet at maturity but does grow fast enough to give good shade in five or six years. The fall color is bright red. It is a good tough shade tree. Pin oak is rapid growing and will give good shade in five or six years from an eight foot transplant. It has beautiful fall color that is much admired. The only fault I know of is the decumbency of the lower limbs. They do require some trimming so you can mow beneath them.

The tulip tree is one of the tallest trees that grows on the Plains. It will reach 80 to 90 feet when adult. It does grow quite rapidly and eight foot seedling will reach 25 to 30 feet in six to eight years. The flowers are tulip-shaped and very fragrant. They are not borne until the tree is 10 or more years old. They are hard to see when the tree is tall but the fragrance is apparent. Also they do not bloom until the foliage is out which hides the blooms. It is a fine shade tree. The sycamore is very easy to grow and does make a shade tree very fast. It is a large tree and needs a large area to grow. A 10 foot young tree will reach 20 feet in five years. The London Plane tree which is a cross between the American and Oriental sycamores is more disease resistant and somewhat smaller in its final growth. I find that sycamore, as a rule, are somewhat on the dirty side as they seem to shed leaves for a long time. They are subject to anthracnose and canker and will shed small limbs. In spite of this, they make good shade very fast.

This is by no means all of the trees that you take your time and pick carefully. If at all possible, look at a full grown specimen so you can see what you will get in a few years. Talk to your local nurseryman or extension expert for more extensive information. Be aware of the fact that the purchase and planting of a tree is a long term investment. It is wise to check carefully and be sure. Give the tree the room it needs. And don't plant a $25.00 tree in a fifty-cent hole.

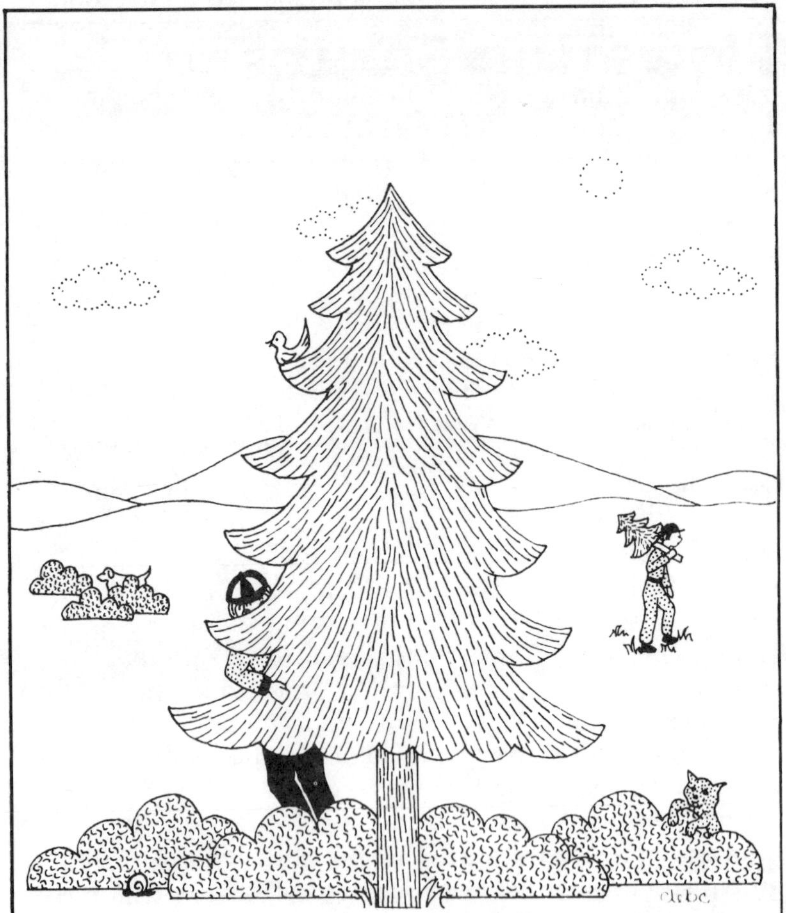

6
Flowering Shrubs and Evergreens

Flowering shrubs and evergreens are extremely versatile plants for many uses in the landscape. There as so many sizes, shapes and textures that it is hard to pick out the best one for a particular use. The ensuing information will give you some of the best for the Great Plains and help you in your decision. The difference between trees and shrubs is sometimes difficult to delineate. Both are woody plants meaning that the stems and branches survive from year to year. a shrub is usually a woody plant with multiple stems that does not grow over 20 feet tall. There are many plants that can be classified as either. By cutting back a small tree you can force it to multiple stems and shorter growth. On the other hand some shrubs can be single-stemmed and be made into a small tree. These are often call standards and have their place in the picture.

SHRUBS

Shrubs can be grown everywhere in the United States. Temperatures lower than 50 degrees below zero will hurt the survival of some, and the hot arid areas fo the southwest and the Gulf States will also curtail use of some of them. The only area in the Great Plains we might have a problem is in North Dakota, although some very good ones will grow there. Be sure to check on the hardiness for your area before selecting.

The varied sizes and shapes of flowering shrubs plus the beauty of the blooms with many colors give you a wide choice. Most require full sun, but some can be grown successfully in light shade. Some do well in moist soil and others can stand a great deal of drought. Some are native plants such as red chokeberry, service berry, bayberry, wahoo, sumac and coralberry. Most ornamental shrubs originated in the Orient or in Europe. China, Japan, Korea, Siberia, and the Near East have been a good source of plant materials found by early plant explorers and brought to America. These have been raised and hybridized, and the results are beautiful hardy plants with a wide variety of colors and textures.

Most shrubs perform many functions, so it is important to look into the adult sizes and characteristics. Some shrubs are best used as single units standing in a prominent place where they can really show their beauty. One of my pet peeves is the trimming of a lone standing shrub to a round or formal shape. Why not let them grow naturally as nature intended? A cropped forsythia looks horrible. One that grows naturally in a cascading free form is a thing of beauty. Hedges may be trimmed formally but with good planning, single plants can be allowed to develop naturally. When you plant, give them room to show the great beauty inherent in them.

The most common uses for shrubs is near the house to accent a point to make the house blend into its surroundings. The next most common use is for border planting or screens. Therefore, it is important to consider the growing habits of the shrubs to be used, as well as the colors involved. A tall growing shrub such a lilac or forsythia planted too close to a house will only detract and not enhance the appearance. There many plants that grow smaller and more compact that can be used. Barberry, Kelsey dogwood, slender deutzia, hypericum, Anthony Waterer spirea, snowmound spirea, coralberry, and dwarf European cranberry bush are examples of some good low growing shrubs.

Another good use for flowering shrubs is in hedges. There are many shrubs that make good hedges. Privet is not the only one. Hedges can be sheared and very formal, or unsheared and spaced to take advantage of the natural growth. Informal hedges need more space but I feel are more attractive and worth the space they take. But there is a place for a formal hedge especially when space is limited. They form a dense screen in a limited area. Some good shrubs for a formal hedge are barberry, winged euonymus, Regal privet, Amur privet, and Pekin cotoneaster. None of these have prominent flowers so adapt them to a sheared hedge.

An informal hedge is very striking when done properly. I like to use a variety of shrugs in an informal hedge of varying sizes, shapes, and textures. Plant taller growing shrubs to the rear and shorter ones to the front. Stagger plantings work very well. Space them so that when they reach full growth there will be a small space between them. They will screen satisfactorily but will let the air circulate. Plant them in groups of three or five for the best effect. Some tall shrubs that work well in this design are Russian olive, forsythia, rose-of-sharon, mock orange, honeysuckle, lilac and weigelia. Shrubs from three to six feet to face with are flowering quince, spreading cotoneaster, spirea, Tartarian dogwood, Persian lilac, and some of the viburnums. Shrubs under three feet for use in clusters in the front are barberry, slender deutzia, Anthony Waterer spirea, coralberry, hypericum and potentilla. In the coves or indentations between the groups of shrubs you can plant perennials, bulbs and many annuals. This will make a delightful border and back ground for your yard.

Mix in some early bloomers with summer bloomers. Don't be afraid to mix colors and textures. This sort of mixing is natural in nature and will be attractive. Early spring bloomers are Cornelian cherry, forsythia, winter honeysuckle, bridal wreath, flowering quince and spice bush. Late spring brings on flowering almond, pearlbush, lilac, Amur honeysuckle, Siberian pea shrub, Persian lilac, and Van Houtte spirea.

In early summer we have beauty bush, mock orange, smoke tree, bottle brush buckeye, hydranqea, and deutzia. Late summer P.G. hydrangea, rose of sharon, and butterfly bush. In fall the bright berries, and foliage are at their height. Some excellent plant for colorful foliage and berries and American cranberry bush, cotoneaster, chokeberry, Cornelian cherry, barberry, sumac, arrowwood, and winged euonymus. Many of the berries hang on into winter and the red bark of red twig dogwood and the yellow of the yellow-twig dogwood show up against the snow. Shrubs for all seasons and for all conditions. Pick them carefully to get the best.

Shrubs attract birds to your garden. The birds pay their way by eating many insects and weed seeds. Birds like to nest in dense shrubs for protection, and they also like the berries and insects that are there. Hummingbirds are fond of the flowers of beauty bush, butterfly bush, and pea shrubs which are all easily grown in our area. Coralberries, sumac, dogwood, cotoneaster, American cranberry bush, and honeysuckle are some that are attractive with their berries. The birds feast on them. Some of the birds that will be attracted beside the hummingbirds are thrushes, finches, robins, waxwings, thrashers, cardinals, catbirds, woodpeckers and flickers. For year I have had a pair of thrashers that live in the shrubs at the back of the yard. The song in evening is a delight. A sassy catbird comes down into the garden when I hoe and picks up the bugs I turn up. He mocks all the other birds and his own song is very sweet. Birds represent a fine asset in the yard, and you should do all you can to attract them. When you see a pert little wren picking squash bugs off the vine, it is worthwhile.

Planting shrubs is more than just digging a hole and dropping in the plant. As I said in the soils portions, it is important that good drainage be provided. The addition of some compost, peat moss, or rotted manure to fill dirt will give plants a better start. If you use peat moss be sure to wet it thoroughly before using. Dry moss will dry out the roots. Do not use chemical fertilizers in the hole when planting but I do suggest watering the plants in with a solution of some Rapid-gro or Miracle-gro. This seems to stimulate them and they will not wilt. On bare-root shrubs be sure to trim off any damaged roots and make fresh cuts on all root ends. This will help make good feeding roots develop. Cut back about one third of the tops and any damaged canes. This will compensate for any root loss.

Container-grown and balled and burlapped plants do not need to be pruned. On container grown plants I find it advisable to remove the plant from the can and loosen up the roots that grow around the outside of the ball of earth. Use your fingers and gently pull the small roots loose. This will give the small roots a better chance to grow out and stop any girdling that could take place. Balled and burlapped plants can be planted in the burlap. Merely loosen up the burlap at the top of the ball and from around the trunk before backfilling. Set the plant at the same depth that it grew in the nursery. When the hole is about filled with the topsoil, settle it down with water. Be sure you do not leave any air space around the roots. After the soil is settled, firm it down with your foot and finish filling the hole. Leave a 2 or 3 inch basin around the plant to retain rain water.

If you water the plant properly when you plant it, you will not have to water again until the plant begins to leaf out. The first year or two it is very important that the new plant gets enough water. Water deeply every couple of weeks. Another thing to do after planting is to cut a three foot circle around the plant and remove all the grass. The strip should be two or three inches deep and can be left as bare soil or mulched. Mulching will keep the weeds down and conserve moisture. The removal of the grass will end the competition for water and food immediately around the plant. It will also protect the plant from mower damage. A mowing strip around the outside of the circle made of bricks or wood makes a very neat looking planting.

One maintainance job with shrubs that seems to bring me a great many questions is how and when to prune. The first thing to do when considering pruning is to obtain good sharp pruning tools. The essential tools are hand shears, lopping shears and a pruning saw. Hand shears will take care of branches up to about three fourths of an inch. For branches three-quarters inches to one and one-half inches in diameter the lopping shears will do the job. Anything over one and one-half inches is better handled with a curving pruning saw.

A pruning saw with a curlving nine to fifteen inch blade with medium coarse teeth is best. The coarse teeth will not bind in green wood. My lopper has an all metal handle and gives me good leverage for the heavier branches. The scissor-type hand pruners are my favorites. Try out the grip when you buy, and it is smart to buy one that fits your hand well. Also, it has been my experience that it pays to spend a bit more and buy good tools. Cheap tools will not stand up and don't put on an edge as well. They will last for many years if you take care of them. Clean off the gummy residue with kerosene after using and wipe with a oily rag to take off the sap and moisture. Store them in a safe dry place when not using.

Dead, damaged or diseased branches should be removed from any kind of shrub. This is the first and most important step. Cut of any branch that rubs against another opening a place for insects and disease to get a start. This remedial pruning should be done at least annually or whenever you see the need.

Timing is important. As a rule, those shrubs that flower in the spring should be pruned right after flowering is over. Summer flowering shrubs flower on new canes so can be pruned in early spring or during the winter. Some spring flowering shrubs to be pruned after they bloom are forsythia, quince, lilac, Beautybush, honeysuckle, and spirea. Summer bloomers are Rose of Sharon, hydrangeas, butterflybush and coralbells. Cut back about a third of the old canes to the ground and remove old flower heads expecially on lilacs. Remove any sucker growth and leave some good strong new canes for future development. Please don't use a hedge shears to round off or square off flowering shrubs. They look so much better and bloom so much better if allowed to grow naturally. If you want a formal hedge or topiary, use plants that do shear well such as privet, barberry, or Pekin cotoneaster. When you shear hedge type plants formally, shear them wider at the bottom and narrower at the top. This allows the sun to get the lower branches and will keep them full and green instead of leggy and ugly. The only flowering shrub I like as a formal hedge is flowering quince. It will bloom on the inner branches and with the glossy green foliage, makes a fine hedge.

EVERGREENS

There are many kinds of evergreens that grow on the Great Plains. They run from spreaders a few inches high to giant pines and spruce. There are needle types and broadleaf varieties. The real definition of evergreen should be a plant that holds its foliage when resting and in winter. This separates them from the deciduous shrubs and trees that lose their leaves in the fall. For our puposes we will divide the evergreens into tall trees, small trees, shrubs, and low-growing shrubs.

Tall trees grow 30 to 50 feet or more tall and spread 20 to 40 feet. Use them primarily as specimen trees for their individual beauty. In large areas it is possible to use them for windbreaks. In this class are white pine, scotch pine, ponderosa pine, Austrian pine, Norway pine, Colorado spruce, Norway spruce, Engellman spruce, Douglas fir, and white fir.

Of all the taller evergreens grown, my favorite is the Eastern white pine. The needles in clusters of five are a soft blue-green and are soft to the touch. It grows well if placed right, and its tall conical shape with horizontal branches is very impressive. It is hardy and insect and disease resistant. Scotch pines are tough, easy to grow and with a more gnarled shape are an asset to the landscape. Scotch pines are widely grown for Christmas trees. Ponderosa pines do better in the western and northern sections of the Plains but not as well in the east. Norway and Colorado spruces do well and the blue selections of Colorado spruce make wonderful specimen trees. White fir does quite well throughout the Plains, but the Douglas fir is better adapted to the north and higher elevations.

Among the smaller evergreen trees an outstanding one is the Black Hills spruce. It is a slow grower that is used for screens, windbreaks and hedges in the Plain states. It withstands heat and cold, wind and drought and can stand crowding. It will made a specimen also. The many selections of both the Eastern red-cedar and the Rocky Mountain juniper do extremely well throughout the Plains. Canaerti juniper is one of the best. The color is a rich dark green and is loaded with pale blue berries. It holds its color all winter unlike most of the juniper that turn brown in winter. It has good cone shaped and will reach 20 feet in 15 to 20 years. Of all the Rocky Mountain junipers, Blue Heaven is outstanding. It is cone shaped with deep blue-green foliage. It will reach 20 feet in 15 to 20 years. All junipers do well in sunny well-drained soil. They are not particular about soil and do well in dry rocky soil either acid or alkaline.

Evergreen shrubs are very diversified and widely used. The most widely used evergreen shrubs on the Plains are junipers of Chinese origin. They grow in a spreading fashion and run from three to 12 feet in height with a spread from four to 15 feet and must be controlled by regular pruning. The best known and most used is the Pfitzer juniper. It has soft green color and is fast growing and will grow in most any soil. It is adaptable throughout the Plains. Its only flaw is that it grows very fast and if allowed to grow unpruned will get too large for most situations. It must be pruned a couple of times each year to keep it in bounds. It is useful for fast results in difficult spots or where there is plenty of room. In close spots its useful life is 15 to 20 years at best. Hetzi juniper is very similar with the same faults. It possesses a good blue-gray foliage. There is a dwarf form of the Pftitzer that is better for confined areas.

The Maney juniper is a medium fast grower that is well adapted to our area. It does not grow as rampant as the Pftitzer and is more erect in its growth. It has a blue-green color and can be kept to a height of four or five feet and a spread of four to six feet for many years with pruning. It is a dandy evergreen for most any landscape. The Armstrong is a very dense compact spreader that has fine foliage. A good choice where three to four feet height and four to five feet in spread are desirable. The light green foliage is fine and extends to the ground.

The Savins juniper is a good choice for hot dry spots. It is a vase shaped, dark-green spreading juniper. It will grow to four to six feet in height and will spread eight to 10 feet. It is a medium grower and can be kept in bounds with regular pruning. The Von Ehrons juniper is related to the Savins, and its globe form is excellent. The Von Ehrons globe makes a fine formal plant that is easy to grow and to control. The Meyers juniper has good blue-green color and an irregular growth pattern makes a fine accent plant. It does beautifully in a Japanese type design. The irregular growth form makes it a most valuable specimen. It does not get very large with a height and spread of four and five feet.

The yew family has some beautiful plants with shiny green foliage, slow growth, and easy control. Yews are sensitive to hot dry wind and should be mainly to the north and east of buildings. They can be used in sheltered locations. The English yews are tender and can only be used in the southern parts of the Plains and only then when sheltered. The Japanese yews are hardier and will do well in most of the Plains. Some of the crosses between the two seem to have much of the hardiness of the Japanese yew. The regular spreading yews sold at most nurseries will grow to six to eight feet in height and will spread eight to 10 feet. they are easily controlled with pruning because they do not grow extremely fast. The dwarf form is even more compact and is very good.

The intermediate yew or cross between the Japanese and English yews has diversified forms and are excellent choices for landscape purposes. The Hicks yew has a columnar form and is good accent plant. If allowed to grow unpruned it can get 10 or 12 feet tall. It is flat-topped so judicious pruning will hold it to desired limits. It gets only two to three feet wide. The Kelsey and Hatfield yews are more conical in growth but can be kept in bounds quite easily. Capitata yews are upright in growth and are great for an accent or corner plant.

One of the best of spreading type is named densiforma. It is very compact, slow growing, and develops a spreading form without pruning. Brown's yew is globular and also makes a good hedge plant. Yews need well-drained soil as they cannot stand wet feet. They will grow in sun or shade if protected from hot winds. Prune a yew with a hand clipper, cutting back only the long branches so no stubs show. They can be kept in bounds indefinitely and still look unpruned. A good point with yews is that they will extend new growth on old wood. This allows a better-looking plant that lasts longer. However, they should be used with caution.

The low growing or groundcover types of evergreens are primarily junipers. There are many that grow from six or eight inches high to some that may reach 18 inches. They have many uses in the landscape, particularly as a ground cover on slopes or difficult spots where taller ones will not work. One of the best of the low growing junipers is the Andorra. It will reach about 18 inches high but will spread six to eight feet. It turns plum colored in winter and is a light green in summer. It will grow all across the Plains but is susceptible to iron chlorosis in alkaline soils. The addition of iron chelates will control it.

The Bar Harbor and Sargent junipers are also excellent. Both grow 10 inches tall and spread six to eight feet. Good green color and tolerant of soil conditions they will withstand dry times. They will thrive much better if given regular waterings. Blue Rug is outstanding because of its blue color both winter and summer. Six to eight inches in height it will spread 6 to 8 feet and is a very good accent plant. Other good horizontal type evergreens are San Jose, Waukegan, Jap Garden, and Hughes. All have similar characteristics but vary in height, spread and color. Check the lists at the end of the chapter. These low growing junipers also have wide useage and should be considered carefully when you want to use them.

The list of adaptable broadleaf evergreens for the Plains is somewhat limited. There are a few that might do well in Oklahoma and eastern and southern Kansas. Boxwood is one of these, and the Korean boxwood will tolerate cold if planted in a sheltered place. Many of the hollies do well in the southern areas but will not go very far north. The hot winds of summer are also a factor to consider. Pyracantha will do well up to about central and eastern Kansas. Your nurseryman may have one of the newer cold resistant selections.

Boxwood makes a fine low growing dense hedge through it may experience some browning of the leaves during a cold winter. Hot summer winds will also hurt them, so use them carefully. The nurserymen are working on better varieties for harsher conditions. The upright euonymus Manhattan is a very fine hedge or specimen plant. It stands cold better than most broadleaf evergreens. In severe weather it may lose leaves but will rebud and come again in the spring. The Corliss selection of smaller variegated euonymus has good cold resistance and is fine small shrub.

Oregon grape holly is one that can be used in all but the most northern areas. Also called mahonia it has very glossy, dark green hollylike leaves that tend to bronze in the winter. The flowers come in early spring at the top of the shrub. They are bright yellow and are followed by blue-black berries with are edible. Mentor barberry is a very attractive dark green shrub that can be used from Nebraska south. It will sometimes lose its leaves in extremely cold weather but comes back. The lists at the end of the chapter give more information. Broadleaf evergreens should be used cautiously in the northern parts of the Plains. Always check with your local nurseryman.

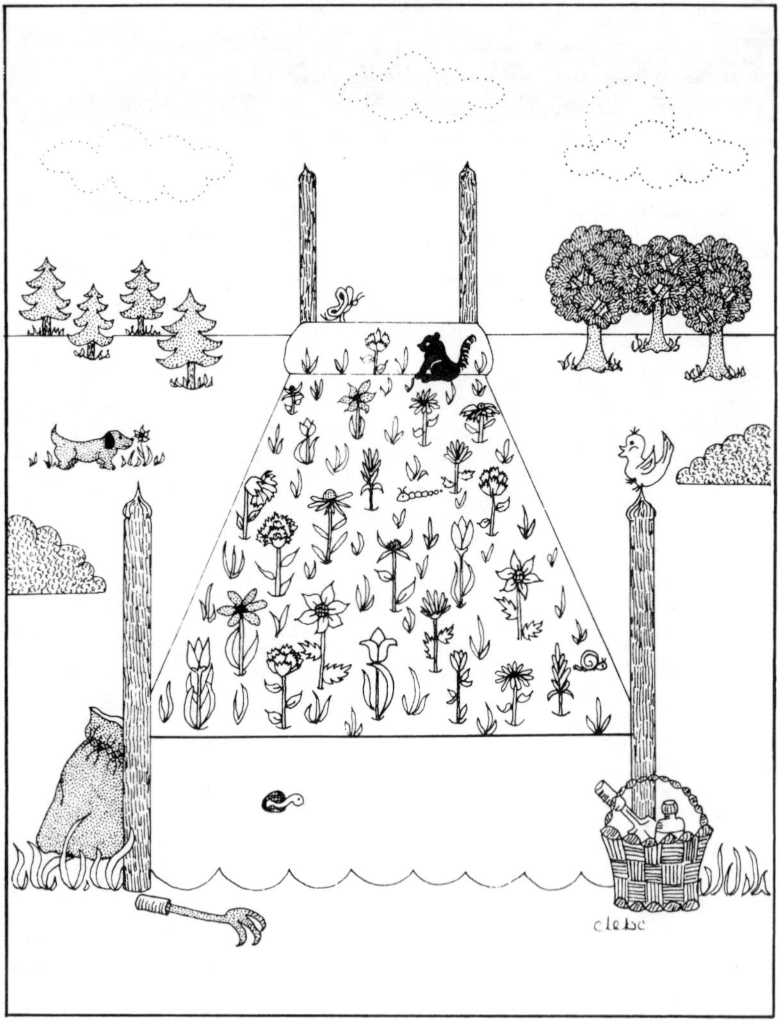
clebc

7
Flower Gardens

"Brighten the corner where you are" the finest and easiest way. Use annual flowers. Growing annuals is one of the most joyous things I know. The satisfaction of planting a seed that will grow into a full grown plant in a single season is beyond measure. Anyone can grow annuals with a wide range of sizes, textures, colors, and blooming times.

An annual, unlike other plants, does not store up energy in its roots but lives and dies in a single season. To perpetuate their kind they produce seeds. As much as 50% of an annual's dry weight may be in seeds at the end of the season. To produce seeds they must produce flowers. If the flowers are cut off before the seeds form, the plant will keep in trying to make up for the loss while there is still time. The more you cut an annual, the more it blooms. Because they are that way, all we have to do is to take advantage of them. If you give an annual plant good soil, enough water and room to grow, you will enjoy spectacular results until frost. A single petunia can have 300 blooms and buds on it at one time.

One thing I like about annuals is that a fairly drab scene can be brightened up so much. They are a yearly event so even a rented home can be made attractive cheaply and very effectively. Many homes have fine evergreen plantings that can be livened up by the use of annuals. Make a drive entrance say "Hello" and "have a good day" with a bright inviting annual bed. Liven up the front of the house. Use pots and planter boxes to accent the entrance. If you have ever visited Europe you may have noticed how every house has bright colorful flowers in great profusion. Here in the United States we have a long way to go to catch up. And we have so many fine flowers that will grow here easily. It has long been a dream of mine to see flowers used here as they are across the sea.

In 1976, I was the state chairman of the Kansas Bi-Centennial Freedom Gardens. I traveled over 9000 miles that year and gave talks in 61 cities to over 11,000 people. We in Kansas got credit for having more red, white and blue gardens than any comparable area. I hope that the start we got then is continuing. Annuals are bright and easy to grow all over the Plains. It would be great for us to be noted for the beauty of our yards as well as for our crops and cattle. Do yourself a favor and give your own area a boost by "brightening the corner where you are."

Flowering annuals are very versatile. There is a wide assortment of colors, many flower forms, heights, growth habits, and textures. Most of them bloom over a long period of them so you can have color from early spring until autumn. New varieties come out each year that have better disease resistance, new colors, and varied growth habits. They can be used in massed plantings or in small beds and containers.

When you select the annuals you want to use, first look at the ones you know are dependable. Pick the ones that appeal to you. Consider where you are going to use them. Don't overpower by using too tall or too heavy flowers. Also be sure they will be large enough to make a showing. Watch what your neighbors use successfully or visit your local park and observe the results they have in their beds. Check with a local Garden Club member or your extension service expert.

It is a good idea to depend on some of the newer improved varieties as they will be better in all ways. The new hybirds now on the market have more vigor and have a lot of the best characteristics of the parents. Almost invariably they will produce more and larger blooms. They are more expensive than the open pollinates as the cost of production is much higher. The F-1 hybrids are made with crosses all done by hand. Almost all annuals today will have hybrid selections, and in my mind they are better.

Be selective when buying seeds and plants. Many people simply pick seed off a rack without paying attention to the name. Before you go to pick up your seed, consult your garden magazine or seed catalogue and select the varieties you really want. Take the list with you and buy both seeds and plants that you have checked. If you order by mail do it early so you get the items you want. The extension service puts out lists of good annuals for your area. They are helpful. Some of the "All-America Selections" are excellent. They are tested throughout the country and will likely do well for you.

Most flowering annuals do best in full sunlight. Keep this in mind when planning your beds. There are a few that will do well in shade. Coleus, lobelia, pansy, sultana, and wax begonias will tolerate quite a bit of shade. Others that do well in partial sunlight or light shade are ageratum, balsam, nicotiana, scarlet sage, and sweet alyssum, However, they will do better in full sun.

Use your flower beds to hide a ugly spot or to enhance a good looking spot. Try to work around the permanent features of your yard such as fences, walks and drives. You can hide an unsightly foundation or make your entrance more inviting. I don't like geometrically precise beds as well as free-flowering curved beds. Along a wall, a fence, or a walk a precise rectangular bed is necessary and looks fine. Make your plantings irregular to give the bed some character. Use bright colored annuals to edge a sidewalk or a facer against the dark green of evergreens. A two or three foot bed following the line of the evergreens will do much to relieve the monotony of solid green.

A three or four-foot wide bed is about as large as you should go in order to facilitate maintenance. If you need to go wider, at least place some stepping stones so you can walk into the bed to pull weeds and clip off spent blooms. A smaller, well-kept bed is much more attractive than an ill kept large bed. When you lay out your plan don't make the mistake of setting the plants in a row like soldiers on parade. Some of the tall ones can be placed in a row in the rear of the bed for background. They appear even more attractive in clusters. Make you groupings large enough to make a showing. It is better to use fewer varieties and plant in groups. Within the beds the groups can be random sizes and shapes.

Place your flower beds where they can be seen easily from inside the house. It is a real pleasure to look out the picture window onto a colorful bed of annuals. Or, when washing dishes to be able to look out the kitchen window on a vista of bright flower beds. Small plots should use fewer colors than large ones. Try to use compatible colors together. Often contrasting colors are very effective. Use your imagination and your good taste to put the picture together. Time of blooming should also be considered as well as height. Perennials and the bulbs have shorter blooming times and can be used with annuals for a great picture. I will cover bulbs and perennials later in this chapter. Don't place tall plants where they will screen lower-growing ones.

Sketch out a plan for each bed taking all these things into consideration. It is simple to make a rough sketch about at scale to decide where you will plant the individual plants. In beds that stand away from a permanent background place the taller plants in the center and graduate them down to the outer edges. Possible you will want to plant some perennials in the center for background purposes. Or plant some spring-blooming bulbs in groups around the bed. They come early enough so that annuals can be planted following their bloom time.

It seems that I always come back to the subject of soils. Good soil and good drainage are very important in producing good flowers. Garden soils can be made good. Deep and fertile soils with good drainage and plenty of organic material are a must. The organic material will retain moisture and allow air and water to circulate. Good soil has many soil bacteria and enzymes that break down the organic material to basic chemical components and makes them available to the plants. Soil is made up of a mixture of rock particles in various stages of weathering plus humus. Humus is a brown or black substance resulting from the partial decay of organic matter. A soil without humus is a barren soil.

There are two schools of thought regarding the treatment of soil for the best production. One side thinks that all the chemical fertilizers are taboo. They claim that everything that goes into the soil should be of organic origin. The other side are the chemical gardeners who think the soil is only a convenient method of holding plants upright, and the food they need should be supplied by chemicals. As long as plants have to have all their food in the basic chemical form to be assimilated, why bother with organics. It is a never ending argument. My opinion is a middle ground between the two ideas. The addition of organic matter to garden soils is essential for making the soil tillable, lets it retain moisture, and allows good drainage. Nevertheless, I think that the moderate use of the chemicals gives good soil even better qualities by supplying plants with the nutrients they need in a faster manner. The best advice is to build up your soils with organic materials but also use a good balanced fertilizer in minimum amounts to give the plants a fast boost. I have operated on this theory for many years with good results. Use a low-nitrogen fertilizer so that you do not overstimulate the vegetative growth at the expense of the blooms.

In tilling the soil, if you use a mechancial tiller, spread two or three inches of compost, rotted manure, or peat moss of the surface before tilling. Apply a light application of 5-10-5 over the organic material. Apply about one pound per 100 square feet. Till it all in, mixing it thoroughly with the soil. In very heavy soil add coarse sand or perlite to loosen up the clay. If you are working the soil with a spading fork, add the extra materials after a first spading and then respade, working in all the material. Rake the surface with a steel-toothed rake until it is very fine. If the soil is very high in clay content spread about one inch of peat moss on the surface and rake it in lightly. This will help prevent crusting.

If you are using started plants be sure to space them far enough apart. I prefer to plant in clusters rather than in straight rows. If I want a row as a background or as a low border for bed plant in a row, I will plant in a row. I use plastic row markers with the names of the plant so I can keep track of the different selections.

Seeding seems as though it would be simple, but because of variation in sizes of the seed it can sometimes be a problem. Large seeds such as nasturtiums or sweet peas can be planted individually quite easily. Medium seeds such as zinnias can be tapped gently from the package. Cut or tear off the top of the package and squeeze the long sides between the thumb and the forefinger so the package spreads open. Tap the packet with the index finger, and the seeds will slide out a few at a time. Very fine seeds like the begonias family are easier to handle if they are mixed with fine sand. I use an old salt cellar to shake the sand and seed mix where wanted. Mark where you have sown the seeds so you can keep track of them. Compress the soil slightly over the seeds. The slight depression will also collect water so the seeds get the moisture they need. If you are planting on a curve or in a cluster mark the ground with a sharp pointed stick. Don't forget the labels.

Be careful of the depth you cover the seed. In early spring sow seeds with a light covering so the sun can warm them. In late spring and summer sow deeper so the sun does not dry them not too quickly. Seeds sown in early spring will need only an eighth to a quarter inch of cover. In summer a quarter or one-half inch will be better. Very fine seeds need no cover at all. They cover themselves by slipping down into the crevices in the soil. I have often used milled spagnum moss as a cover for seed and it works well because it retains moisture. Rub the moss through a sieve so it is fine. Firm the soil after planting and water gently but thoroughly with a fine spray. The seeds won't wash out if you are careful. The seeds must be kept moist without fail until they germinate. If they are allowed to dry after germination has started you are in trouble. It does not take heavy watering but on bright sunny warm days you may have to sprinkle lightly a couple of times. This is absolutely essential. That is one reason I like the spagnum moss as it helps retain the moisture.

Most annual seeds take a week or so to germinate. First will come the embryonic seed leaves. About a week later the true leaves will emerge. After the true leaves are through, it is time to thin them out. Select the strongest plant in a cluster to remain and remove the weaker plants. Be sure the soil is moist so the plants pull out easily. Always pull them by the leaves and not the stems. You can often use some of the removed plants for transplanting to a desired spot. Keep the roots moist. I often start zinnias in a row, and when I move the small plants they will come along fast. Be sure to handle the little plants by the leaves and get the roots into the new spot as soon as possible. Firm the soil around the plant and water it. Easy does it. I move zinnias all around the yard in this way. Many other plants can be handled the same way. Late in the afternoon or some cloudy day is the best time.

When the plants are about four inches tall it is time to pinch them back. Use your thumb and forefinger to nip out the top just above the top pair of leaves. this forces the plant to send out side branches and makes a sturdier plant with many more flowers. An unpinched plant tends to get lanky and sparse looking. This is a most neglected job so get with it. The same is true of plants bought at a nursery. Some of them have been pinched and will be stocky and healthy looking. If they are tall and spindly, pinch them back even at the expense of a few early blooms. The few that should not be pinched are balsam, cockscomb, and poppies.

Many of the smaller seeded and tender plants are better started indoors early. Time the plantings so they get into

PLATE I

Many flowering annuals, such as impatiens, can be grown indoors in a sunny window.

FLOWER GARDENS

the garden after all danger of frost. Don't get impatient and start them too early. Six or eight weeks before the last frost date is about right. Most packets give you that time to start inside as well as outside. Some take a bit longer to reach transplanting size and can be started sooner.

The following flowers are best seeded inside and set out after any danger of frost. Ageratum, annual dahlias, annual phlox, coleus, coneflower, cosmos, cockscomb, impatients, petunia, pinks, salvias, snap dragon, sweet alyssum, and verbena are all flowers that do better if started inside. By the same token these are the plants to purchase at your garden center when you are ready for them.

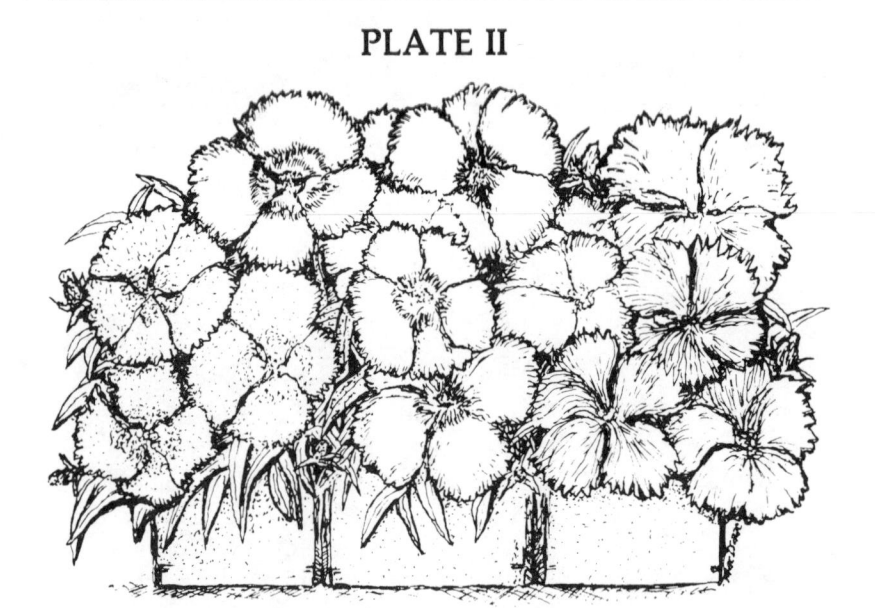

PLATE II

The special magic of bedding plants is the "instant" garden they make possible in all climates.

Ordinary garden soil is a poor medium for starting seeds inside. The easiest and safest way to have the right medium is to buy a sterile prepared mix from your garden store. You can make your own mix if you prefer, but you must sterilize it before using. Sterilizing gets rid of weed seeds, soil-borne diseases, and insects. A mix can be made of two parts rich loam, one part peat moss, and one part sharp sand. It helps to add one and a half ounces of superphosphate and 1 ounce of ground limestone to each bushel of mix. Stir it up thoroughly and screen it through a half-inch hardware cloth screen. To sterilize this mix, it should be heated in the oven to 180 degrees for 30 minutes. It is rather smelly and messy, so I feel the prepared mixes from your garden shop are easier and are very good.

For containers you have a wide choice. Clay or plastic pots, plastic or wooden trays, half a milk carton - in fact almost any sort of tray or container. Just be sure there are drainage holes in the container. An eight inch pot will start enough plants of one kind for most yards, and it is easy to keep track of the varieties. I use a starter tray with a heat cable in it because my basement is really not warm enough. It is thermostatically controlled to 75 degrees and works great. I also use some plastic trays for seeds that do not need the extra heat. In the plastic trays I line the bottom with a couple of sheets of newspaper. It allows the water to drain but holds the mix better and seems to hold moisture better. After filling with dirt, I moisten the mix throroughly. With the pots and plastic trays, place them in a pan of water and let the water work its way up through the mix. Drain well before planting the seeds.

Mark off the surface with tiny furrows by pressing it lightly with a ruler edge deep enough to accomodate the seeds you are going to sow. Seeds are planted about two or three times their diameter. This is not a hard and fast rule as some seed need little or no cover. Most seed packets will give you proper depth. With very fine seed I like to use spagnum moss that has been rubbed through a fine screen for a cover. It works best on very fine seeds although I have used it on many with good results. The seeding is done as explained on outdoor seeding. Use a marker of some sort at the end of each row to mark the variety. This is very important. It is very discouraging to plant something and then not know for sure just what it is.

After the seed is sown, be sure the medium is thoroughly damp. You may have to mist spray the surface to get enough moisture to the seeds. Place the container in a plastic bag to retain moisture. Prop the bag up so it does not lie on the surface. You make a minature greenhouse and will probably not have to water again until the seeds sprout. The containers must be kept warm is most cases. Shade is the one other thing of which to beware. With few exceptions, seeds germinate better if kept from bright light. Read the directions on the packets.

   When the seeds have sprouted the plastic cover should be removed and the container moved to bright light. I have a table in the basement where I grow my seedlings. It has a fluorescent light hanging above it. I use Gro-lite bulbs but regular bulbs are fine. For the newly sprouted seedlings I set the light six or eight inches above the soil in the flats. This tends to keep the plants shorter and stockier because they don't have to stretch for the light. A good sunny window works also. You must turn the container every couple of days as the little plants will bend toward the light. Keep the plants moist. I use a plastic spray bottle and mist the plants and the soil. You will not wash the soil by doing this way.

   As soon as the seedlings show the first true leaves it is time to transplant to separate containers. The first leaves that show are seed leaves so wait until the true leaves appear before transplanting. I transplant into 2½x2½ inch peat pots, the same size plastic pots and small clay pots using the same mix used in germination. An old skewer or a pencil works well for tranplanting. Push down under the little plants and loosen up the soil. Use the end of the pencil to make a hole in the mix in the containers. Take the seedling by the leaves and pull it out gently. Lower the roots into the hole in the pot and firm the soil around the plant gently but firmly. Put the pots in a plastic flat, keeping varieties marked and then immerse the whole flat in a pan of water so the pots can take up the water. After they are well watered, placed under the light or in a sunny window. The light can be eight or ten inches above the plants but no higher. Place them where they will have cooler temperatures. Too much heat will make them gangly. When I ran a greenhouse we set all the transplants in a cool house a few days after transplanting. Cool temperatures will make much sturdier plants. Be sure when transplanting to put the seedling at the same depth it grew in the germinating container. Deeper planting will result in some rotting at ground level.

A week or so before you are ready to plant outside, take the plants to cooler location and harden them off. I have a covered patio that does well for hardening off. It gets east sun, and if freezing weather is forecast it is easy to move them in for a night. Be sure they get sunlight while they are being tempered. One thing that can be done during this period is to pinch back the tips to force side branching and bushier plants. When planting peat pots in the garden it pays to tear out the bottom of the pot and tear along the top edge. The peat in the pot will draw water from around the plant if the top edge is above ground like a wick. Another thing to help is to give each transplant a teacup of a liquid fertilizer such as Rapid-gro or Miracle-gro. They will not wilt at all with the extra help.

A perennial is a plant that lasts three years or longer in a given place. Biennials are plants that grow through one season, flower the second, then die. Perennial gardens are very good for those who wish little maintenance as they continue for many years. Most perennials are easy to grow and require only a small amount of maintenance. The only fault they have is that the blooming time of most of them are short. Some of the new selections that are now on the market have a better blooming period. Cutting off spent blooms will make new ones appear and will extend the bloom period.

Perennials are many and very diverse. Tall and short, all colors of the rainbow, vigor and good disease and insect resistance. Even here on our windy hot Plains states we grow some superb ones. Peonies flourish, and so do Oriental poppies, garden phlox, bearded iris, day lilies, chrysanthemums, and others.

The main challenge of a perennial garden is its correct layout. It is a long range project with both permanence and constant change. The objective is to have bloom from early spring into the fall. Another point is to plant so each seedling has room enough to reach its best size and appearance. Some spread very fast, like mums that require digging annually and separating. Some never need extra room, such as the peony. In the planning you must take these things into consideration. Your planning before planting will pay off in both appearance and in reduced maintenance.

The location of the bed is important. Ample sun plays a big part as it does with annuals. A few perennials will tolerate some shade, but for the most part sun and good air circulation will make stronger and better plants. It is not necessary to have a bed completely perennial. I have had success mixing perennials and annuals. Plan the plantings to have some bloom throughout the season. One of my beds is along the south edge of the lawn, and I have blooms from crocus very early to the mums in the fall. It really is a mixed bag as I think of it, but it does have color all season. It is a bed about four feet wide and about 40 feet long. One end is shady in late afternoon, but the rest is sunny all day. At the shady end I plant impatiens and fibrous begonias. I use ageratum and small marigolds for the borders. In the bed are iris, peonies, coral bells, columbine, daisies, mums, gaillardia, phlox, and snap dragons. Quite a mix but very attractive all spring, summer, and fall.

Another bed is a five foot wide bed on the east side of the house. One end near the kitchen door is for herbs. It has easy access from the door so we always have fresh herbs for cooking. It seems to arouse much interest in our guests. The herbs are mostly perennial and fit into the picture. There are some cosmos at the back of the bed that self seed and come up each year. They make a good background. This bed is a mixture also with penstemons, daisies, mums, and others with a border of ageratum and petunias. There are some bulbs that come each year also. There is color all season. It seems I continually add something I want to try or that has caught my fancy. The great thing is that you can always change, add, or take away.

Come to think about it, I guess all the flower beds are a mixture of perennials, annuals and bulbs. At the front of the house I have a few yews, Japaness holly, mums and some ivy that climbs on the brick. I fill in the bed with petunias, salvia, alyssum, mums, and ageratum. There is a built-in planter at the entrance and I fill with with geraniums, browallia and cascading petunias. It sets off the front of the house with good color.

Choose your plants carefully. The lists at the end of the chapter will give you colors, sizes, and blooming times. Some bloom briefly so they can be surrounded with others that bloom at a later time. It is possible to start most perennials from seed as explained earlier. The methods are the same. It is better in the long run and easier to purchase good started plants or beg some from a friendly gardener. The amounts of any one variety involved are usually not great, so it is not really practical to raise a lot of seedlings unless you want to share. You will find plenty of takers. The divided clumps available a the nurseries come along fast to help get a good-looking bed much faster.

When planning a bed it is usually easier to start at the back of the bed and work forward. The taller and later blooming plants make a pretty background. Don't plant in a straight line but instead irregularly with some forward of the others to give a more natural effect. The tall ones should include hardy asters, tall mums, sunflower, and hollyhocks — I have used goldenrod effectively as a background plant. As you come to the front, Shasta daisies, day lilies, foxglove, Japanese iris, and phlox will fit nicely. Don't plant in rows — bunch them in clusters. Plant shorter ones to the front. Spring bloomers are shorter as a rule. One of the biggest kicks in a perennial bed is to experiment, and if that doesn't look right, try something else. Changing and experimenting to get the combinations you want is a challenge and you will truly enjoy it.

For a succession of blooms consider iris, lupines, peonies, pansies, bleeding heart, coral bells, and columbine in early spring; for early summer sweet William, delphinium, English daisy, sundrops, poppies, phlox, coneflower, and veronica; midsummer has bee balm, salvia, feverfew, sedum, yarrow, hollyhock, butterfly weed, painted daisy, coreopsis, mist flower, gaillardia, day lily, and liatris; for fall blooming try dahlias, chrysanthemums, asters, and goldenrod. Some of these will extend from one season to the next if the blooms are removed when they are spent.

I have debated with myself just where to add roses. I finally decided that they are primarily grown for the flowers even though they are shrubs and are widely used for landscape purposes. And of course, they are perennial. Roses have universal appeal because of their charm, strength, delicacy of colors, fragrance, and assortment of colors, sizes, and shapes. Too many folks are a bit afraid to try roses because they think they are difficult.

First, and most important, the soil must be well-prepared before planting. A sunny location is a must and away from the competition of tree roots. They must have five or six hours of full sun each day. Morning sun is preferred. The ground must be well drained. Roses cannot stand wet feet.

PLATE III

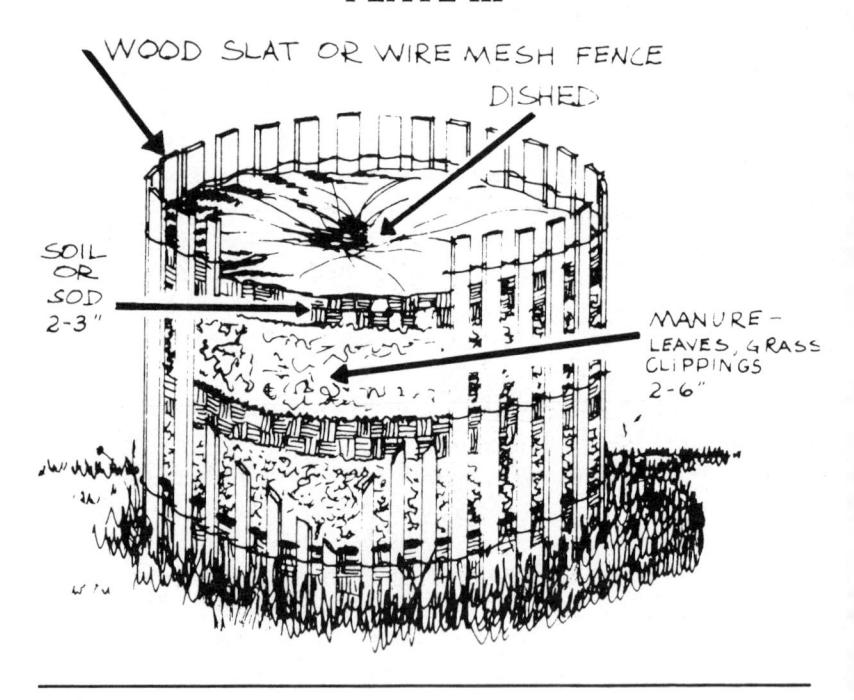

Diagram labels: WOOD SLAT OR WIRE MESH FENCE; DISHED; SOIL OR SOD 2-3"; MANURE — LEAVES, GRASS CLIPPINGS 2-6"

Work lots of organic material in the form of well-rotted manure, compost, or peat moss to a depth of 18 to 24 inches. Roses like heavy soil so this is not problem if you add organics. In sandy soil it is necessary to add even more organic material to prevent too fast a loss of moisture. It will help if you add some superphosphate to the soil at about three or four pounds per 100 square feet when you are working the bed. This permits stronger roots on the new plants and encourages bloom. Roses prefer a soil that is slightly acid, so in much of our area peat moss would be a fine additive because it makes the soil more acid. I have found that roses do better for me if they are planted in spring. This is true particularly in the northern Plains.

Second, I feel that it is important to buy high quality plants. Roses are all graded and will be marked Number 1 or Number 1½s. The number 1 roses will perform much better for you and are worth the higher price. Number 1½s will do well but take a year or two to catch up. Third, water is one very essential factor to which we sometimes do not pay enough attention. Water deeply when you water and keep the moisture off the foliage as much as possible. If you do the watering early in the morning the foliage will dry before nightfall. Mulching probably comes next. A good mulch is one of the best things you can do for roses. Rather than peat moss which tends to crust, I suggest shredded bark, ground corn cobs, wood chips, or any coarse organic material. Spread the mulch two or three inches deep. The mulch will conserve moisture and hold down the weeds, and it looks a lot better. It is one way to avoid blackspot. The splashing of the rain on plain soil carries the spores of the backspot up to the leaves. The mulch will prevent the splashing.

In planting bare-root roses, take the wrapping off as soon as you get them and plunge the roots directly into a bucket of slightly muddy water. The roots must never be allowed to dry out. A little Rapid-gro or Miracle-gro in the water is also a help. They can be left in the water for 24 hours or so. You will want to plant as early as possible in the spring, so be sure the roots do not get frozen in a late freeze. Just before planting trim off any broken roots. If there are many you may have to trim the tops to compensate for the loss of the roots.

Space the roses about three feet apart in this area. In a rose bed I find that staggering them makes a better looking bed. Make the holes 18 inches deep and about 18 inches across. You may have to go a bit deeper or wider for heavier roots. The bud union or knot that is on every rose plant should be placed so it is about an inch below the ground level. You will find the roots are funnel shaped. To compensate, make a mound in the center of the hole so the roots will slant down over it naturally. The mound should be high enough to raise the plant so the bud union is at the correct height. The bud union is vulnerable to severe cold so by planting it at the proper depth it can be protected better when you mound up in the fall. In the spring pull the dirt away from the bud union so the sun can get to it. This stimulates more and stronger growth.

With the plant placed properly, backfill six inches of soil, making sure the soil gets on and under the roots so there will be no air pockets. Firm the soil down with your foot but go easy so no roots get broken. Fill the hole on up to three inches from ground level and water it all down. Using some of the solution from the bucket will help. When the water has settled down continue filling and mound up the soil over the stems for a few inches. This will keep the plant from drying out and keep it warm so the buds will break out sooner. When the buds are a quarter inch long, carefully rake away the mound from around the plant. Rake it so you form a dish that will hold water and put it where it can do the most good. Potted roses can be planted the same way except you will not have to make a mound in the hold. Be sure the bud union is set right. Remove the roses carefully from the pot so the roots are not disturbed. Tar paper pots can have the bottom pulled off before setting in the hole. When the plant is positioned, tear away the sides of the pot in a way that will not disturb the ball of earth. Most potted plants will be leafed out so you will not have to mound soil around it. Just be sure of the correct position of the bud union.

Regular maintainance is not difficult but must be done on a fixed routine. Watering is important. Keep the water from the foliage as much as possible. Early morning watering gives the foliage a chance to dry before nightfall. I have a routine of spraying my roses every Saturday morning. A spray is more effective than dust. Use a hose-end sprayer and make sure you get under the foliage with the spray. There are a number of excellent rose sprays on the market containing both an insecticide and a fungicide. There are some rose fertilizers available that have a systemic insectide built in to them. A feeding once a month with this mixture does a good job, although I also spray once a week. The fungicide Benlate or Benomyl is a systemic that works well also. It keeps down the incidence of disease. I would caution you that you should not feed roses after the middle of August. This allows the plant to go into a natural dormancy as fall approaches. Over-stimulating the plant late in the year subjects it to cold damage.

The only pruning needed during the summer is to remove all spent blooms as they fade. Cut the stem off just above the first side shoot with five leaves. Always make your cut on a slant so the rain will run off and not soak into the stem. You can trim back any stems that get too long or cross over another and rub on it. The rubbing of the stems together will make a good spot for disease and insects to get going. Cut off any damaged canes and thin out some of the more vigorous bushes so air and light can reach the center of the plant.

Winter care is simple. Have a supply of soil nearby so that you can mound up the soil on the bush for eight or 10 inches. Don't rake up dirt from the bed for mounding but use soil from the supply you have on hand. Do the mounding after the ground has frozen a bit and the foliage has died back. Prune only the long canes that may whip around in the wind and only to about 18 to 24 inches. A rose cane dies from the tip down so by covering the bud union with soil and leaving longer canes you can be sure the rose will Winter over. In the spring you cut back all the dead canes down to just above a good healthy bud. Any serious pruning is done is early spring. It is amazing how soon the buds will burst out and the canes start to stretch. You can usually expect bloom by mid-May.

Roses are divided into a number of types, but we are interested mainly in six classifications. The hybrid tea is a rose grown for a large individual flower on a long stem. It is the most popular type because of the vigor, range of color, fragrance, and flower size. It is good for cutting and just for decoration in the garden. Floribunda roses are usually somewhat shorter with many flowers growing in clusters. They bloom from early spring until frost and come in many colors from white to yellow to deep red. They fit in well with other plantings and make excellent hedges. Floribundas are tougher than teas and are very adaptable.

Grandifloras are about what the name says. They are, as

a rule, taller and hardier than hybrid teas with more blooms. There are a number of them that are really spectacular. One of my favorites is Queen Elizabeth, a deep pink large flower and a sturdy bush. Climbers are in a class by themselves that have long arching stems or sometimes upright that don't really cling to anything but must be trained on a trellis, up a porch, or along a fence. Some of the newer varieties, such as Don Juan, have large flowers like tea roses. Some of the teas have developed long canes and are used as climbers. They come mostly from selections or sports that show up. They must be tied up to a support to get the right look.

One other class that is often overlooked is the shrub rose. They are usually wild roses, very hardy, vigorous, and low-maintenance. I have used them mostly for landscape uses. They are great in a shrub border or as a specimen plant. I might also mention the little beauties, minatures. There has been great interest in them in recent years, and there are some beauties on the market. Most of them grow one foot or less with flowers about the size of a fingernail. They are fine for rock gardens, window boxes and pots. I have grown one in a pot in a kitchen window that bloomed all winter. I could write a whole book about roses, but I am trying to cover some basics so you can have a starting place.

Many All-America Rose Selections are superior in most cases. The non-profit organization has been testing roses since 1930 in some 26 test gardens all around the country. In order to get an All-American award they must perform well in all the test gardens. This is really a sign of superior quality, and I recommend you try them. Use your roses in beds and for landscape designs. They are very satisfactory.

Bulbs are another fine addition to your garden. They are easy to use and give you great returns for small effort. Corms, tubers, tuberous roots, rhizomes and true bulbs will all be covered in this section. True bulbs are like daffodils, tulips, lilies and hyacinth. A corm is the swollen base of a stem like crocus and gladiolas. Tubers have no covering of dry leaves but just a tough skin and are usually short, fat and rounded. Tuberous begonias, anemone and caladium are in this group. Tuberous roots are fleshy swollen roots that produce roots and buds. Dahlias are the

PLATE IV

1. Prepare and fertilize bed. Dig 15" to 18" wide and as deep. Add quart of peat moss mixed with ½ cup of fertilizer. Mix well with soil. Form a mound in center and position rose on mound.

2. See that roots are spread out naturally and that bud union (swelling at base of stems) is level with ground. Scatter several inches loose soil over roots and firm well with foot.

3. Fill remainder of hole with water and allow to drain. See that the bud union remains at ground level.

4. Fill remainder of hole with soil and tamp. The plant is now ready for the mound of soil which will protect it against rapid freezing and thawing during the winter.

5. Mound soil around and over plant to a height of 12". Remove protective mound in the spring after growth starts.

All-America Rose Selections

(E-5. Glossy photo.)

best known of these. A rhizome is really a rootstock. Cannas and lily of the valley are good examples.

Most bulbs do best in bright sun and with good drainage. Some will do well as long as they get a few hours of sunlight or strong diffused light each day. I have found that the addition of peat moss or compost to the soil when spading the ground is helpful. Use bonemeal for a long lasting fertilzer to promote root growth and blooming. Five and six pounds per 100 square feet is about right. You can also use phosphate, but my experience has been good with bonemeal.

The spring flowering bulbs are most commonly used and have delighted people for many years. The early spring bulbs are so delightful pushing up through the last remnants of the snow. Snowdrops and crocus are the first to come along, and their bright colors after a drab winter are most welcome. I have planted my crocus in drifts along the edge of the lawn and under the trees. The ones in full sun come first, followed by the bulbs partially shaded. There is a longer period of bloom when they are planted this way. Most of the early bulbs respond this way. As spring advances, the early daffodils, grape hyacinth, and early tulips show up. A little later along come the large hyacinths, late daffodils, late tulips, and anemones that extend the spring blooming until late May. I have always planted spring flowering bulbs in the annual beds. It works great because when the annuals come along they hide the old foliage left after blooming. Be sure that you do not cut back the foliage after blooming. Cut off the flowers stalks but leave the foliage because as long as it is green it will be making food for the bulbs by the process of photosynthesis. Bulbs will bloom for many years if you follow this rule. Just add a little bonemeal each year.

One thing that I have learned is to plant bulbs in clusters or groups and not in a straigh row. It is far better to buy a

PLATE V

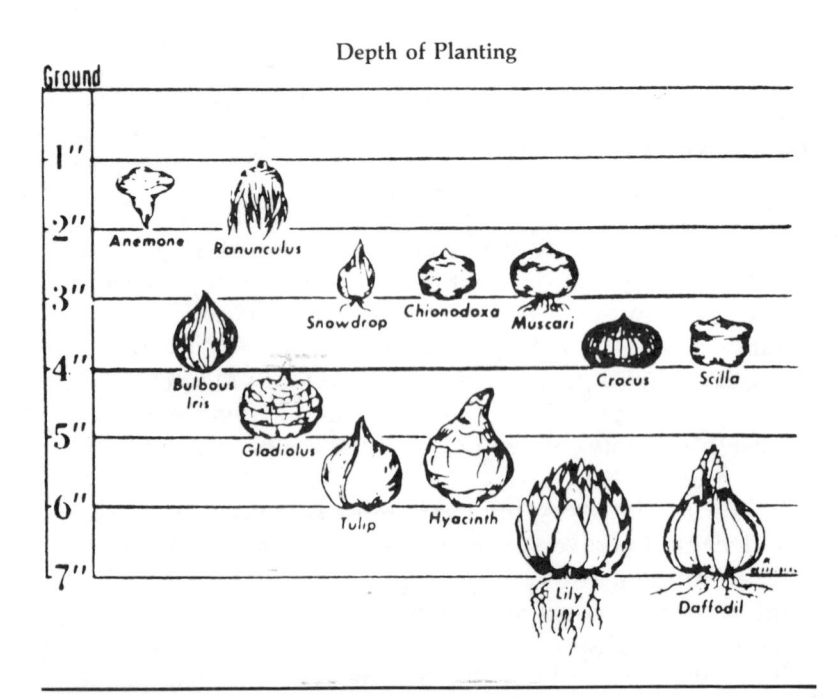

Depth of Planting

dozen tulips of one size and color and plant them in an irregular clump. They are far more effective this way. In a naturalistic garden stand with your back to the bed and toss the bulbs over your shoulder and then plant them where they land. You will be surprised how good they will fit into the picture. Small bulbs like crocus, grape hyacinths, dwarf iris and snowdrops are great in a rock garden. Larger ones like tulips, daffodils and hyacinth look better in a large bed.

Summer bulbs like the gladiolas, lilies, allium, cannas, dahlias, and Dutch iris are better in open beds. As with spring bulbs, plant them in groups. There are so many colors available in glads, dahlias, and lilies that you must use care in getting them in a compatible setting. I use glads primarily as cut flowers and have often planted them in a row at the end of the vegetable garden for easy cutting. They are fine for beds, but their best use is for cutting. Dahlias must be dug and stored for the winter as are most summer bulbs. Lilies are an exception as most of them can be left in plant if they are mulched. In the spring divide the dahlias to get good eyes for new growth. Start them inside in peat moss before they go out for earlier blooming. Handle cannas this way also. Dahlias have so many colors, flower shapes, and heights that they have many uses. The tall ones make marvelous cut flowers. The dwarfs are fine for beds as a border. The following list are some of my favorite bulbs and most are hardy in our area.

Spring blooming - in order of bloom:
Snowdrops - white delicate flower - light shade - in groups - 3" to 9"; Crocus - many colors - full sun - spread naturally - group - 2" to 6"; Squill - blue mostly - sun or shade - naturalize well - group - 6" to 12"; Grape hyacinth - blue white - sun or light shade - naturalize - 6" to 9"; Early daffofils - yellow white - sun light shade - group - 12" to 18"; Early tulips - many colors - sun - shorter than late ones - 9" to 16"; Daffodils - yellow white - many sizes and shapes - sun - 12" to 36"; Tulips - many colors and sizes - sun - group - 9" to 30"; Hyacinth - blue, pink, white - fragrant - sun rock gardens - beds - 8" to 12";
Summer blooming
Allium - blue yellow - sun - tall for accents - 6" to 5";

FLOWER GARDENS 87

Caladium - great foliage - sun shade - dig in Fall - 6" to 24"; Lilies - many colors - sun - last for years - 2' to 5'; Canna - white, yellow, red - full sun - dig in Fall - 1½' to 5'; Gladiola - many colors - full sun - dig in Fall - 1' to 5'; Dahlias - many colors and shapes - sun - dig in Fall - 1' to 7'; Autumn Crocus - white, lilac, yellow - sun - naturalize - 4" to 8".

The summer bloomers that must be dug in the Fall should be stored carefully after drying in a place that will not freeze. Keep dry until time to start out again.

This is by no means all the choices. There are many fine bulbs available at your dealers. Try some. These I have named are all hardy for our area except the ones noted that must be dug in the Fall. Use bulbs for a balanced garden with bloom from early spring until frost.

CHART A

Color Key B - blue Lav - lavender O - orange P - Pink Pur - purple R - red Y - yellow W - white

NAME	HEIGHT	FLOWER TIME	COLOR	USES	REMARKS
Ageratum	4-15"	June-Oct	B-W-P	Border, edging	Sun - seed inside 3/1 outside in May
Annual Dahlia	18-36"	June-Frost	Various	Border, Beds	Sun - seed inside 3/1 outside in May
Annual Phlox	6-12"	June-Frost	W-P-Lav	Border, edging	Sun or shade - seed outside
Balsam	8-24"	June-Sept.	W-P-Pur-R	Border, edging	Sun or shade - seed outside
Blanket Flower (Gaillardia)	12-30"	July-Oct.	R-Y	Border	Sun - seed out in late April
Poppy	10-12"	June-Frost	Y-O-W-P.R	Border, beds	Sun - see outdoors
Coleus	12-18"	May-Frost	Foilage	Border, beds	Sun or shade-seed inside 3/1 outside in May
Coneflower	12-24"	July-Frost	O	Border, cut flower	Sun - seed in Sept. self sow
Cornflower	12-20"	May-Frost	W-B-P-Pur	Border, beds	Sun - seed in Sept. self sow
Cosmos	30-48"	June-Frost	W-P-R	Border, background	Sun - seed inside - outside in May
Cockscomb	6-24"	June-Frost	Y-R	Border, beds	Sun - seed inside - outside in May
Four-O'Clock	18-30"	July-Frost	Various	Border	Sun or part shade - seed ouside-self sows
Marigold	6-36"	June-Frost	O-Y	Border, beds	Sun - seed outdoors after frost
Gazania	8-12"	July-Frost	O-Y-W	Border, beds	Sun - seed inside - outside in May
Globe Amaranth	6-24"	July-Sept.	W-Pur	Border, cut flower	Sun - seed inside - outside in May
Impatiens	6-24"	June-Frost	R-P-O-W	Border, beds	Sun or part shade-seed inside-outside in May
Larkspur	24-48"	May-July	W-P-R-B-Pur	Border, cut flower	Sun - seed outside in spring or fall
Morning Glory	CLIMBER	July-Frost	W-B-P	Screen, trellis	Sun - seed outside in Spring

continued on next page

FLOWER GARDENS 89

CHART A

Color Key B - blue Lav - lavender O - orange P - Pink Pur - purple R - red Y - yellow W - white

NAME	HEIGHT	FLOWER TIME	COLOR	USES	REMARKS
Moss Rose	4-12"	June-Frost	W-P-R-Y	Rock garden, beds	Hot sun - seed outside in spring
Nasturtium	10-18"	July-Frost	O-Y	Border, beds	Sun or part shade - seed outside in May
Nicotiana	12-30"	June-Frost	W	Border	Sun or shade - seed outside in spring
Periwinkle	10-14"	July-Frost	W-P-Pur	Border, beds	Sun - seed inside - outside in May
Petunia	12-24"	June-Frost	Various	Border, beds	Sun or part shade-seed inside-outside in May
Pincushion Flower	24-36"	July-Aug.	W-R-B	Border	Sun - seed outdoors in spring
Pinks	3-12"	June-Frost	W-P-R	Border, beds	Sun - seed in fall or inside early
Plains Coreopsis	18-30"	June-Forst	Y-O-R	Border, cut flowers	Sun - seed inside - outside in May
Scarlet Sage	10-30"	Aug.-Sept.	R	Border, beds	Part shade - seed inside - outside in May
Shirley Poppy	24-26"	June-Frost	W-R	Border, beds	Sun - seed in fall - self sows
Snapdragon	6-36"	June-Sept.	Various	Border, beds	Part shade - seed inside - outside in May
Spider Flower	36-60"	July-Frost	P-W	Border	Sun - seed outdoors in spring
Sunflower	30-72"	July-Sept.	Y	Background, screen	Sun - seed outside in spring
Sweet Alyssum	4-10"	June-Oct.	W-Lav-P	Border, edging	Sun or part shade - seed inside - outside May
Verbena	8-18"	July-Frost	P-R-W-Pur	Border, rock gardens	Sun - seed inside - outside in May
Zinnia	6-36"	July-Frost	Various	Border, beds	Hot sun-seed outside after frost danger

CHART B

22 Good Annuals for the Great Plains

Color Key B - blue Lav - lavender O - orange P - pink Pur - purple R - red Y - yellow W - white

NAME	HEIGHT	COLOR	USES	REMARKS
Ageratum	4-15"	B-W-P	Borders, bedding, edging	Sunny location - start inside
Alyssum	4-10"	W-P-Lav	Bedding, borders	Sun or part shade - start inside
Asters	24-30"	Pur-W-P-Rose	Cut flowers, borders	
Bachelors Button	12-15"	Pur-P-W-Lav-Rose	Cut flowers, beds	
Celosia Cockscumb	6-48"	Y-R	Bedding, border, background	Start inside - sun - plumed & crested
Cleome Spiderflower	48-60"	Magenta-W	Cutting, background	Sun - withstands adverse conditions
Coleus	12-18"	Colored foliage	Borders, bedding	Start inside - sun or shade
Dusty Miller	18-24"	Silvery foliage	Border	Start inside - sun & dry - good accent conditions
Gazania	8-12"	O-Y-W	Borde, bedding	Start inside - good for dry sunny sites
Helianthus Sunflower	30-70"	Y	Screen, background	Sow direct - dry sunny sites
Impatiens	12-15"	R-Rose-W-P	Boxes, bedding	Start inside
Marigold	8-24"	Gold-Lemon-Spotted Maroon	Beds, borders, cutting	Sow direct - sun - use as a border for vegtables - discourages insects

continued on next page

FLOWER GARDENS 91

CHART B
22 Good Annuals for the Great Plains

Color Key B - blue Lav - lavender O - orange P - pink Pur - purple R - red Y - yellow W - white

NAME	HEIGHT	COLOR	USES	REMARKS
Nasturtiums	8-10"	R-Y-O-Mahogany	Borders	Sow direct
Petunia	12-24"	Many shades & blends	Boses, pots, versatile, bed borders	Dependable, start inside - sun partial shade
Phlox	8-10"	R-P-W-Pur-Rose	Beds, borders	
Poppies	10-12"	W-P-R-Y	Rockgarden, beds	
Portulaca - Moss Rose	4-12"	W-P-R-Y	Rockgarden, beds	Sow direct - Hot dry site - self sow
Rudbeekia - Coneflower	30-36"	O	Background, cutting	Sow direct - sunny site - native
Salvia	10-30"	R-P-W	Beds, cut flower	Start inside - sun - part shade
Snapdragon	6-36"	Many shades	Beds, cut flowers	Many sizes & colors - start inside - partial shade
Verbena	8-18"	P-R-W-Pur	Rockgarden, beds	Very dependable, start inside, sun
Zinnia	6-36"	Many shades	Beds, cut flowers	Small flowered varieties dowell - sow direct - sun - M.G.P.

CHART C

My Favorite Roses
HYBRID TEAS

NAME	COLOR	HEIGHT	BLOSSOM SIZE
Charlotte Armstrong	deep pink	4'	3-4"
Chicago Peace	pink-yellow	2½-4'	4-6"
* Chrysler Imperial	crimson	2½-4'	3-5"
Crimson Glory	Deep crimson	2½-4'	3-4"
Eclipse	Golden yellow	2½-4'	3-4"
* Garden Party	white to pink	4'	3-5"
* Kings Ransom	golden yellow	2½-4'	5-6"
* Mirandy	deep red	4'	4-6"
* Mister Lincoln	dark red	2½-4'	5-6"
* Mojare	apricot orange	4' +	3-5"
* Peace	yellow to pink	2½-4'	5-6"
* Tropicana	coral orange	2½-4'	4-5"
* White Knight	white		3-4"

continued on next page

CHART C

My Favorite Roses

NAME	COLOR	HEIGHT	BLOSSOM SIZE
FLORIBUNDA			
Betty Prior	Mealium pink	4-5'	Single petals 3-4"
* Circus	yellow with variations	2-3'	2-3"
* Else Poulsen	Bright pink	3'	Semi-double 1-2"
Europeana	crimson	2-3'	2-3"
* Eutin	Dark red	2-3'	2½-3½ Good for Hedges
* Fashion	coral-peach pink	2-3'	2½-3½"
* Floradora	orange red	3'	1-2"
Frensham	Deep scarlet	3'	2-3' - Hedges
* Gold Cup	golden yellow	2-3'	3-4"
* Jiming Cricket	coral orange * pink	2-3'	2½-4"
* Roman Holiday	deep red & yellow	2'	2-3"
Spartan	Orange-red	3'	2½-3½"
* Vogue	pink	3'	3½-4½"
GRANDIFLORA			
* Apricot Nectar	apricot pink	3'	3½-4½"
* Camelot	salmon-pink	4'	3½-4"
* Duet	deep pink	4'	3-4"
* John S. Armstrong	dark red	4'	3-4"
* Mount Shasta	white	4'	4-5"
* Queen Elizabeth	medium pink	4'	3-4"

continued on next page

CHART C
My Favorite Roses

NAME	COLOR	HEIGHT	BLOSSOM SIZE
CLIMBERS			
Blaze	scarlet	15-20'	2-3"
Climbing Crimson Glory	crimson	8-12'	3-4½"
Climbing Peace	yellow to pink	15-20'	2½-4½"
Coral Dawn	coral pink	6-12'	4-5"
Don Juan	red	6-10'	4-5"
Golden Shower	yellow	6-12'	3-4"
New Dawn	double pink	15-20'	2-3"
Paul's Scarlet	scarlet	10-15'	2-3" Spring bloomer
White Dawn	white	6-12'	2-3"
SHRUB ROSES			
Grootendorst Supreme	red	4-7'	¾-1" Blooms Spring or Fall
Harrison's Yellow	yellow	5-8	
Rosa Hugonis	light yellow	6-8'	½-2" one bloom a year
Rosa Rugosa	red	5-6'	2" one bloom a year
			2½-3" Spring & Fall
MINATURES			
Baby Darling	orange-pink	12-14"	1-1½"
Cinderella	white & pink	12-15"	¾-1"
Pixie	white & pink	8-10"	¾"
Red Imp	crimson	8-9"	¾-1"
Tinker Bell	pink	8-10"	1-1½"

There are many more choices but I have found all of these to be **tough** & very colorful. Try some new ones & you may fine one you like better.

FLOWER GARDENS 95

CHART D
Perennials

NAME	COLOR	HEIGHT	BLOOM TIME	ZONE	NOTES
Yarrow	white-yellow-red	2-4½'	Summer	All	Good for drying
Hollyhock	white-pink-lav-purple	5-9'	Summer	All	Backgroung
Columbine	white-red-pink-yelow-blue	1½-3'	Spring	All	New hybrids ver good
Silver Artemesia	silver foliage	3'	— —	All except 3	Good for accent
Butterfly Weed	orange	2-3'	Summer	All except 3	Wildflower
English Daisy	red-pink-white	6"	Spring to Summer	All	Mulchin Winter
Chrysanthemum	many	from 1' to 4'	Fall	All	Fast growing - tough
Shasta Daisy	White	3'	Summer	All except 3	Great Hybrid
Coreapsis	orange-yellow	2-3'	Summer	All except 3	Very colorful
Delphinuam	blue-lav-purple-white	2-4'	Summer	All	Bothered by heat
Bleeding Heart	pink	2½-3'	Spring	All except 3	Light shade
Coneflower	coral-red-white	3'	Summer	All	Dark center cone
Mistflower	blue	1½-3'	Summer	All	Spread rapidly
Gaillardia	red-yellow	2'	Summer	All	"Indian Blanket"
Sunflower	yellow	4'	Summer	All	Background
Day Lilis	yelow-pink-red	1-2'	Spring thru Summer	All	Many selection
Coral Bells	white-red	1-2'	Spring thru Summer	All except 3	Tolerate light shade

continued on next page

CHART D

Perennials

NAME	COLOR	HEIGHT	BLOOM TIME	ZONE	NOTES
Hosta-Mountain Lily	white-variegated foliage	1-2'	Summer	All	Likes shade
Iris	wide selection	2-3'	Spring	All	Bearded hardiest
Liatris	lavender-white	4-6'	Summer	All	Welldrained soil
Lythram-Loosestrife	pink-red	2-5'	Summer	All	Good Background
Berganot-Bee Balm	red	2-3'	Summer	All except 3	Wildflowr
Peony	white-pink-red	2-4'	Spring	All	Some good selection available
Poppy	orange red-pink-white	2-4'	Spring	All-	Dies down in summer
Phlox	many	2-4'	Summer	All	Many selections
Rudbeckia	yellow with dark center	2-4'	Summer	All	Gloriosa daisy in some family
Sedum	ivory-pink-red	1½'	Summer	All	Good for rock gardens.
Golden rod	yellow	2-3'	Summer	All	Great Backgroundk
Veronica	blue-violet-white	1-2'	Summer	All	Full sun

FLOWER GARDENS 97

CHART E
My Favorite Bulbs

Spring Bloom - in order of blooming
Snowdrops - white delicate flower - light shade - group
Crocus - many species & colors - full sun - spread naturally - group
Squill - blue & some other colors - sun or shade - naturalize well - plant in drifts
Grafe Hyacinth - blue & white - sun or light shade - naturalize well - group
Early Daffodils - yellow & white - sun or light shade - plant in clusters
Early Tulips - many colors - sun - early tulips are shorter - borders
Daffodils - yellow & white - many sizes & style - sun - many types - plant in clusters
Tulips - many colors - sun - tall & short - many tupes - plant in clusters
Hyacinths - blue, pink, white, fragent, sun-rock gardens & beds

Summer Blooming
Alluims - blue & yellow - sun - tall ones as accents - small in beds
Caladrum - great foliage - sun to shade - will not winter - dig in fall & restart in spring
Lilies - wide range of colors - sun - small groups along a fence or hedge - last for years
Canna - white, yellow, red - full sun - against green background - dig in fall
Gladiola - many colors - full sun - mostly for cutting - must be dig in fall
Dahlias - many colors & shapes - sun - many uses from bedding to cutting - dig in fall
Autumn Crows - white, lilac, yellow - sun - naturalize in clusters - last for years.

This is by no means all the choices. There are many fine bulbs available at your dealers. Try some. These I have named are all hardy for our area except the one noted that must be dig in fall. Use bulbs for a balanced garded with bloom from very early until frost.

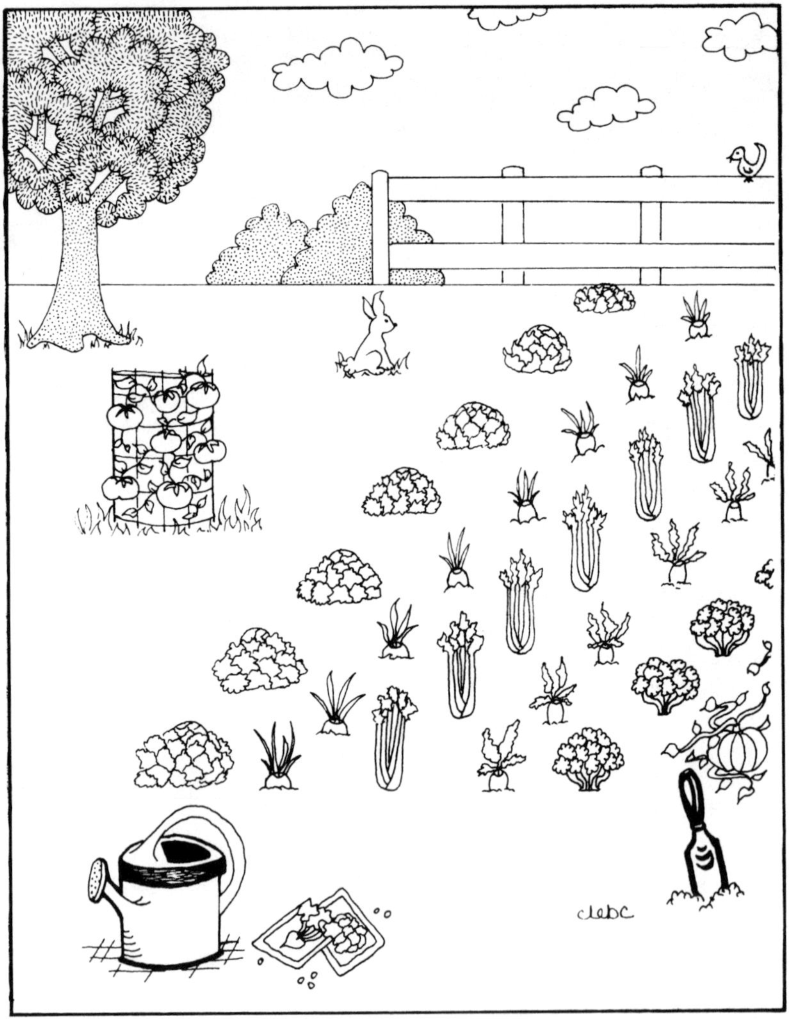
clebc

8
Vegetable Gardens

If you want a thousand dollar bonanza in your own back yard, plant a vegetable garden. They are important in these days and times even more than they used to be. With the times as they are, and with the energy crunch, it is a well-paying proposition. Beside that, the exercise will do you a world of good. The food provided by the garden is only one of the good things. It is a dandy family project, as you can see and eat the products of your efforts. It is a fine project for young and old. Retired persons can take advantage of the time that is so available to many. It can be a good fund-raising project for the youth or retired person who wants to make some money selling surplus crops to those who do not garden.

The big plus is the savings that can be realized with the ever-increasing cost of food. Some researchers have found that a 30' x 40' garden can raise over $900.00 worth of vegetables. They arrived at this figure by averaging the price of the produce at several super-markets and using that as a base. Also, the garden produce you grow is far superior in quality. A batch of fresh green beans from your own garden, cooked within minutes of picking, has flavor that cannot be matched. If you don't garden you would probably spend a great deal of time and money on more expensive recreations.

One year on a 16' x 32' garden I raised over $500 worth of very tasty vegetables. My seed cost was about $15 and I used about eight dollars worth of fertilizer and another five dollars covered the cost of insecticides. Sure, I had some hours of labor. But the good eating we had plus some frozen and canned vegetables were ample pay for the effort. I have always had fresh vegetables from the garden from early spring until almost Christmas. Following are some tips on how to do it and the better varieties to plant.

It is important to plan your garden so you can get the most from it. The chart in this chapter shows ideal spacing, planting times, varieties, and additional information. The column on the amount of crop that can be expected is average, and in a good year can be higher. Also, in a bad year they can be lower. The summer of 1982 I had nearly a total bust. My garden drowned out twice because of the excessive rains. I hadn't paid enough attention to the drainage and learned a hard lesson. Don't overplant some of the items that produce heavily. Most of us overdo the tomato planting. A single plant will produce 15 pounds or more, so if you don't plant to can or sell some, be careful. One year I raised over 150 pounds of tomatoes from five plants. You can stagger your planting to extend the season. Plant late-maturing crops between early ones. As the early ones are used up the late ones will have room to grow. Plan to replant some of the early plants for a fall garden. You know best what your family likes and needs are, so plan to provide them the best way.

Many of our areas have heavy clay ground with poor drainage. Lighter soils need treatment to retain more water. Good drainage comes first. I found out the hard way, so give it some serious thought. If water lies on the surface for very long you must do something to improve the drainage. The addition of organic material to the soil is a big help. Rotted manure, compost, green manure, or any organic matter will help. In sandy soil it is even more essential, In heavy soil sharp sand, Nitron, and gypsum will all help. Don't use fine sand. Sometimes it is even necessary to put in drain tile. This is extreme but can cure a very wet garden. Organic material and the other treatments will loosen up the clay so root vegetables will make better crops. I recall one garden I had some time ago that was heavy clay, and I failed to add enough organics to correct it. The carrots were awful short and deformed because they could not penetrate the clay. Think drainage and soil additions of organics.

Organic material will build a biological situation with literally billions of living organisms. They break down the organic material and change the elements into forms that the plants can absorb. This is an simplification of the

PLATE I

Planting Guide

Crop	Planting Date	Days to Germination	Weeks to Transplant Size	Transplant Date	Days to Harvest	Seeds per Foot	Planting Depth	Distance Between Plants	Distance Between Rows	Yield per 15 feet of row
Beans, Bush Snap	May 1-7	6-14	—	—	50-60	6-8	2"	3"- 6"	18"-30"	7 lbs.
Beans, Pole Snap	May 1-7	6-14	—	—	60-75	4-6	2"	6"- 8"	36"-40"	12 lbs.
Beans, Lima	May 1-7	7-12	—	—	60-80	5-8	2"	4"- 8"	36"	4 lbs.
Beets	March 25-30	7-10	—	—	55-65	10-15	½"	2"- 4"	18"-24"	12 lbs.
Broccoli	March 1	6-8	5-7	Apr. 10-15	60-80	—	½"	12"-18"	24"-36"	10 lbs.
Cabbage	March 1	6-8	5-7	Apr. 10-15	65-80	—	½"	10"-12"	24"-36"	40 lbs.
Carrot	April 7-15	10-12	—	—	70-80	15-20	½"	3"	18"-24"	8 lbs.
Cauliflower	March 1	6-8	5-7	Apr. 10-15	95-140	—	½"	18"-24"	36"	10 heads
Corn, Sweet	Apr. 25 - May 10	6-8	—	—	60-100	4-6	2"	14"-18"	36"	30 ears
Cucumbers	Apr. 10-15	5-8	4	May 10-15	50-60	—	½" - 1"	in hills	48"	45 lbs.
Eggplant	April 1	8-12	6-9	May 10-15	75-90	—	¼" - ½"	18"-24"	36"	40-60
Lettuce	March 15-20	6-8	—	—	45-50	8-12	¼"	2"- 4"	18"	2½ lbs.
Muskmelon	Apr. 10-15	4-8	3-4	May 10-15	75-100	—	1"	12"	48"-72"	6-10
Okra	May 1 - 7	7-14	—	—	50-60	6-8	1"	18"	24"-36"	10 lbs. per 2 wks.
Onions, Seed	March 15	7-12	—	—	50-60	10-15	½"	2"- 3"	12"-24"	10-15 bu. 15 lbs. dry
Parsnip	March 15-20	15-25	—	—	100-125	8-12	½"	3"- 4"	18"-24"	15 lbs.
Peas	March 15-20	6-15	—	—	65-85	6-7	2"	2"- 3"	18"-30"	5 lbs. per week
Peppers	April 1	10-20	6-8	May 15	65-80	—	¼"	18"-24"	24"-36"	9 lbs.
Potatoes	March 15-20	sets	—	—	70-90	1 set	4"	12"	36"	15-25 lbs.
Radishes	March 15-20	3-10	—	—	25-30	14-16	½"	2"- 3"	12"-18"	8 lbs.
Spinach	March 25-30	5-10	—	—	40-45	10-12	1½"	2"- 3"	12"-18"	4 lbs.
Squash	May 10-15	3-12	—	—	50-60	4-6	1"	16-24"	36"-60"	16 lbs.
Tomato	April 1	6-14	5-7	May 15	55-85	—	½"	24"	36"	15 lbs. per plant
Turnip	March 15-20 Early Sept.	3-10	—	—	45-65	14-16	½"	3"- 4"	12"-18"	15 lbs.
Watermelon	April 10	3-12	3-5	May 10-15	80-100	—	1"	12"-16"	60"	6-12

VEGETABLE GARDENS

process but easier to understand. Just know that the process will grow stronger plants. The use of some chemical fertilizer is also helpful, and the combination of the organic materials plus some of the chemicals makes good sense. Organic material will deplete the nitrogen in the soil in the breaking down process. It is important to add some nitrogen to make up for the loss of available nitrogen. A good balanced fertilizer is 10-10-10 and 4-10-6 at the rate or one to two pounds per 100 square feet. The phosphate is very helpful for strong roots and for flowering. The potash builds up the strength of the plants so they stand better and helps in disease resistance. A plant will only use the nitrogen or other elements when they are converted to a form that the plant can use. Whether it comes from organics or from chemicals, the useable element is the same.

Another important factor for vegetable garden soils is the pH factor or the acidity or alkalinity. Get a soil test throughout the county agent or get a simple test kit at your garden center. Most garden plants do best with a neutral soil. That means that on the pH scale between 5.5 and 7.0 is neutral. One vegetable that prefers an acid soil are potatoes. Never use lime where you are going to plant potatoes. If your soil is either way from the range of 5.5 to 7.0 it will pay to alter it. Add lime if it is too acid. Five pounds of fine ground limestone per 100 square feet will raise the pH from a half to one unit. If the soil is alkaline, add one-half pound of ground sulfur or three pounds of iron or aluminum sulfate per 100 square feet to lower the pH by a half to one unit. These should be worked into the soil to get the most benefit.

I have prepared a list of recommended vegetable varieties for the Great Plains. Most of these I have checked myself, but I have checked with the extension service for verification. If you have varieties that perform well for you in your own back yard, stick with them. Try some new ones in a small way and you may be surprised. There are times when none perform well and other times when all do well. Part of the fun of a garden is trying to grow new vegetables that you have never tried before. This list of mine is by no means fail-safe, but to the best of my experience these will do well. Gardens and other conditions vary. One tomato that was highly recommended and did well most places was a fiasco in one garden. Local variations make you experiment with different varieties until you discover the right one.

The seeding chart I have prepared is based on the area of northeast Kansas. Southeast Kansas and Oklahoma dates will be two weeks or more earlier. The last frost date for your area is the standard to go by. It takes from four to six weeks to grow the transplants, so if you figure on that basis from the frost date you will be on the money. Northwest Kansas and southern Nebraska frost free dates are two weeks later. Western and northern Nebraska. four weeks later. South Dakota, six weeks later and North Dakota, six to seven weeks later. Some of the dates for seeding outside may seem late to you, but from experience it does not pay to hurry these dates. You can plant earlier, but it will be a gamble.

The soil must be warmed to at least 65 degrees for some hot weather seeds to germinate. A soil thermometer is a good investment. Setting out tomatoes early can be done by using hot caps or some kind of protection, but you really don't gain much. The plants set out when the soil is warm will catch up and pass the earlier plants. If you want to do the extra work, go to it.

Depth of planting is very important. In early spring there is usually enough moisture for germination at the top of the soil, but when the soil gets warmer and drier it pays to plant deeper to take advantage of the moisture. Seed has to be kept moist for germination to take place. Early in the season you can plant shallower, but later the seeds must go deeper. A rule of thumb is to plant the seeds twice their diameter. On the chart you will find the depths to plant.

Spacing plants is one of the most neglected aspects of vegetable gardens. We are all too generous with seed when we plant and it is difficult to pull out the extra plants. They look so nice. But if we let them grow so close together that they have no room to develop we are just kidding ourselves. For instance, if we do not thin radishes to a two or three inch spacing, there is no room for the radishes to grow. Most of them will grow to one and one half to two inches in diameter. If they are not spaced apart there is no room for them to grow. It is simple, logical, and the right way to go at it. I know I am often remiss in doing the job right. The little plants look so nicely spaced when they are little, and I just hate to uproot healthy looking plants. By the way, it would be far better to snip off the surplus plants with a scissor. Pulling them will disturb the roots of the ones you leave. On the chart proper spacing is shown so the plants will have the room they need.

We have our garden started so now we can think of how to take care of it to get the best from it. First priority goes to watering. Nothing is more important in garden production. Water stress affects various vegetables in different ways. A cucumber under stress just stops growing but will resume when water is applied. Tomatoes, as they near harvest stage, will ripen all the fruit when put under stress. Blossom end rot of tomatoes is a result of water stress, Lettuce is shallow rooted and needs frequent watering to keep its good quality. As a rule, one inch of water a week will keep plants going well. Water deep. Shallow watering brings roots to the surface and evaporates rapidly. A good watering soaks the ground to a depth of six or eight inches. The roots will go down to the water and be a great deal stronger. The new drip systems are fine. It will pay you to look into them. They conserve water by putting it where it will do the most good. Each garden has its own problems and experience will show you how to win out.

Watering brings up an important point. **MULCH** - mulching pays off in several ways. It conserves moisture, keeps weeds down, and protects crop from the soil. There are many mulches that can be used. Straw, prairie hay, wood chips, rotted sawdust, peat, compost, dry manure, and newspaper are all good organic mulches. If you use any of them, add some nitrogen to help in the decomposition. Two or three pounds of 4-10-6 per 100 square feet will help. Dark-colored mulches absorb heat and warm up the soil better in the spring. I do not like to apply any mulch until the soil has warmed to 70 degrees or so. Light-colored straw will keep the ground cool in summer. Clean straw and prairie hay are good summer mulches. They should be four to six inches deep in the aisles between the rows and lighter up around the plants.

Ground corn cobs are a dandy mulch if you can get them. The use of combines has made them hard to come by. Newspapers are fine for between the rows. Four or five layers of newspaper laid on the soil with a bit of dirt thrown on them to stop them from blowing about. It holds moisture well and keeps down weeds. It can be tilled into the soil in fall and has organic content. There are shredders on the market now that chew up the paper so it can be used around the plants much better. Do mulch.

If you don't mulch, you must cultivate. You can cut off the weeds and loosen the surface for better water penetration and air circulation. Always cultivate shallowly. Most vegetable roots are fairly shallow so deep hoeing can cut off some of the feeder roots. I like to use a scuffle hoe or any light sharp hoe that will pull naturally at a shallow depth.

A word about chemical weed controls. Use carefully. Follow directions very closely. There is no single material that will control all the weeds in a garden. Treflan and dachtal are most commonly used. They control grasses well but not all the broadleaf weeds. They must be applied to clean ground because they do not hurt weeds that are growing. It is really better to use mulches or to cultivate.

One reason I like to start some of my own seeds is because I can be sure to have some varieties I want. Commercial growers do not always have the newer selections. The same procedure I outlined in the flower chapter holds true for the vegetable plants. Most vegetable seeds are easier to grow then the flowers. Use the sterile soil mix for best results. Melons, cucumbers and squash are very easy. Plant two or three seeds of each in individual pots. When the seeds have germinated and have their first true leaves, take a scissors and snip off the weaker plants, leaving a single strong one. Snip the unwanted plants and don't try to pull them. The roots of the one remaining are not disturbed, so will be stronger when set out. Be sure to put started plants where there is adequate light and cooler temperatures. This makes much stronger plants.

In your garden layout you should have the location of each variety well thought out. In the chart I show the distance betweens rows. This is based on the used of mechanical equipment for cultivation. In my own garden, because of lack of space, I plant my rows much closer. Even this has to depend on the size of the mature plant. I plant radishes, carrots, beets, lettuce, and other small early crops only 12 inches apart. I can still do a good job of cultivating with a hoe, and I get a lot more varieties in the garden. Tomatoes, okra, corn, and larger crops have to be spaced farther apart. One idea that I have tried and liked was that instead of making furrows on the level, I mound up the loose soil into a ridge four to six inches wide and three to four inches higher than the regular ground level. I then scatter the seeds along the mound instead of in a row. This way I get more plants in each row, and by raising it I get better drainage which my garden needs. The only problem that I have found with the idea is that you must be careful to see that the mound does not dry out. Some extra watering is necessary. This is especially true in the germination period and when the plants are small.

A few notes on some of the vegetables you will want to use. Beans, especially snap beans, are one of the best crops

PLATE I

you can grow. You will get a bigger return for your effort than with most other plants. Dry beans are a good crop particularly in the north. Lima beans have always been hard for me to grow, but you may find them doing well for you. My wife is very fond of Kentucky Wonders so we try to grow some. They have great flavor. There is a new bush type on the market that doesn't take up as much room, has the good flavor, and is easier to grow. In the north be sure to plant early maturing varieties.

Beets are a good crop as they have a double purpose. When you thin them, the small beets with the tops make a tasty dish. Broccoli is one of my favorites. They are comparatively easy to grow. Cut the heads before the buds start to open. They will put out side shoots with smaller but good heads. Cabbage is a favorite with everyone. Plant a selection of varieties that mature at intervals so that you won't have a glut. If you are going to make kraut, it would be right to have enough that mature at the same time to

PLATE II

Courtesy Burpee Seeds

make the kraut. About the only problem with cabbage and other cole crops are the cabbage worms. They are easy to control with bacillus thuringensen that is sold as Dipel or Thuricide. It is a biological control that is quite safe to use.

PLATE III

Carrots are good if you have loose well-drained soil. In hard clay they get twisted and dwarfed. Be sure your soil is right if you are going to attempt them. Sweet corn is a favorite crop, but it occupies considerable room in a small garden. If you have the space it is a fine crop, and I sure love to eat fresh sweet corn right from the garden. There are many new varieties now that mature early and are very sweet. Fresh picked sweet corn is in a class by itself, and if I had the room I would surely grow some.

Cucumbers are one of my favorite vegetables and there have been some improvements in them. The newer sorts are not as sprawling but more a bush type and do not need so much room in the yard. They are a warm season crop, so plant them after all danger of frost is over. Some of the new ones have a tender skin and excellent flavor. Many of the fruits run 10 to 12 inches long. There are also new varieties developed specifically for pickles that are smaller, although they can be eaten fresh as well. Keep the cucumbers picked so the plants will constantly bear. Wilt is a problem that is spread by the cucumber beetle. Control the beetle and you will have no problem. I spray weekly with diazinon, making sure to get up under the foliage. It does the job and is a fairly safe insecticide to use.

PLATE IV

Make successive plantings of bunching onions to insure a continuous supply.

Lettuce is one of the easiest vegetables to grow. You can raise either looseleaf or semi-head plants in our area. The easiest to grow is the looseleaf, and there are a number of good ones to try. I like the Bibb type or semi-head lettuce the best of all. Start the plants inside early and transplant to the garden early since lettuce can tolerate low temperatures. Buttercrunch is a favorite and make a tasty dish fresh from the garden with a home-made dressing. Onions are essential in the garden. They can be grown from seed, sets, or plants. The sets make green onions fast. Always get your sets and plants in early since they like cool weather. Seeds take longer to produce results, but you can have a wider selection. Plants of Sweet Spanish and Bermudas make the best large onions. I plant fairly close and thin out using the pulled plants for green onions. The large onions need four or five inches space for room to mature.

Peas are a cool-season crop. Plant peas in northeast Kansas about the last week of February so the plants can produce before hot weather. The seeds will germinate in cold ground. Soak the seeds overnight before planting for a faster start. The new edible pod peas such as Sugar Snap are a great thrill. You can eat pods and all for a delicious dish. There are some new selections that are bush form and don't take us as much room as the climbers. They do a good job.

PLATE V

Courtesy Burpee Seeds

PLATE VI

PLATE VII

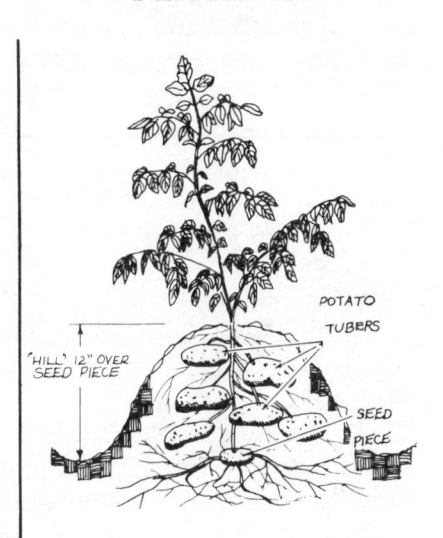

Peppers come in a wide variety of shapes and glossy colors, from the large, blocky sweet Bell peppers to the long tapered form of cayenne peppers.

Either sweet or hot peppers are a hot weather crop. They cannot be set out until the ground temperature is 60 to 65 degrees and all danger of frost is past. Big fat bell type sweet peppers have a taste all their own. I like them fresh in salads and I dearly loved stuffed peppers. Hot peppers are a bit easier to grow, and if you like them there are many different choices.

Potatoes are a good crop if you have a large enough garden. They take room, but new potatoes are a real delicacy. They like an acid soil so if your ground is alkaline you may have to amend the soil by increasing the acidity. It is possible to raise potatoes by setting the seed pieces on the surface of the soil and covering them with a foot or more of clean straw. As the straw settles down from the rains add straw to keep the potatoes covered. The potatoes will develop in the straw, are easy to harvest, and will be clean. Be sure to get one of the varieties suitable to your area.

VEGETABLE GARDENS

Radishes are hardy, easy to grow, and quick to mature. You can be eating them four weeks after planting. They like cool weather and will get pungent as the weather gets hot. I make successive plantings every 10 days for a longer season.

PLATE VIII

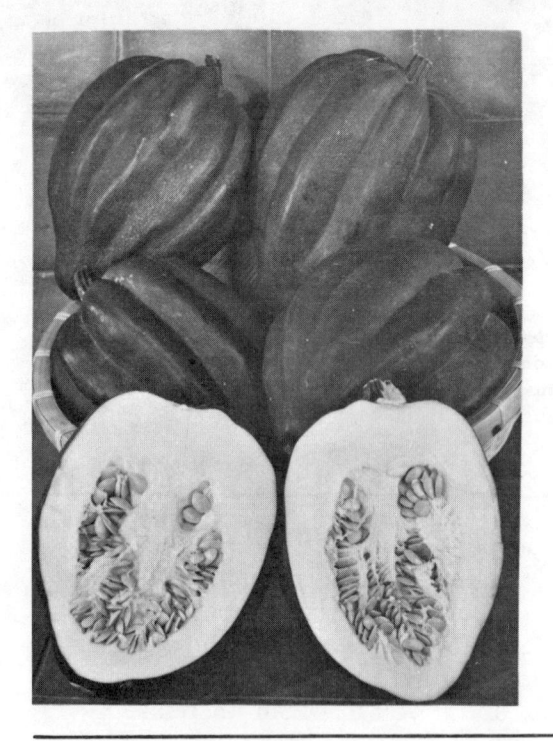

Courtesy Burpee Seeds

Both summer and winter squash make a very good crop. the winter types are Acorn, Butternut, and Hubbard. They have hard skins and will keep well for winter use. The most popular summer squash is zucchini. The skin is soft, and they can be eaten raw in salads if picked when six or eight inches long. I am very fond of them sliced and sauteed in butter. They come mostly in green colors, but there is a yellow one that is good. There are bush types now that are excellent for small gardens. They don't require much rooms, and if you keep them picked they will supply you with a spate of fruit. Don't plant too many or you will be flooded with more than you can handle. Squash borers and beetles are in the main problem to keep under control. I have found that a weekly spraying of diazinon will keep them at bay. The beetles spread the wilt that is a killer. Control the beetles and you are home free.

PLATE IX

VARIETY	F Aristocrat	F Ball's Zucchini	F Early Butternut	F Goldbar	F Sundance	F Table Ace	F Scallopini	F Gold Rush
SHAPE								
LENGTH	6-7"	7-8"	9-11"	6"	6½-7"	5"	1"	7-8"
TYPE	Summer	Summer	Winter	Summer	Summer	Winter	Summer	Summer
MATURITY	52 days	50 days	85 days	50 days	50 days	70 days	50 days	52 days

Tomatoes are everyone's number one crop. They are very easy to grow and produce great quantities of fruit. There are so many uses for them either fresh, cooked, juiced, or canned that they are more widely grown than any other vegetable. There are so many different varieties and forms that it would take a whole book to detail them. We have early, mid-season, and late producers. We have tiny ones and large ones. Some can be grown in pots while others will grow forever all over a garden. It is smart to stick with hybrids that have more disease resistance and bear heavily. In the northern parts of the Plains it would be better to stick with early producers. Your local center or greenhouse is likely to have the varieties that do best in your area. Check with the extension service for good sorts. Tomatoes are a hot weather crop and like peppers should not be set out until the soil is warm and all danger of frost is past. You can set them out early if you want to protect them from the cold, but you don't gain enough for the extra effort. Tomato crops should be rotated around the garden to avoid a buildup of disease in the soil.

I like to stake up tomatoes or ring them so they don't sprawl on the ground. It is my belief that they produce better fruit this way even though they may produce heavier on the ground. And it is so much easier to pick them.

VEGETABLE GARDENS

PLATE X

PLATE XI

Hybrid Tomato Guides

HYBRID TOMATOES—MOST POPULAR GARDEN VEGETABLE
BRED ESPECIALLY FOR DISEASE RESISTANCE, HIGHER YIELDS AND BIGGER SIZE

VARIETY	Sweet 100	Early Girl	The Juice	Sunripe	Floramerica	Golden Boy	Pink Panther	Super Fantastic	Champion"	LaRoma (Roma Hybrid)	Better Boy	Beefmaster
SIZE	1"	4-6 oz	6-8 oz	8-10 oz	8-10 oz	8-10 oz	8-10 oz	9-12 oz	10 oz	4 oz	10-14 oz	Over 12 oz
GROWTH	Indeterminate (Pole)	Indeterminate (Pole)	Determinate (Bush)	Determinate (Bush)	Determinate (Bush)	Indeterminate (Pole)	Indeterminate (Pole)	Indeterminate (Pole)	Indeterminate (Pole)	Determinate (Bush)	Indeterminate (Pole)	Indeterminate (Pole)
MATURITY (DAYS)	65	52	65	75	75	80	70	70	62	62	70	80
DISEASE TOLERANCE	—	V	VF	VFN	VF	—	F	VFN	VFNT	VF	VFN	VFN
NOTES	Extremely sweet	Earliest yet. Smooth. Good flavor. A Ball Exclusive	Bred especially for juice. Smooth. Good taste. A Ball Exclusive	Widely adapted. Good taste. Tolerant to blossom-end rot.	Widely adapted. Grow in cages or on short stakes.	Golden yellow fruit. Very mild flavor. Only hybrid yellow.	Pink fruited. Crack-tolerant. Smooth. A Ball Exclusive.	High yields. Good flavor. Continuous cropping. A Ball Exclusive.	Large fruited. Medium-early tomato with good disease resistance. A Ball Exclusive.	Heavy yielding Italian-type tomato. A Ball Exclusive.	Most popular. Excellent flavor. Smooth. Grow on stakes or sprawled.	Beefsteak type. Rough. Good flavor. Tolerant of cracking or splitting.

HYBRID TOMATO—MOST POPULAR GARDEN VEGETABLE!

VARIETY	Sweet 100	Small Fry	Early Cascade	Patio	Sunripe	Floramerica	The Juice	Early Girl	Golden Boy	Pink Panther	Super Fantastic	Better Boy	Beefmaster
SHAPE													
SIZE	1"	1"	3-4 oz	4-5 oz	8-10 oz	8-12 oz	6-8 oz	4-6 oz	8-10 oz	8-10 oz	8-10 oz	10-14 oz	Over 12 oz
GROWTH	Indeterminate	Determinate	Indeterminate	Determinate	Determinate	Determinate	Determinate	Indeterminate	Indeterminate	Indeterminate	Indeterminate	Indeterminate	Indeterminate
MATURITY	65 days	65 days	55 days	70 days	75 days	75 days	65 days	52 days	80 days	70 days	70 days	70 days	80 days
DISEASE TOLERANCE	None	VFN	VF	F	VFN	VF	VF	V	None	F	VFN	VFN	VFN
NOTES	Extremely sweet! 6-8 ft. tall	Cherry type. Good flavor. Grow in container	Clusters of 7-9 fruits. Tolerant to promoted	24-30 in. tall. Containers or small gardens.	Widely adapted. Good taste. Tolerant to blossom-end rot	78 AAS winner. Widely adapted. Grow in cages or on short stakes	Bred especially for juice. No staking	Earliest yet. Smooth. Good flavor	Golden-yellow fruit. Very mild flavor. Only hybrid yellow	Pink fruited. Crack tolerant. Smooth	High yields. Good flavor. Continuous cropping	Most popular. Excellent flavor. Smooth. Grow on stakes or sprawled	Beefsteak type. Rough good flavor. Tolerant of cracking or splitting

Credit Ball Seed Co.

Tomatoes must be watered regularly to produce best. They respond well to a good mulch. The last couple of years I have had good results with the Judd Ringer System. This is a six-sided wire frame that is filled with compost and the tomatoes planted around the outside of the frame. Water once a week. I let the hose run for 15 or 20 minutes inside the frame on the compost. The nutrients run down and spread out to the plants. One year I raised 150 pounds of tomatoes from five plants. Try it and from this one frame you can raise enough tomatoes to supply a large family. Your dealer will have information about this system.

These are a few notes on some of the most commonly grown vegetables and one that most of us will grow. There are many more you may grow or want to try. That is part of the fun in gardening. The following lists have information that will help you. The varieties named are ones that I found to be good. A few are on the recommendation of the extension service. Each year will see more varieties, and they will be worth a try. Don't be afraid to experiment, but don't go too strong. Stick with the varieties that do well until you find a better one.

CHART A
Good Vegetables for the Great Plains

Asparagus - Martha Washington - Waltham
Beans, Snap - Toperop - Buch Blue Lake
Beans, Wax - Pencil pod. - Goldcrop
Beans, Pole - Kentucky Wonder - Blue Lake
Beans, Limas - Ford Hook - difficult
Beets - Detroit Dark Red - Early Wonder
Brocoli - Green Bud - Green Comet - Green Goliath
Cabbage, Early - Machel Prize Hybrid - Marchel Topper - Golden Acre - Red Acre
Cabbage, Mid-season - Stonebead - Marion Machel - Flat Dutch
Carrots - Scarlet Nautes - Redcored Chanteway - Waltham Hi-color
Cauliflower - Snowball
Sweet Corn, Early - Marcross Nothern Belle - Hytime
Sweet Corn, Mid-season - Gold Dup - Gold Eagle - Midway - Kandy Corn
Sweet Corn, Late - Loyal Gold - Jochief - Golden Cross Banctam - Illini Extra Sweet
Sweet Corn, White - Silver Queen - Country Gentleman
Cucumbers, Slice - Burpee Hybird - Poinrett - Hybird Sweerap
Cucumbers, Pickling - SMR 58 - Earli - Pih - Pioneer - Brava - Spartun Dawn
Cucumbers, Bush - Patio Pik - Spacemaster - Streamlines
Egg Plant - Black Magic Hybird - Black Beauty
Lettuce, Leaf - Salad Bowl - Ruby - Bibb - Grand Rapids - Oah leaf - Cheat resistant
Lettuce, Head - Ithica - Butter Crunch - Great Lakes (Fall)
Muchmelons - Burpee Hybird - Super mashed hybird - Harvest Queen - Triqirois - PMR 45
Honey Dew Melons
Mustard - Southern Curled - Green Wave
Okra - Dwarf Green - Emerald - Clemson Spinelers
Omons - Yellow & White Sweet Spanich - Red Hamburger - Bermuda - Walla Walla
Parsnips - Hollow Crown

118 IN YOUR OWN BACK YARD

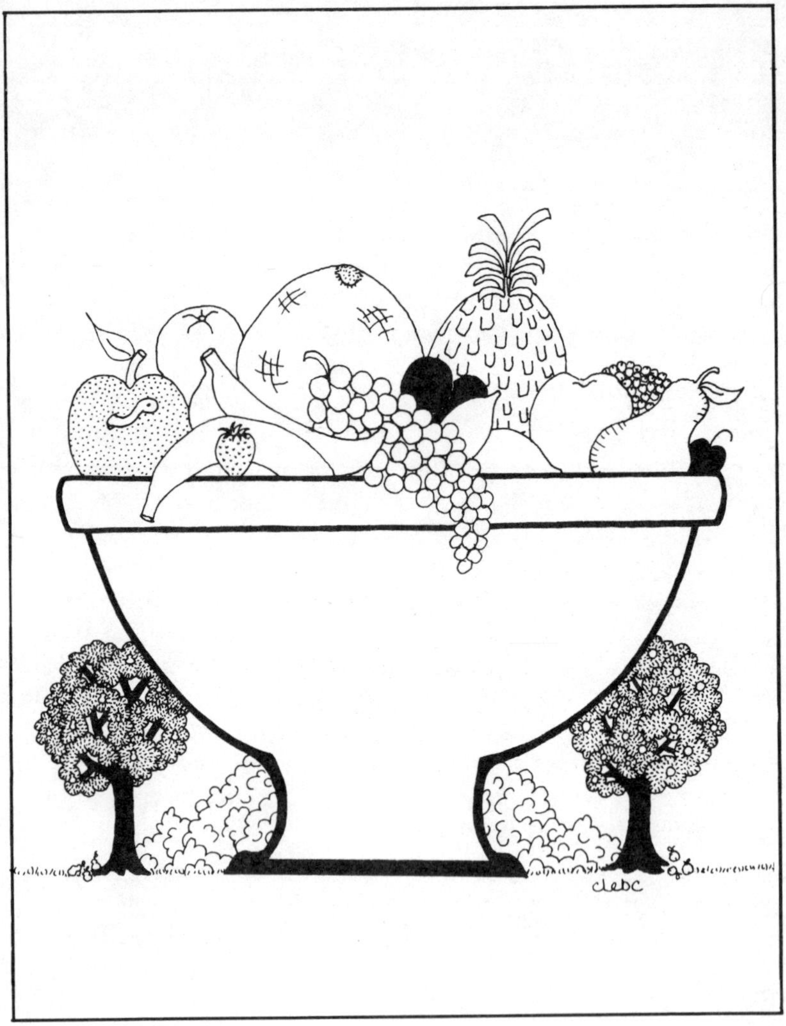
clebc

9
Home Grown Fruits

The most neglected item in our home food production is the raising of fruits and berries. There has been little done to stimulate the use of them. It is true **that** the production of fruits and berries is a bit more difficult than vegetables, but the difficulties are not hard to overcome if you may pay attention to some of the basics. One of their benefits is that once you have them producing, they will go on for years. Fruits and berries are nutritous, but it is even more important to enjoy the delightful flavor of tree-ripened fresh fruit and berries. Can you think of a better taste than that of a fresh picked, sunripened peach? Or the taste of a fresh crisp apple right from the tree.

As a boy in New England I liked to go out in the old orchard with a book and lie under the Red Astraken tree eating apples right from the tree. They were a delightful crisp summer apple that is hard to find today. When I was a lad the tree was over fifty years old and still produced bushels of apples. I imagine that they were passed up because they were not good keepers. It remains as one of my great childhood memories.

To have fruit in your yard you must have some patience. Most fruit trees need from two to eight years to get established before you get good crops. Dwarf types bear sooner, usually in two years. If your yard is small the best bet is a dwarf. You can get them in a much smaller space. I have often used dwarf fruit trees, usually apples, in a landscape plan. Many of them are very beautiful in bloom and you have the added feature of the fruit. I have used cherries, peaches, and pears as border line accents points, shade for a patio and a corner planting. The semi-dwarf trees grow over 14 to 18 feet tall and are good for both

PLATE I

Courtesy Burpee Seeds

production and for landscape purposes. If you have a very limited space the real dwarf that grows from six to 14 feet is very good. A big yard can use standard trees. They are excellent shade trees in addition to the beauty of the blossoms and the fruit.

The different climatic conditions of the Great Plains make it essential to take pains selecting the varieties you plant. Peaches do not grow well from southern Nebraska north. Pears, with a few exceptions, are the same. There are some varieties that are much better adapted to northern areas. If you are in an area where hardiness is questionable, the location of the planting can make a difference. Trees planted on a slope can often escape late spring frost that could kill the blossoms. Hill tops and low valleys are most apt to give trouble. A north-facing slope is preferred as the buds will not swell as early. Partially swelled buds are hurt the most. I recall one year when the south sides of apple trees had no fruit but the north sides bore a normal crop. The reason for this was a warm spell in February, and the buds on the south side began to swell while the north side buds were still tight. A late frost caught the buds on the south that were swollen while the tighter buds on the north were not injured. It pays to be careful where you plant.

Work the ground up with organic material added to it. Most trees need good drainage so be sure to check this. Fruit trees can be planted in either spring or fall, but I prefer spring planting. I feel that this allows the tree to get well established before cold weather. Fall planting can gain a year on fruit production if you are fortunate enough to have a mild winter and keep the tree well watered. Most fruit trees will be bare root when you get them. They are packed in a material to keep the roots damp. The first step when you remove them from the pack is to prune off any broken roots or any that are going in the wrong direction. Roots growing in a circle around the plant can strangle the tree when grown. Prune off any broken limbs and cut back all but the leader about one third. Place the roots in a bucket of muddy water for a few hours until you have the hole ready. Never let the roots dry out.

Make the hole deep enough to set a standard tree two inches deeper than it grew in the nursery, with the bud union or the graft two inches below the surface. On dwarf trees the bud union must remain above the soil level so the top will not take root and defeat the dwarf. Put two or three inches of topsoil and organic material in the bottom of the hole to set the bud union at the proper depth. Keep the tree as straight as possible. With dwarf trees a stake will help. Dwarf trees roots are shallow so extra support is necessary. Fill the hole about two-thirds with the topsoil mix and tamp it down. Pour a bucket of water into the hole to settle the soil. I use Rapid-gro or Miracle-gro in the initial bucket of water because it will get the tree off to a better start. After the water has drained away, finish filling the hole. Make a saucer-like depression around the tree to catch the rain.

Strip the sod from the ground around the tree for about two feet. This does away with the competition from the weeds and grass. A mulch will help keep the soil moist and also hold back weeds. Keep the tree well watered the first year or two until the roots get well established. It is not necessary to fertilize the first year, but from the second year on an annual fertilization makes good growth. Use one of the fruit tree fertilizers that are on the market.

All fruit trees will benefit from pruning practices. The extension service has some excellent bulletins that give you step-by-step procedure. The general purpose of proper pruning is to make a healthier, more productive tree. Thinning to allow air and sunlight to reach the center of the plant is the most important step. The removal of diseased limbs or those that will cross others and cause rubbing is good maintenance. The water sprouts and suckers should be removed. They take a lot of nutrition from the tree that can be better used in the production of fruit. Narrow forks should be corrected. The best angle for side branches is 45 degrees or flatter. These have more strength than the narrow forks eliminating the chance of splitting. It will often pay to use spreaders to force some of the branches to a better angle. This is all detailed in the extension bulletins.

Timing is important. Apple trees can be pruned when the foliage has dropped and the tree is dormant. A good warm day in winter gives you a chance to get outdoors and perform a worthwhile chore. Pear trees need less pruning, mostly the removal of diseased or crossing limbs and suckers. Peach and nectarine should be pruned after the danger of frost or any severe freeze is past. Mid-March to early April would be about right for our area. Cherries and plums are pruned in late winter or early spring. Apricots respond better if pruned after blooming as the blooms are often hit by a late frost.

A regular spray program will supply you with much better fruit. The first, and I think, the most important spray is the dormant spray. This is applied before the buds start to open and the tree is semi-dormant. Lime-sulfur with a miscible oil produces good results. This clears out most of the over-wintering insects and disease spores. It is important to thoroughly drench the plant and the soil around it. Spray on a day when the temperature is about 45 degrees and there is no freeze predicted for 24 hours. You can get a spray schedule for your area from the dealer or from extension. Timing varies with different climatic areas. For a home fruit grower the prepared home orchard sprays at the garden centers are very useful. There is no bothering to mix various chemicals as they have to right combinations for your plant. It is less expensive, too, if you have only a few trees. Cover the foliage and the limbs thoroughly when you spray. A hose-end sprayer will do a good job on small trees, but the larger trees a trombone type sprayer will reach higher. If you have many trees it will pay to buy a power sprayer. If you have tractor there are some good P.T.O. pumps that will do a good job. Consult your local folks for the best timing.

 Strawberries are very popular home fruits. I cannot think of a more delightful treat then fresh picked strawberries in a shortcake with rich cream. Oh, those calories! But, oh, that delicious flavor. If you have room in your yard they are one of our better crops. They are short-lived perennials but will produced for four or five years and by allowing the runners to root in can be renewed easily. Although there are June-bearers and everbearers, the June bearers seem to have more flavor. There is a new strawberry on the market now that I believe has a great future. It is the Sweetheart stawberry that is grown from seed. Seeds started inside in February and transplanted outside in April will be bearing ripe berries by late July. They will keep bearing until frost stops them. They are perennial and with normal treatment will keep going for years. They will bear better if the runner production is restricted. Sweetheart may be better used as an annual started fresh every year or every other year.

 Of course, there are many good berries in use that you can obtain easily. There is one adapted to each area. If you start with plants it is advisable to pinch off the blooms the first year and not pick any fruit until the second year. Strawberries do best in a highly organic soil made by mixing compost or manure into the soil. Good drainage is most important. Raised beds are a big help with drainage. Do not plant where tomatoes, potatoes, okra, melons, and egg plants have been grown. Disease organisms can be left in the soil. Stay away from freshly tilled sod unless you treat for grubs.

 Depth of planting is important. Only about half of the

crown should be covered. Water in each plant with a cupful of liquid fertilizer such as Rapid-gro or Miracle-gro at half strength.

Space plants 12 to 18 inches apart in both directions with each bed about two feet wide and raised six inches above the garden level. Keep runners cut back the first year and pinch back the blossoms for better production the second year.

The second year allow about six runners per plant to grow. Allow them to grow into the area between the rows so the old plants can be removed, and the runners will set up a new bed. The plants from the runners will produce the next year.

In the fall to renovate old beds, especially if weedy. mow off the older plants and weeds with the mower set high enough that it will clear the crowns. Where the plants from a solid mat, spade, hoe, or till an open area between rows to form renewed beds. Make an application of 10-10-10 fertilizer in late summer. Three or four pounds over 1000 square feet of bed is the right rate. Wash the fertilizer from the foliage. Remove weeds by pulling or hoeing. In the spring apply Dachtal or Treflan to the clean soil to control weeds. A second application is needed in about six weeks. Irrigate to supplement rainfall so the berries get one inch of water per week.

Mulch the bed with clean straw or prairie hay three to four inches thick when night temperatures fall below 20 degrees. The purpose of the mulch is to stop the alternate freezing and thawing that will heave the plant roots out of the ground. Uncover in the spring when new growth starts to show. Do this gradually as the plants green up. Leave enough mulch under the plants to keep the fruit from resting on the soil. It makes much cleaner and tastier berries.

Grapes are one of the oldest of cultural fruits and are used for wines, jellies and just good table eating. You have to consider local conditions when selecting varieties. Some are not winter hardy, especially in the northern Plains. Most of the French grapes are not hardy, but the American varieties are much tougher. The hardiest grapes for the north are Edelweiss, Beta, and Swenson Red. Most of the others are hardy from Zone 5 on south. Muscadine are southern grapes and do best from Zone 7 on the south. Talk to your local experts for the best advice.

Grapes do best in sandy, high organic soils made by adding compost and rotted manure. Heavy clay soil must be modified with organics for best results. Plant two year old plants in early spring. It takes several years to reach full production but they do bear some in two or three years. Plants should be spaced about eight feet apart. I think the easiest method for the home gardener is to train them to wires. The first wire is set about three and one-half feet above the ground and the second two feet above that. The first year after planting, cut back to two buds, and they will sprout laterals or side branches. Cut off the weaker ones and tie the stronger one to the stake holding the wire. The next spring tie the vine to the wires and cut off the tip three inches above the top wire. The third spring tie four laterals to the wires and then prune to five or six buds each. Cut the other canes away. Leave a spur under the laterals to sprout some renewal canes for the next year. The detail sketch details this method.

The brambles or cane fruits have some of the most delicious berries. The thorniness of most of them discourages many people from growing them. If they are pruned and thinned properly they are not so bad. Raspberries, blackberries, gooseberries, and currants will be considered in this group. Raspberries come in both red and black. I personally like the taste of the red raspberries, but the blacks are tasty too. Both are succulent and delicate when allowed to ripen on the plant. You will seldom see them in the market as they are hard to ship and the ones they do have are drier and not as tasty. Check with your local garden shops for the right variety for your area.

You don't need a large garden to grow raspberries as they do not take up much room if handled correctly. The easiest method is the hedge row system. Set the plants about two feet apart after working the soil deeply adding some slow release fertilizer. Prune the plants to eight to 12 inches from the ground. Cultivate as shallow as possible to avoid cutting off roots and suckers. After the first year cut off all but four or five of the best canes. Canes should be kept four to five feet tall. Setting stakes and running wires on either side of the canes will give them enough support for easier picking and management. Buy virus free stocks in all brambles. Blackberries are planted three feet apart and treated the same as raspberries, except that they should be headed back in late June or early July. This is done to force side branching and to increase the crop. Canes only fruit one year so the canes that have borne bruit should be cut to the ground. New shoots will replace them.

Gooseberries and currants are closely related and need the same culture. Both plants are hosts of the white pine blister rust so check to see if they are banned in your area. If there are white pines in your vicinity they should not be grown. They like some filtered shade most of the day, but an hour or two of direct sun morning and evening will be fine. They are heavy feeders so use compost or rotted manure in preparing the soil. Fertilize each year after they have had fruit. Space them four feet apart. Trim out weak canes in May. They do best in clay loam soil. The best varieties are listed on the table at the end of the chapter.

Stone fruits are short-lived. Peaches, plums, apricots, and cherries do not last long but are great eating. Most of them have landscape value as well as for fruit. Peaches cannot be grown very well north of southern Nebraska except for a few hardy selections. Even in northern Kansas I had an old time orchardist tell me that he got a crop of peaches about one year out of five as late frosts killed the blooms. Apricots have the same problem. They bloom very early and the flowers get nipped. There are some hardy sorts that will do fairly well. Sweet cherries are less hardy than the sour varieties. Bush cherries are very hardy and will grow farther north than the tree types. Hansen's Improved is a good one. You need two plants to get pollination. The fruit is tart and good for pies and jellies. There are some hardy plums that will do well far to the north. In fact, there are plums that will grow in every state.

All the stone fruits like a soil well mixed with organic material and have to have good drainage. Most should be planted on a slope, preferably north facing, to help avoid frost damage in the spring. If the foliage shows some yellow and doesn't have good dark green color, fertilize with some 10-10-10 scattered on the ground around the plant. Pruning of stone fruits is largely thinning out in the center of the plants, removing sucker growth and any diseased or broken branches.

All these home-grown fruits need a regular spray program for the best fruit. A dormant spray in early spring followed by a regular program of a home orchard spray. Your local dealer and extension agent can help you with a program. The extension service has some fine bulletins with all the necessary timing. If you want high quality fruit, do carry on a good program.

The following tables will be of assistance in making good selections for your area but I caution you to check with local experts to be sure the selection is correct.

CHART A
Fruit Varieties

Apples	Summer Apples - Red June - Lodi - Anoka - Red Duchess Fall Apples - Wealthy - Red Baron - McIntosh - Cortland Winter Apples - Johathan - Haralson - Honey gold - Red Delicious - Golden Delicious - Fireside - Granny Smith
Pears	Hardy Pears - Lincoln - Douglas Regular Season - Kieffer - Bartlett - Magness - Seckel
Cherries	Hardy Sour - North Star - Metcor - Montmorency Sweet - Zone 5-7 - Black Tartarian - Lambert - Napoleon Bush - Hansen's Improved - Black Beauty
Plums	Hardy - Sapa - Kaga - South Dakota Regular - Stanley Prune - Waneta - Green Gage
Peaches	Best South of South Dakota - Reliance Hardiest - can stand 24° below. Zones 5-8 - Halehaven - Redhaven - Sunhaven - Sunapee
Apricot	Moorpark - Early Golden - Moongold - Sungold - Scout
Strawberries	June Bearers - Cyclone - Dunlap - Trumpeter Everbearers - Ogallala - Superfection - Ozark Beauty
Raspberries	Red - Latham - Heritage - Fall Red - Indian Summer (everbearer) Black - Cumberland - Black Hawk - John Robertson
Blackberries	Darrow - Eldorado - Ebony King
Gooseberries	Pixwell - Wilcome - Poorman
Currants	Red Lake - Wilder - Perfection
Grapes	Concord - Himrod - Fredonia - Steuben - Niagra - Beta - Edelweiss - Swenson Red - Van Buren

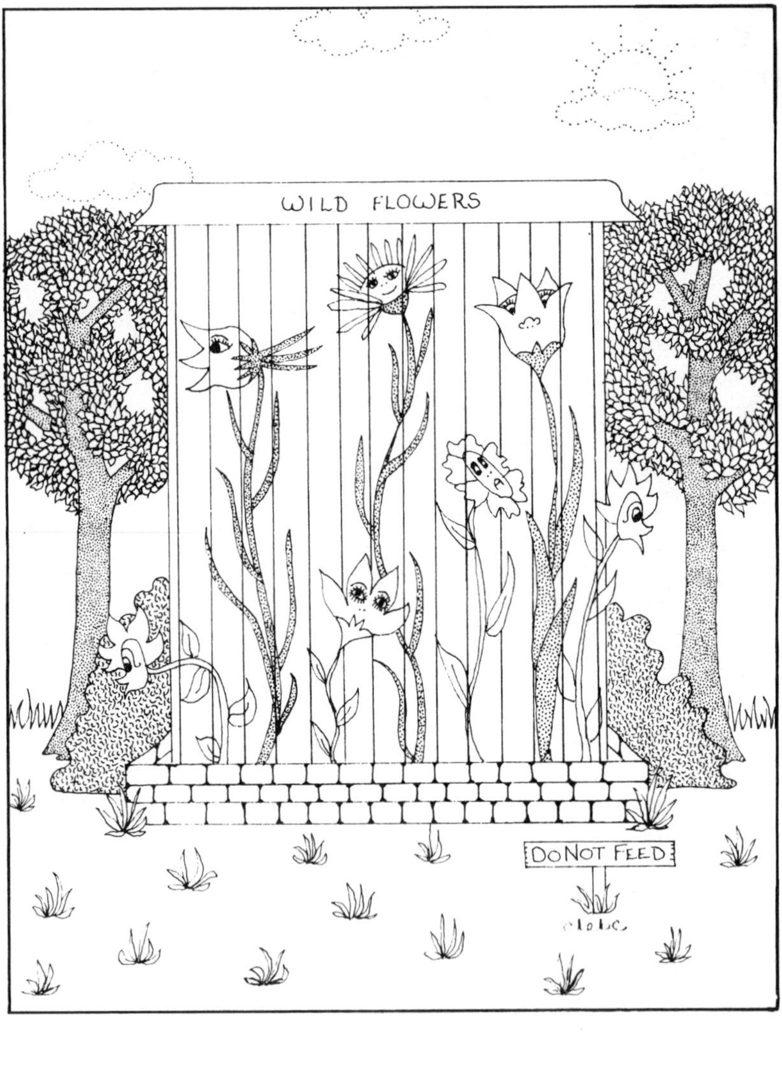
WILD FLOWERS
DO NOT FEED

10
Wildflowers

Remember when you were young, walking along a country lane on a summer day, with all the beautiful flowers growing in the ditches and in the fence rows? Butterfly weed, Queen Anne's lace, and goldenrod? In damp spot, violets, cardinal flower, and lobelia? It was as pretty, if not more so, than any formal garden. There is a great resurgence of interest all over the country in wildflowers. If the idea seems strange to you, consider the fact that very few man-made gardens can compare to the beauty of a field of wildflowers in bloom. Most wildflowers have the built-in advantage of being better suited to the local conditions of climate and soil. For centuries they have adapted to local conditions and are better able to cope with weather extremes such as drought and extreme cold. Consider planting a wildflower garden in your yard. Once started, they require minimum maintainance and reward you with great beauty.

To have a good wildflower garden you must make an environment similar to the native habitat. There are five major habitats, but we are concerned mainly with two of them and in spots a third. Prairie environment covers most of the area, but in the eastern and western sides of the area there is considerable woodland environment and there are pockets of wetlands everywhere. Prairie wildflowers grow mostly in full sun on rich soil. These flowers are sturdy because they compete with the tough prairie grasses, hot dry summers, and cold winters. Because of the value of the farmlands on the prairie a great many areas are bare of wildflowers, although you will find them along old roads, tucked in corners of farmlands and in pastures. If you live on prairie ground you can grow many of the prairie flowers with a small amount of effort.

The flowers of the deciduous forest will grow any place where there has been timber even though it is gone. We have many former woodland areas scattered through the area. The soil will be more acid and the drainage is usually good. Any woodland flowers will do well in these spots. Many farms and town yards have boggy spots where it is possible to grow wetland plants. It is possible to look at the possibilities in one's own ground when deciding what to plant. Thee are over 15,000 flowering plant species growing wild in the United States, but only about 6000 are favored by wildflowers growers. Many are considered weeds but are so pretty that they can be grown as flowers. Some of our wildflowers are strays from old cultivated planting. Queen Anne's lace and day lilies are good examples. Others are mustard, sorrell, chicory, purslane, plantain, and peppermint. Yarrow is a delightful escapee while the dandelion is detested. Ox-eye daisy and orange hawkweed are attractive but very difficult to remove from a good lawn.

Don't try to go too far in planning your wildflower garden. Start easy and work up. Get some of the most adaptable and easiest to start and plant them in with your other plants for a start. They work well in a perennial bed. Be sure they are compatible to the environment. If you have a boggy, badly drained spot it is not too hard to start a bog garden. If you have a shady area partially enclosed by shrubs and trees, try some of the forest plants. It will take some patience as many wildflowers are slow to develop but last for years when established. This is true especially when you start from seeds. It is easier to get plants to start with. The prairie flowers, although tough, can use some protection from strong southwest wind. If you are going to use some shrubs or trees in your plans, fit them into the plan as naturally as possible with an eye to giving the flowers some protection. Beware of heavy foot traffic. Most wildflowers will not do well on compacted soil but need loose well-drained soil. Layout paths if needed, and use some stepping stones or a gravel base for trails in your wildflowers. It is possible to have a long season of color by good planning. In an open space start out for spring with blue-eyed grass, violets, columbine, May apple, and Virginia bluebell. Bee-balm, yarrow, butterfly weed, and wild lupines bloom in summer. Joe Pye weed, goldenrod, asters, and turtlehead carry on in fall. Pick what you want and try to achieve a long blooming season.

Soil is the important thing with wildflowers, as it is with all gardening. Wildflowers need a stable growing medium, and the requirements vary with the type of garden. Wildflower soil needs to be very porous. Prairie flowers will thrive in soil very like your regular garden soil. They do need a mulch of dead grasses and neutral soil such as is good for lawns and most domestic plants. Woodland plants need an acid soil and a very porous soil. Lots of organic material to make a humus will do fine. Woodland flowers take a bit more doing but are well worth it. Field flowers are not as finicky and will grow in a wilde range of soils. Mulches are important. Woodland gardens can use a mulch of leaves from your trees but the prairie flowers will do better with lawn clippings or prairie hay.

Once a wildflower garden is planted it will not require much maintenance. Some water may be desirable even though the plants are drought resistant. If the plants show signs of wilting some water will help them. If we have no rain for a couple of weeks, the deeper rooted plants can use a good soaking and for the shallow rooted ones, a half hour shower with a sprinkler will do. The plants will reward you with a longer period of bloom if they get water when needed. About the only other chore is to watch for insect pests. Wildflowers do not have many diseases, but some insects can cause trouble. Most can be put under control by using insecticides cautiously. Borers, slugs, aphids, and cutworms are the worst offenders. Slug bait will control the slugs, and diazinon will help with the others. The mushrooms and toadstools that will appear are actually a sign of health among plants that like an acid soil. If they grow the woodland plant will flourish.

There is an increasing number of seedhouses that are supplying seeds of plants you may wish. For many of the plants you will have to collect the seeds, transplant some plants or propagate by division or by rooting cuttings. It is also possible to buy some started plants at garden centers and greenhouses. This is a good way to get good stock as the potted plants are usually tougher and will start off well.

Transplanting from the wild should be done sparingly. Too many plants are lost from the wild by over digging. Check the protected plants in your area before you do any transplanting from the wild. Growing your own plants is more complicated and time-consuming but relatively inexpensive. It is very interesting and challenging. Raising from seed is sometimes difficult as some of the seeds take a long time to germinate. Rooting cuttings or dividing clumps is often easier. Just be sure you do not dig up plant without looking to their future.

The list of flowers I show is by not means all the ones that will do well but are some of the easier ones to get going. The Prairie group need humus, well-drained soil and prefer sun. The woodland group needs humus soil also, with more moisture and a higher acid soil. Most of them want shade or partial shade. The use of native mulches is strongly urged. I hope I have created an interest in the use of wildflowers, and also native grasses, to help maintain our heritage.

I will try to give the best information I can find for growing selected plants in your back yard. It is difficult to find cultural directions for many plants, although there are some good sources of identification. I am indebted to Edwin F. Steffek for *Wildflowers and How to Grow Them* and Marjorie J. Dietz for *Favorite Wildflowers* for much good information. Some of the tips have come from asking questions and from my own attempts. It is complex and a subject about which little is written. The cultural directions given are not infallible, but at least they're an effort in the right direction.

The plains region has its share of wildflowers, and because we have a wide range of climate, topographic and geological conditions there is a great variety of native plants. The largest number are prairie flowers as a large area is prairie. In the eastern and western areas there are woodland areas similar to Eastern Woodlands where the woodland plants flourish. In the southeastern area many plants common to the Ozarks and Ouchitas are found. In southwestern areas we will find plants from the arid southwest and the plains of Colorado. This gives us a very wide divergence of choices for the different areas. Prairie wildflowers grow mostly in full sun and on thin rich soil.

These flowers are sturdy as they have competed under adverse conditions for survival. In many of the old pastures and in corners here and there you will find native wildflowers that have been around forever.

In some sections you can find areas that were or still are woodlands. The flowers of the forest will grow there. The soil is usually more acid and the drainage is good. You must study your ground and learn what plants will adapt to it. I learned from experience that moving some prairie flowers to an improved flower bed can be disastrous. They just can't stand prosperity after generations of fighting adversity. Some that I tried soon ran rampant and took over the beds. They got taller and more dense than in the wild, and I had trouble controlling them. You must be sure the plants you want are compatible to your conditions. You can do a certain amount of soil conditioning that will help. Use some of the native shrubs and trees that will fit into the overall picture. Redbud, crabapple, hawthorn, Osage orange, rough dogwood, wahoo, and even buck brush will fit in.

There are getting to be more sources of seeds and plant material each year. These sources are fine to get a start with wildflowers instead of trying to collect them from the wild. I will give you some directions for some plants that will help and also a list of sources for seeds and plants.

The following list is for some plants that I feel will do well and are fairly easy to obtain. With the common name there is the botanical name, color, bloom time, height and best uses. The botanical name is because some dealers sell by that name. There are many more than these but these are easy to grow and to obtain.

1. Columbine - (Aquilegia canadensis) - varied colors - blooms in late spring - 1½ to 2½ feet tall - likes light shade - a woodland type that does best in well-drained slightly acid soil of average fertility - old clumps can be divided in early spring on in fall, but it is easier to sow seed outside in the summer - mulch lightly - leaf miner is its only problem and can be controlled with lindane borer spray.

2. Bergamot - (Monarda pistulsa) - called Beebalm and Horsemint - lavender flowers in drifts - blooms early summer and for many weeks - three to six feet tall -

tolerates most any soil - if given soil too rich will go rampant so be careful - good in a perennial border - full sun or part shade - divide clumps in the spring or in fall - can be moved any time.

3. Black-eyed Susam - (Rudbeckia hirta) - brown, cone-shaped center with golden yellow petals - two feet tall - blooms a long time starting in early summer - upright clumps that like dry poor soil in full sun - seeding is easy - biennual that acts like a perennial very often - use in clumps in small wildflower gardens.

4. Butterfly Weed (Asclepeas tuberosa) - bright orange, apricot or yellow flowers from early July through August - from one to three feet tall - tolerant of soils, even dry ones - can be seeded in fall or early spring - transplant when small as large plants are difficult to move because of a long taproot - use in perennial borders or naturalized as a foreground planting for shrubs.

5. Blue-eyed grass (Sisyrinchicum augustifolium) - blue or purple flowers on six to 18-inch stems - flowers do not last long but the plant blooms from early spring into summer - forms a tuft of long iris like foliage - tolerates a wide variety of soils from wet meadows to dry sandy soil - full sun or partial shade - increase by separating clumps - seeds available - self sows.

6. Bleeding Heart (Dicentra exima) - rosy pink, short-spurred flowers, roughly heart shaped - up to two feet tall - fernlike foliage - tolerant of widely variable soils - from sun to partial shade - self sows freely - blooms all summer - likes soil that is moist but well-drained and rich in leafmold - clumps can be divided in early spring or just after flowering (Dutchman's breeches is the same family and needs the same treatment - both ideal for woodland gardens, around shrubs, on shady banks, and along paths - they do well together).

7. Gayfeather (Liatris pycnostachya) - rich purple flowers along stiff stems - three to five foot stalks - blooms in late summer-grow in full sun in a moderately rich soil - propagate by seed in the fall or divide clumps in early spring - use around ponds or at the edge of woodlands - flowers last into fall - also called Kansas gayfeathers.

8. Goldenrod (Solidago canadensis) - yellow to gold flowers close together in panicles or racemes - five to seven

feet tall - blooms in late summer into fall - full sun - so tall it can be used in speical places as a background - grow in average soil, even dry and poor - plants can be moved in spring - old clumps can be divided - goldenrod does not cause hay fever.

9. Cardinal Flower (Lobelia cardinalis) - scarlet blooms in a clump two to four feet tall - blooms in midsummer into fall - likes moist, humus rich and acid soil - does fairly well in average garden soil if given plenty of water in dry periods - full sun to partial shade - self seeds - sow seed in spring or fall - can be divided in spring - very effective along a stream or beside a pool - can be grown in semi-shady parts of perennial beds.

10. May Apple (Podophyllum peltatum) - fragrant white flowers 1½ to 2 inches across about 12 inches tall - blooms in early spring - moist humus rich soil but tolerates some variation - grows from a rhizome and is easily transplanted - self-seeds and spready by rhizomes - light shade - use as a ground cover in shade along fences, walls, walks and drives.

11. Partridge Pea (Cassia fascillata) - bright yellow blooms to 1 inch across - long seed pods - 8 inches to 2 feet tall - blooms in early summer into fall - very drought tolerant - grow in a dry sunny area - best grown from seeds but can be transplanted in early spring - use in dry sunny areas on banks and slopes or in the rock garden.

12. Mist Flower (Eupatorium coelestinum) - also called perennial ageratum - purple to blue flowers in fuzzy heads on a 2 to 3 foot stalk - flowers in late summer - rich moist soil that is slightly acid - obtainable in nurseries - spreads by stolons - plant in light shade or sun - use in perennial beds or as accents.

12. Phlox (Phlox divaricata) - also called wild Sweet William - lavender blue flowers on 8 to 12 inch stems - rich humus soil in sun or light shade - divide clumps after flowering - blooms early to late spring - obtainable at nurseries - use as a foreground for perennials in rock gardens or in front of walls.

13. Solomon's Seal (Polygonatum biflorum) - flowers are yellow-green bells hanging along stem in mid to late spring - from 1 to 4 feet - tolerates a wide vareity of soils and deep shade to bright sun - berries can be planted in the fall

(remove the pulp) and will grow in the spring - can be transplanted in early spring - very effective in shady spots.

14. Turtle-head (Chelone glabra) - white flowers looking like a turtle head on 1 to 4 foot stems - prefers moist rich soil in partial shade - nurseries have plants - clumps can be lifted in spring or fall and divided - self sow - bloom in late summer when other flowers are scarce - very effective around pools.

15. Vervain (Verbena canadensis) - flat clusters of rosy purple fading to rose colored flowers 1 to 2 feet tall - bloom midsummer to fall - moderately acid soil enriched with leaf mold or peat moss- full sun - divided in spring - will self sow - use on sunny slopes or rock gardens.

16. Virginia Bluebells (Mertensia virginica) - true blue flowers on 2 foot stems - clusters of funnel shaped flowers 1 inch long and pink in bud - humus rich soil in semi-shade or light shade - plant the fleshy roots in early spring or while dormant in summer or fall - will self sow - lift and divide old large clumps - grow in clumps among daffodils and ferns in open woodland setting - the tops die back after the seeds ripen so be careful to mark the location - flowers from early to mid-spring.

17. Wild Geranium (Geranium maculatum) - clusters of rose-purple flowers 1 to 1½ inches across on 10 to 24 inch stems - a good colonizer in partial shade with rich humus soil but does well in average soil - self sows - can be divided in spring or fall - effective among ferns and other spring flowers - good in a shady rock garden - blooms in late spring.

Here is a list of some sources for seeds and plants. Many garden centers are stocking wildflower plants and seeds. Most of the major seed companies list some also.

Applewood Seed Co., 833 Parfet, St., Lakewood, CO 80215
Claude A. Barr, Prairie Gem Ranch, Smithwick, SD
Far North Gardens, 15621 Auburndale Ave., Livoni, MI 48154, catalogue - 50¢
Ferndale Nursery & Greenhouses, Askow, MN
Green Horizons, 500 Thompson Ave., Kerrville, TX 78028
Lounsberry Gardens, Box 135, Oakford, IL 62673

Midwest Wildflowers, Box 644, Rockton, IL 61072, catalogue 25¢
Northplan Seed Producer, Box 9107, Moscow, ID 83843
Olds Seed Co., 722 Williamson, St. Madison, WI 53707
Orchid Gardens, Rt. 1, Box 290, Grand Rapids, MI 55744
Parks Seed Co., Greenwood, SC 29647
Frank H. Rose, Missoula, MT
Sunshine Seeds Co., 310 N. Madison Ave., Wyoming, IL 61491, catalogue $1.00
Woodland Acres Nursery, Crivitz, WI

Some Good Books on Wildflowers
Wildflower Gardening, James Underwood Crockett & Oliver E. Allen, Time-Life Books, 1977
Gardening With Wildflowers, Brooklyn Botanical Gardens - 1974
How To Grow Wildflowers, Wild Shrubs and Trees In Your Garden, Hal Bruce, Alfred A. Knopf, 1976
The Women's Day Book of Wildflowers, Jean Hersey, Simon and Schuster, 1976
Wild Flowers and How to Grow Them, Edwin F. Steffek, Crown Publishers, 1963

CHART A

NAME	COLOR	SEASON	HEIGHT	ENVIRONMENT
Columbine (Aquilegia Canadensis)	R-Y	Spring & Summer	over 3'	Woodsy
Jack-in-the-Pulpet (Arisgema triphyllum)	W to G	Spring & Summer	1-3'	Damp - Woodsy
Butterfly Weed (Asclepias tuberosa)	Y to O	Summer	1-3'	Prairie - Grassland
New England Aster (Aster novge anliae)	B-W-R	Summer & Fall	over 3'	Woodsy - Edge of Woods
Coreopsis (Coreopsis lancolata)	Y to O	Summer	1-3'	Prairie - Grassland
Bunch berry (Cornus canadensis)	W to G Berries	Summer	under 1'	Woodsy - Damp
Shooting Star (Dodecatheon meadia)	W-R-B	Spring	1-3'	Prairie
Coneflower (Echinocea augustifotia)	P	Summer & Fall	over 3'	Prairie
Fawn Lily (Erythronium americania)	Y	Spring	under 1'	Woodsy
Indian Blanket (Gaillardia arista)	Y to O	Spring	1-3'	Prairie
Kansas Gay Feather (Liatris pyenostachya)	W-R-P	Summer & Fall	over 3'	Prairie
Cardinal Flower (Lobelia cardinalis)	R-W	Summer & Fall	over 3'	Wet ground
Virginia Bluebell (Mertensia vivginica)	B	Spring	1-3'	Woodsy
Bergamot (Monarda fistulosa)	W-B	Summer & Fall	over 3'	Prairie
Sundrop (Oenothera fruiticosa)	W-B	Summer & Fall	over 3'	Prairie
Prickly Pear (Opuntia)	W-Y	Summer	under 1'	Prairie - Dry Grassland
Penstemon - many	W-Y-R-B	summer	over 3'	Prairie - Grasslands
May Apple (Podophyllum petlatum)	W	Spring	1-3'	Woodsy
Solomon's Seal (Polygonatum commutatum)	W	Spring	1-3'	Prairie
Blackeyed Susan (Rudbeckia hirta)	Y-Black Ctr	Summer	1-3'	Prairie
Violets - several	W-B-R-P	Spring	under 1'	Woodsy
Adam's Needle (Yucca filamentosa)	W	Summer	over 3'	Prairie - Grasslands

Color Code- Y - Yellow   B - Blue   O - Orange
R - Red   W - White   G - Green   P - Purple

Woodsy indicate a shady spot with loose spongy

142   IN YOUR OWN BACK YARD

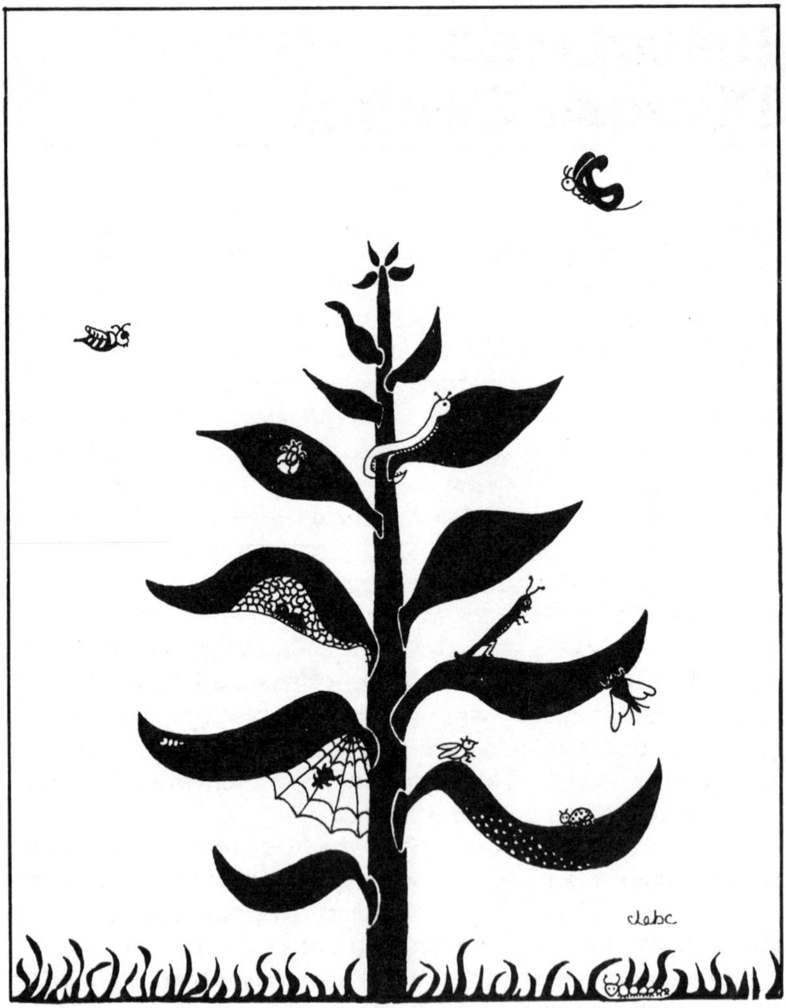
clabc

11
Insect and Disease Control

If we were in the commercial production of fruits and vegetables the problem of insect and disease control would be an almost daily fight. In order to achieve saleability, the produce has to be nearly perfect. I feel that in most magazine articles and garden books too much has been made of pest control. There is no question that it is a factor, but by a few positive steps control before problems occur is possible. The first step is to buy those plants that have been bred resistant to insects and diseases. Our plant scientists have done a great job by providing us with better plants. The vigor of the new hybrids make insects and disease less of a problem. Even with the better plants, you can get an invasion of both which by numbers alone becomes a serious problem. Weather plays an important part in these things as well. I believe in biological controls whenever possible, but I am not going to stand by and have a crop ruined. There are times when chemical control is the only way to get the job done.

One of the more contraversial methods of natural control is companion planting. The basic principle is that odors or juices of certain plants are a deterrent to some insects. Another theory is by planting a plant beside another plant the insects will be attracted away from the other. This is the case where radishes are planted with or beside carrots. The weevils that can raise hob with carrots will attack the radishes be preference. Radishes are cheaper and easier to grow. I am not sure that there is scientific proof that companion planting works, but many folks have told me that they have success. It is certainly worth a try.

I have planted radishes in my cucumber, squash, and melon hills for several years and feel that it helps keep away the beetles that infect them. I don't have complete trust in it, so I watch the plants for signs of the beetles. If I find them I do spray with diazinon. I plant marigolds all through the garden and also nasturtiums and cosmos. It seems I have less trouble with insects. The following list is some ideas for companion planting. Try it. You may like the results.

LIST

There have been many steps made in the last few years toward biological controls. One of the best that I have used is bacillus thuringiensis, commonly sold as Dipel or Thuricide. It is the spores of a disease that kills the larva of moths and butterflies. It is very effective on cabbage-type plants in controlling the pesky cabbage worms. The bacillus lives over and after a couple of years of use will build up enough to give sufficient control withou more spray. It does get the cabbage worms. It also gets any caterpillar-type insect. There are other botanical sprays that are effective for some insects. Pyrethrum, rotenone, and nicotine and three of them. They are made from plants so are less dangerous although nicotine should be used cautiously.

A new control on the market is Safer's Insecticidal Soap. I have found it to be deadly to a wide range of insects. I remember as a young lad, my father raised and bred dahlias. As a spray he took a bucket of hot water and shaved Fels-Naptha soap and plug tobacco into the water. This was stirred us and made a frothy, smelly mixture. As I recall it, there were no aphids, larva, or red spider that survived this spray. Safers have concentrated the soap so that a small quantity suffices. It did a good job for be on aphilds, red spider, and even scale.

One thing that I must stress is that in the control of insects and disease, cleanliness is the number one answer. You must keep the weeds cleared away from garden areas. They harbor the insects that will carry disease from the weeds to the good plants. Always pick up and remove any dead or diseased foliage. Put it in the compost pile or, if diseased, burn it up. In the autumn, when production has ceased, till the garden and turn under all the debris. The freezing of winter will take care of many over-wintering insects, eggs, and some disease organisms. Leave the surface rough for best results.

There are many ways of tabulating diseases and insects and the controls. I am tabulating the insects and diseases that are most troublesome in our area with suggested controls. If I would go into every insect and disease, it would take a whole book by itself. I feel it will be more helpful to you to show only the ones that will trouble you as a home gardener. If you run into something not covered, I suggest that you contact the county extension agent or your local garden center. They will know your local conditions and will be better able to help you.

Additionally, there are new controls coming on the market every year, so keep up by reading the garden papers and magazines. Try companion planting for a start.

If you have a problem, take a large enough sample to your expert for better analysis. I have been dismayed at times when I received one leaf from a plant for diagnosis. Take a large sample so that we can really help. If you can isolate an insect take one in. It is amazing how often we have figured out a problem with scant evidence. More luck that brains. I welcome your letters if you have problem. Maybe I can help. I am not infallible, but I have resources that help. Please send a stamped self-addressed enveloped for a fast answer.

CHART A

COMPANION PLANTS

Combinations of vegetables, herbs, flowers and weeds that are mutually beneficial:

PLANT	PLANT WITH
ASPARAGUS	tomatoes, parsley, basil
BASIL	tomatoes (improves growth and flavor, repels flies and mosquitoes)
BEANS	most vegetables and herbs
BEETS	onions, kohlrabi
CABBAGE FAMILY	potatoes, dill, sage, tyme, mint, beets, rosemary, onions, aromatic plants repel
CARROTS	peas, lettuce, onions, sage, tomatoes
CATNIP	in borders, repels flea beetles
CHIVES	carrots, plant at base of fruit trees to repel some climbing insects
CORN	potatoes, peas, beans, pumpkin, squash
CUCUMBERS	beans, corn, radishes, (repels cucumber bettles), sunflowers
EGGPLANT	beans
GARLIC	plant throughout the garden to deter pests
LETTUCE	with radishes and carrots make good companions
MARIGOLD	discourage many insects and nematodes, plant freely
NASTURTIUM	deters aphids and pests of cucumbers
ONION	protects against slugs
PETUNIA	beneficial throughout the garden
RADISH	lettuce, cucumbers, repels many insects
ROSEMARY	deters cabbage moth, bean beetles, carrot fly
TANSY	deters many pests
TARRAGON	good anywhere in garden
THYME	deters cabbage worms
TOMATO	chives, onions, parsley, marigold, carrots

CHART B

GENERAL PESTS

PEST	CONTROL
Aphids, multiply fast, attack most plants	Diazinon Safer's Soap, malathion
Cut Worms, cut plants off at ground level	Use shields, spray soil with toxaphene or diaxzinon
Flea Beetles, eat holes in the foliage	Diazinon, rotenone, safers soap
Grasshoppers, eat anything	kill them when small in the weeds, Methoxychlor, diazinon
Borers, bore into many plants	keep the weeds down, spray the plants & ground with lindane
Slugs, eat anthing, nasty	slug bait, clear hiding places, pie tin or beer, they drown
Spider Mites, attack many plants	Kelthane, Safers soap, spray with strong steam of water
Sowbugs, eat roots and decayed matter	slug bait, clear hiding spots, diazinon, malathion
White Grubs, eat roots	treat soil with chlordane or diazinon
Powdery Mildew, mold on leaves	dust with sulfur, Karathane
Chlorosis, iron shortage, turns foliage yellow	spray with iron sulfate at 2 tsp. per gal. water, soil and plants

continued on next page

INSECT AND DISEASE CONTROL   149

CHART B

SPECIFIC PROBLEMS

PLANT PEST	CONTROL
Beans, bacterial blight dead areas in leaves red cankers	Plant Western grown beans, don't touch wet plants, avoid water on foliage
Cabbage family, cabbage worms, yellows, stunts plants blackleg - black rot	spray with Dibel, Thuricide, use resistant varieties, don't plant in infested soil seed from Pacific NW free of disease, avoid infected soil
Carrots, weevil, burrow in roots	treat soil with chlordane or diazinon
Corn, earworm	Spray silks with Sevin, 4 times at 2 day intervals, mineral oil on silks
Cucumber and related plants, squash bugs, carry disease	plant radishes in hills, spray with diazinon
Beetles, carry disease	same as squast bugs
Squash-borers	use lindane
Bacterial wilt	control beetles
Anthracnose, cankers	change location each year, spray with zineb or captan
Onion, thrips, blotches on the leaves	Malathion
Peppers, blossom, end rot	too much nitrogen and too little water, apply phosphate
Potatoes, Colorado potato beetle	spray with methoxychlor or lead arsenate
scab	do not apply lime or wood ashes or fresh manure
Strawberry, leaf rollers	spray with diazinon or methoxychlor before bloom and after harvest
Tomato, stink bug, white, spots benath skin	Sevin, thiodan
hornworm	pick off by hand
Fruit rots	fertilize, mulch, spray with maneb or zineb
Septoria leaf spot, lower leaves yellow and die	stake and mulch, spray with zineb or bordeaux, mix keep water from foliage
Virus, rolling and twisting, yellowing	plant resistant varieties
Fusarium wilt	plant resistant varieties.

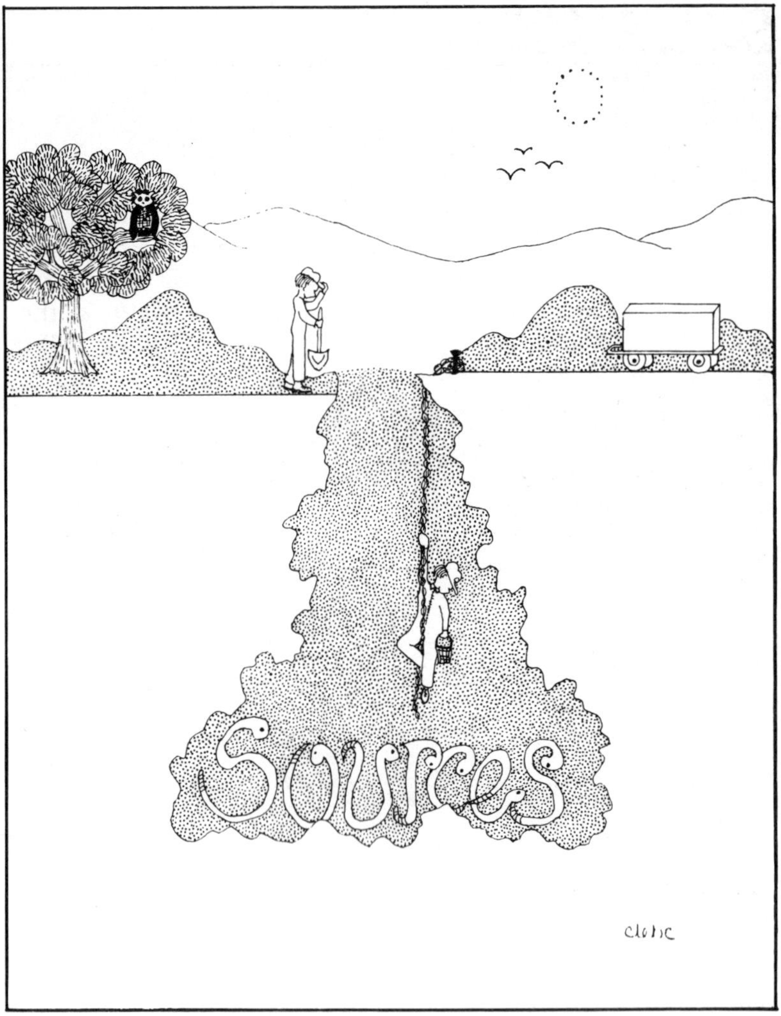
Sources

SOURCES

I think that you will do well to go to your local garden center, nursery, or greenhouse for most of your garden needs. These people are better informed about your local conditions and will have most of the things that you want. Some of the newer seeds and plants you can get only from the mail-order houses. My suggestions is to order from the ones that belong to the national or state associations. All of the associations have high codes of ethics, and you will find them fair to deal with.

SEED COMPANIES

Applewood Seed Co. - Wildflowers - herbs - catalogue
Box 10761, Edgemont Station, Golden, CO 80401

W. Atlee Burpee Co. - General Seeds - catalogue
300 Park Ave., Warminster, PA 18974

Comstock, Ferre and Co. - old time company - general - catalogue
263 Main St., Weathersfield, CT 06109

Farmer Seed & Nursery - Northern grown seed - general - catalogue
818 NW 4th St., Fairbault, MN 55021

Herbst Brothers Seedsmen, Inc. - general - catalogue
1000 N. Main St., Brewster, NY 10509

J.W. Jung Seed Co. - general - catalogue
339 S. High St., Radolph, WI 53956

Henry Field Seed & Nursery - general - catalogue
407 Sycamore, Shenandoah, IA 51602

Gurney Seed & Nursery Co. - Northern grown - general - catalogue
Yankton, SD 57059

Otis Twilley Seed Co. - general - catalogue
Box 65, Trevose, PA 19047

George W. Park Seed Co. - general - good selections - catalogue
Box 31, Greenwood, SC 29647

Stokes Seeds, Inc. - general - catalogue
737 Main St. Buffalo, NY 14240

Joseph Harris Co. - general - catalogue
Moreton Farm, 3670 Buffalo Road, Rochester, NY 14624

Johnny's Selected Seed - excellent for north - catalogue
Albion, ME 14910

Nichols Garden Nursery, Inc. - many hard to find seeds - catalogue
1190 N. Pacific Hwy., Albany, OR 97321

Earl May Seed & Nursery Co. - general - catalogue
100 N. Elm, Shenadoah, IA 51603

Vermont Bean Seed Co. - Veg. seeds - Northern grown
Garden Lane, Bomoseen, VT 05732

NURSERY STOCK

Inter-State Nurseries - general nursery stock - catalogue
504 East St., Hamburg, IA 51640

Jackson and Perkins - Roses - fruit trees - catalogue
Medford, OR 97501

Kelly Brothers Nurseries, Inc. - fruit trees - catalogue
602 Maple St., Dansville, NY 14437

Stark Brothers Nurseries - fruit trees - catalogue
Louisiana, MO 63353

Wayside Gardens Co. - ornamentals - catalogue
Hodges, SC 29695

For Your Lawn & Garden Needs See Holwick Farm & Home Supply

Lawn & Garden Supplies

Grass Seeds
Fertilizers
Weed Control
Insect Control
Bulk Garden Seeds
Fruit Tree Spray

Garden Hoses
Sprinklers
All types of Sprayers
Gypsum/Lime
Bone Meal
Many Other Items

Household Supplies

Insecticides
Water Softener Salt
House Plant Supplies

Rat & Mouse Control
Mole Traps
Live Traps

Pet Supplies

Cat & Dog Food
Rabbit & Pet Feed
All Types Bird Seed
Fly Control

Waterers & Feeders
Cages & Feeders
Fencing

Wild Bird Seed

Wild Bird Seed
Sunflowers
Bird Feeders
Humming Bird Feeders

Finch Feed
Sunflower Bits & Hearts
Quail Feeders

Weather Vanes

Trailer Hitches

All types of Chicken-Cattle-Hog Feeds
Mineral Feeders-Fencing-Cattle Waterers
Fly Control and Feed for Horses

If you want to save come in and see us!

Holwick farm·home supply

1209 N. Kansas Ave.   (913) 235-2966

BIBLIOGRAPHY

Besides the many excellent bulletins of the extension service, numerous services have been used as references in preparation of this text. I recommend any and all of these for fine information and for just good garden reading.

Abrahams, George and Katy. *The Green Thumb Garden Handbook.* Englewood Cliffs, NJ: Prentice-Hall.

Carleton, R. Milton. *The New Vegetable and Fruit Garden Book.*

Flemer, William, III. *Nature's Guide to Successful Gardening.* New York: Thomas Y. Crowell.

Gardening for Food and Fun. U.S.D.A. Yearbook, 1972.

Landscape for Living. U.S.D.A. Yearbook, 1972.

Reilly, Ann. *Park's Success with Seeds.* Park Seed Company.

Shurtleff, Malcolm C. *How to Control Plant Disease.* Ames, IA: Iowa State University.

Taylor, Norman. *Taylor's Encyclopedia of Gardening.* Boston: Honghton, Mifflin.

Wescott, Cynthia. *The Gardener's Bug Book.* Garden City, NY: Doubleday.

YOU UPLIFT PEOPLE

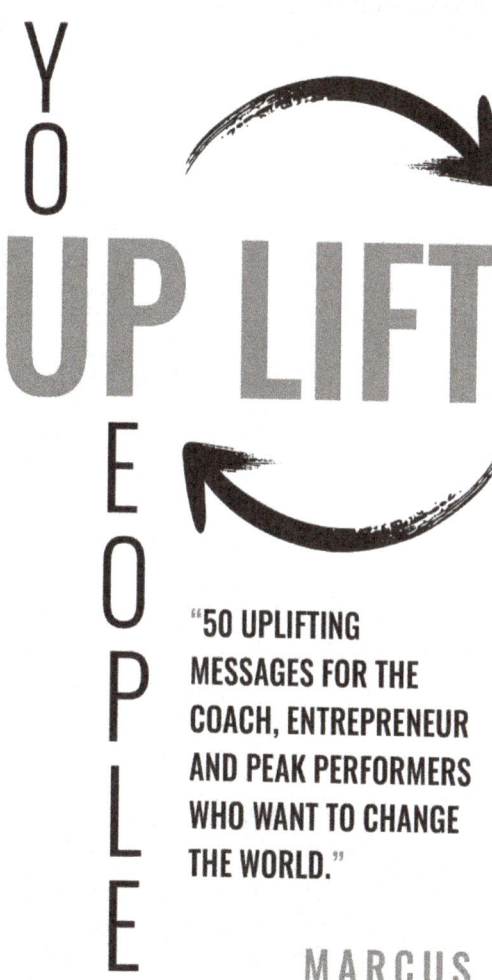

"50 UPLIFTING MESSAGES FOR THE COACH, ENTREPRENEUR AND PEAK PERFORMERS WHO WANT TO CHANGE THE WORLD."

MARCUS BRUGGER

Copyright © 2021 Marcus Brugger

www.marcusbrugger.com

Limits of Liability and Disclaimer of Warranty

The author/publisher shall not be liable for your misuse of this material. The author and/or publisher shall have neither liability nor responsibility to anyone with respect to any loss or damage alleged to be caused, directly or indirectly, by the information contained in this book. This book is strictly for informational and educational purposes.

Contents

Acknowledgements 6

Introduction 7

The Call That Will Change Your Life Forever............ 11

Faith Over Fear 16

The Thing about Dreams 20

A Scary Solution 25

If You Love Something, Let It Set You Free 29

Big Goals 34

You're F-IN Powerful! 38

Fully Commited Dreams 41

Fully Focused 46

Mental Muscle 53

Get Moving! 61

Habit Stacking & How It Can Change Your Life 66

Choose OUT-STANDING! 71

Forget Fear 76

The New Way 81

Your Motivational Fire 86

Forget Normal 93

YOKWYK 97

Why Are You Stuck? 102

The Hard Truth.. 105
How to Fight Resistance? 110
Tomorrow Is Going to Be Better! 114
Traveling Up, Up & Away! 118
Have a GREAT Day!... 122
Stretching for Success....................................... 127
"I Don't Feel Like It!" 131
The Power of Resistance 135
It's Time to Fight Back 139
Rise UP 142
Your Heart Is Gold... 145
Double Down... 149
The Sun Will Come Out Tomorrow..................... 153
People Need You.. 157
Alone Syndrome... 161
Redo?.. 166
Why Your Energy Matters................................. 170
Just BREATHE 176
Turn On Your Light 180
Replace the Lies 186
How to Be Driven in Your Destiny 193
Screwed Over... 199
Your Big JUMP! 203
2.5 Seconds 209

Please Unsubscribe! 215
Mission Impossible 221
What's Right? 226
Rebuild 230
Where Does My Story Go from Here? 234
30 Thousand 237
So, Who Do You Think You Are? 241
Who Are You Going to Uplift Next? 249
Pay It Forward 251
About the Author 252

Acknowledgements

I could never list all of the people who have made it possible for me to write this book. I have been blessed with such a wide variety of support from different areas of my life. From family to friends, from mentors and colleagues and to every client and each person in between. The continued support has been massive and deeply appreciated. To my wonderful wife Tara and to all of my children, Hannah, Jacob, Clark & Marcus Jr., thank you for providing me with so much support, sacrifice and endless love. To my awesome mentors Pat Rigsby, Linda Decker, Linda Nedlisky thank you for your direction, bluntness and simplification but also the multitudes of wisdom you have brought to my life. To my tight-knit, best-year-ever group of men, I thank you for your friendship, accountability, encouragement and faithfulness to grow into a better Christian, Husband, Father, Entrepreneur, Writer and Man. To all of my Clients I have had the opportunity to work with, thank you for trusting me, allowing for my mistakes and motivating me to serve each of you in a better way. Finally, this book would not be possible without God putting the idea, the pages and the words in my heart. I thank God for being able to not only take my next breath but also to try to do something special with it!

Introduction

I believe we need more people in this world that can Uplift others.

Uplift the people around them.

Not just the people you like but each person that you come in contact with.

Our modern world is filled with more "opinions" and "what's in it for me" attitudes than ever before.

This is creating a culture of negativity towards any person that doesn't fit into our ideal. The idea that if there is nothing you can gain from someone, then they are not worth your time, is widely accepted in our modern world.

This ever growing culture is more impressed by titles, high dollar luxuries and social scroll attention.

These compounding attitudes are creating a vacuum of less than ideal empathy for their fellow neighbors and community members.

The gap between people's quality of caring and what's best for others is growing at an exponential rate.

The lack of caring in a single individual person just for being them without any strings attached is becoming eroded by the day.

This is leading to a more disconnected and less empathic world.

A world that is becoming less about doing things for others, and more about taking from others to improve your position.

All of us are missing opportunities to create a true life-changing moment in the people around us.

It's time to do something different.

It's time to be an Uplifter.

Someone who lifts up people because it's the right thing to do.

No hidden agendas.
No hidden rewards.
No hidden profit.

Just putting in meaningful actions for the benefit of others.

To do this...

We need you.

We need you to Uplift others.

We need you to be the leader that can Uplift one person at a time, the difference-maker who cares enough to change the world.

You can't Uplift others if you are stuck in the wrong lane of life.

Through this book we will be working on Uplifting you, also.

When you experience something that Uplifts you, it activates a powerful energy that motivates you to be an Uplifter.

Not just an Uplifter to everyone, but to certain specific people who you were put on earth to truly help and serve.

It doesn't matter what place in life you are in right now.

What matters is you are still here, and that means you have a specific purpose.

This purpose is for you to be your best, so that you can Uplift each person around you!

When you Uplift someone, you meet them where they are and help them move up in their life.

It can be as simple as a smile, a hug or you slowing down and listening.

It can be more complex, such as coaching, parenting or supporting someone's dream.

No matter what you will do to Uplift the people in your life, you will have to be able to be available and willing to be at your best.

When you are at your best, you become an Uplifter. An Uplifter is just who you are.

You condition yourself to Uplift others without thinking.

You see the need and show up in the best way possible for them.

You don't need anything but you!

As you read through this book, you will automatically develop this ability.

By reading each message, you will gain the clarity needed to not only be an Uplifter to others but also yourself.

Are you ready to become an Uplifter?

The Call That Will Change Your Life Forever

"When your destiny is calling, answer that call."
~Janet Coron

You have a fire inside of you that wants to grow.

It is literally fighting inside of you to explode.

You have what it takes to go where your heart is calling you!

You have the…

Strength
Skill
Support
Ability
Attitude
Affectiveness

…Needed to accomplish your calling. All you have to do is answer it.

Pick up the phone and say "Hello?!"

When you do, the rest will unveil itself to you.

The problem is you are scared to answer the phone.

You let it ring each day with no answer.

Over and over again you get the call.

The first call, you actually think about answering it.

You stare at it and think, "What if I answer it?"

Then all of the thoughts in your head tell you why you can't.

You believe the thoughts and hit "Decline".

The next day you will get another call but this time you will not even think about it.

You will just hit "Decline".

On the next day you will get another call but this time you won't even look at the phone.

You will just hit "Decline".

On the next day, you will get another call and this time you will be annoyed.

Annoyed that you keep getting the call.

You will angrily hit "Decline"!

On the next day you will get another call and completely ignore it.

You won't do anything, just let it go away without even taking the time to hit "Decline".

On the next day you will get another call and "Think what a waste of my life this is."

You will not only hit "Decline" but also go in and "Block" any future calls.

Now you have "Blocked" any of your calls going forward.

You do this because it's easier and less scary for you to "Block it" than press "Accept" to your calling.

When you make this mistake, you will feel as if something is not right inside of you.

You will have this "Something's Off" feeling.

This "Something doesn't feel right" feeling.

That feeling is…

Your fire is out.

It's your purpose to answer your call.

It's what makes life feel real.

It's what brings fulfillment, gratitude and contentment into you.

Once you realize the special gift, that call is each day, you will wish you would have never "Blocked it".

You will wish you had answered the call and enjoyed the moment.

The moment you figured out what lights your fire.

What makes you so passionate about each of your days.

What makes you realize and understand the true reason you were put on this earth.

The "Why" behind each and everything you have tackled in life and how it has set you up for the next moments.

No matter what you think, your calling is still there.

You might not see it or hear it anymore but it's there in the background calling each day hoping you will just answer.

Hoping you will "Unblock it".

Hoping you will say "Hello!"

The world needs you to say "Hello!"

You have a specific purpose that has been placed inside of you.

It's calling you each and every day.

It's there for a reason.

It's there for a season.

It's there for someone.

It is there for you.

Don't waste another day ignoring the next call.

The next opportunity.

The next person that needs you.

Are you ready to change everything and say "Hello"?

Faith Over Fear

"Faith will take you to a far greater place than fear ever could." ~Neil L. Anderson

Everyone has FEAR in their life, PERIOD!

FEAR can paralyze.
FEAR can stop.
FEAR can disrupt.
FEAR can derail…

YOU!

But FEAR can also bring out the best in you.

It can make you do things that produce the magical kryptonite to FEAR.

This kryptonite is a much more powerful source than FEAR.

It's a gift given to everyone, but very few people actually use it.

It will take you further than you ever thought possible, and it's a renewable resource always at your disposal.

The FEAR killer is FAITH.

FAITH in tomorrow.
FAITH in people.
FAITH in success.
FAITH in the next step.
FAITH in…

YOU!

When you have FAITH in any aspect of your life, you will win.

Guaranteed!

It's DONE.

Automatic WIN!

The stronger your FAITH is in anything, the less chance that FEAR builds up to cripple you or stand in your way.

FAITH isn't something that you have to figure out.

It's simply there to use and build into your life.

When you consistently use FAITH, you start to have a reserve of it built inside of you.

It works like a hybrid car that runs on gas and electricity.

When you're driving, the hybrid car is using gas, but when you stop at a light, the gas turns off and the electricity kicks in to power the car.

The moment you tap the gas pedal, the electricity turns off but still works in the background, and the gas kicks in for the car to start accelerating.

This is exactly how FAITH works.

It's in the background running and supporting you.

When you let your foot off the gas and are unsure or FEARFUL, FAITH takes over to allow you to put your foot back on the gas and accelerate forward toward your goals.

The more you develop FAITH, the better your life gets.

FAITH combats FEAR.

The moment you feel any FEAR, is the moment you must choose FAITH.

When you do, you will see FEAR subside, your FAITH grow and be replenished and your overall mood and energy improve instantly.

FAITH is growth. FEAR is a chance at growth by using FAITH.

FEAR is the single biggest stopper of people in the world, but luckily for us, FAITH is the single biggest supporter of people in the world.

Today is not like any other day. It's a new day that starts with you reading this message and having the opportunity to choose FAITH or FEAR!

The thing about opportunity is…

Are you going to have FAITH in the opportunity or FEAR it?

The Thing about Dreams

"If you give up on your dreams, what's left?"
~Jim Carrey

Most if not all people have a DREAM they want to accomplish in their lifetime.

It could be a variety of different things.

Graduate College
Win a Race
Get Married
Have Children
Get That Dream Home
Land Your Dream Job
Start a Business
Get into Shape

And so on.

Whatever your DREAMS are, you must work towards them to feel and be fulfilled.

The longer you put it off or discredit the DREAMS, the more you become unhappy and look at yourself and the world in a negative light.

The missing piece standing in your way of pursuing your DREAMS is TIME.

TIME doesn't stand still, it continually moves whether you like it or not.

You cannot stop it or start it but you can manage it.

When you manage time, you make a conscious decision to go after your DREAMS.

You deliberately set aside a specific time to go all in on your DREAMS.

In the next 5–10 years, you will see everyone talk about the next big thing. It will be TIME.

With technology speeding everyday lives up, there will be a huge emphasis on TIME.

The most successful people will accomplish their DREAMS by managing their TIME and putting full focus into their days.

I'm going to give you a sneak peak to how to make more out of your TIME and accomplish your goals faster and with more ease than ever before.

5 Steps to Making Time Work for Your Dreams

Step 1 – Recognizing

Recognizing that you need to improve on using your TIME wisely is #1. Understanding that the goal is to improve, which means make better. Don't feel as if you need to be perfect or tear off the bandaid and change everything over night. Start with a small goal of improvement in mind and stay focused on each step below.

Step 2 – Measurement

If you don't track it, you won't know what you need to improve on or if you are improving.

Measure your current use of TIME. You can write it down or even keep a running stopwatch when you're working towards your DREAM.

Remember we are going for Full Focus, not distracted doing 2–3 things at once.

After addressing how much TIME you are actually working on your DREAMS, it's time for you to start a routine.

Step 3 – Routine

A routine is a bunch of habits you do on a predetermined time and place consistently. Routines can be done either daily, weekly or monthly.

Start out with something so simple you will easily do it, and then you can make it slightly more challenging as you go. The best practice in routine is to do the 1-2-3 habit method. 1—Pick a habit. 2—Pick a specific time. 3—Pick a place to do the habit.

Step 4 – Ritual

Once you get your routine set in, all you have to do is do it for a 90-day period and it will turn into a Ritual automatically.

The beauty of a ritual is that you do it without putting a ton of thought into it.

The Ritual pretty much happens automatically and if you miss it, something feels off in your life. The power in Ritual is it becomes automatic and you rely on it to feel good.

Step 5 – Breaktime

Scheduling 10–20 minute breaks throughout the day will actually make you more productive with your TIME and happier in general.

Another big one is scheduling Big Breaktime.

Vacations! Take extended weekends, a week off, and the biggest game changer out of all of them... a Value Vacation.

A Value Vacation is 10 days or longer. This type of vacation is a supercharger for you and your TIME.

There are countless studies showing that when on a vacation, it takes at least 3 days for you to detach from normal life once you get to your destination, and then another 5–7 days to actually reap the benefits of the vacation.

When you take a Value Vacation, it allows you to really recover.

The bottom line in all of this is to schedule the time off and start to do it, no matter what. Once you schedule it, you'll figure out how to make it happen.

TIME is moving each day and your DREAMS are either coming closer to you or moving further away.

You are in a perfect position to get moving towards your DREAMS.

It's TIME for you to become your best and live your best life.

The thing about TIME is we always think we have more of it than we really do.

Don't waste another day wasting your TIME or your DREAMS.

A Scary Solution

"It's okay to be scared. Being scared means you're about to do something really, really exciting."
~Mandy Hale

Who likes to be scared?

Not me.

Probably not you either.

No one really likes to be scared.

Being scared makes you feel small and uncomfortable.

It makes you question yourself and if you will be okay.

But the tough thing for most people to understand is that the solution to your problem in life is scary.

It's scary to think about.

It's scary to take the first step.

It's scary to take the next step.

And…

It's scary to go after your dreams.

What isn't scary is…

Procrastinating
Being Comfortable
Putting it off another day
Starting tomorrow
Wishing for different
Believing You Can't

All of these and more are not scary.

They are comfortable and you can relate to them too well.

They will also make you feel unpassionate, unfulfilled and unhappy.

The solution to your problem and life goals is to be scared.

I'm not talking about being so scared that you freeze, pee yourself or develop a tick.

I'm talking about just being a little scared.

Just enough to move 1% toward your goals and dreams.

Wake up each day and ask yourself, "How can I be 1% scared today?"

Feels wrong, huh?

But guess what?

If you don't do it, another day will pass, and then another, and then another, and then you will wake up wondering, where did all the time go?

Where did the person I know go?

Where did my life go?

When you are scared, you are on the way to a life full of happiness, fulfillment and passion.

You simply get to live a life better than you had ever thought possible.

Once you embrace this scary solution, you will gain a higher perspective that is vital to your development.

This development is needed for you to accomplish your dreams.

Your dreams do not magically just happen.

They are a representation of who you are and what you have become.

When you understand this, those scary solutions do not seem as intimidating as you once thought.

Get scared today so you have the solution to tomorrow's aspirations!

If You Love Something, Let It Set You Free

"If you love something, set it free; if it comes back it's yours, if it doesn't, it never was."
~Richard Bach

I don't know where the above quote came from but a version of it was written by Richard Bach.

Today, I wanted to talk to you about setting yourself FREE.

When I talk about FREE, I'm talking about a better and happier life.

A life you could only dream of, that is filled with wonderful attributes, characteristics and talents including but not limited to…

High Energy
Extreme Motivation
Passion
Great Health
High Focus

Confidence
Fulfillment
Strength
Happiness

The best and fastest way to develop all of these attributes is through LOVE.

LOVE can change everything.

You can be at rock bottom and LOVE can flip it upside down.

You can be depressed, unhappy and have extremely low energy but the moment you do something you LOVE, everything improves immediately.

My true question for you is, "What are you doing each day that you LOVE to do?"

The sad fact is that in our current lifestyles most people go days, weeks, months or years without doing even one thing they LOVE to do.

You've heard it before.

I'm too busy.
I'm advancing in my career.
The kids have a lot going on.
I'm grinding for a better future.

All of these are just bull$#%& excuses.
The way to be FREE is to do things you LOVE to do!

I'm going to say that again so it really sinks in. The way to be FREE is to do the things you LOVE to do!

The way to get...

High Energy
Extreme Motivation
Passion
Great Health
High Focus
Confidence
Fulfillment
Strength
Happiness

Is through doing the things you LOVE.

When you do something you LOVE, you improve and recharge YOU.

Sometimes you can be so detached from LOVE, you don't know how to get it back.

This can happen from years of grinding, setbacks or simply from inactivity.

The two best ways to get back to doing the things you LOVE are to Reconnect and Connect.

1. **Reconnect**

   Reconnect with the things you used to LOVE to do. The things that gave you happiness, energy and peace.

   If you are having trouble identifying them, just think back to your childhood and look at what types of things you enjoyed doing. The beauty about childhood is you got to choose on the basis of fun without anything else altering your decision. Most of the time, the things you did as a child brought happiness to you which you automatically were wired to LOVE.

   An example would be playing a sport as a child and now as an adult going back and playing that sport again in some facet.

2. **Connect**

   Another great way to recognize and find things you will LOVE to do is by connecting with others. It could be your current friends or joining a group of likeminded people who already have something that they LOVE to do.

   The chances are high that you might LOVE what they LOVE to do, too. You could join a friend or group to try anything, you really never know what you will become passionate about or grow to LOVE.

A couple of things that I personally LOVE to do that recharge me and bring me true fulfillment are playing basketball and crocheting.

Yes, two complete opposites and a fun fact about me.

Both came from my childhood.

Playing basketball allows me to turn off everything else that's going on in my life and allows me to kick it back to being a kid again.

Crocheting came from going to my grandma's house as a kid each week and crocheting a blanket with her. There is something so peaceful and stress-relieving about it.

The bonus is, it reminds me of my grandma and the time we spent together.

Which I LOVE!

The next step is ultimately up to you. It's time to set yourself FREE and get back to developing yourself through LOVE.

They say LOVE what you do and you will never work another day in your life.

I say LOVE something you do each day and never work another day without being FREE again.

Are you ready to LOVE today again?

Big Goals

*"If you do not get chills when you set a goal,
you're not setting big enough goals."*
~Bob Proctor

Big Goals are something special.

They tell a lot about what you think you can accomplish.

The funny thing is you might not think you have a Big Goal but you do.

A Big Goal is one of those wishes you have in your mind that you have always wanted to do.

"I wish I could do _____!"

"I wish I had the time for _____!"

"One day I want to _____!"

It's something that you have put off or have been scared to do.

It's the thing you just haven't figured out how you are going to do it or create the time to do it.

There is massive power in a Big Goal.

A Big Goal makes you do things you typically wouldn't do.

It makes you more motivated and wakes you up from the monotony of daily life.

A Big Goal also gives you tons of fulfillment and confidence.

The one problem most people see with their Big Goal is it takes work and can be scary.

And...

Most of the time the work needed is something you just haven't done before. It's normally something that you have to learn, which makes you uncomfortable and fearful.

3 Steps to Accomplishing Your Big Goals

1. Set Your Big Goal.

You have to have and recognize your Big Goal to accomplish it. A lot of people will try to ignore their Big Goal in hopes it just goes away, but it won't. It will pop into your head over and over until you recognize and understand you must go after it.

2. **Get Big Goal Support.**

   Since you will need to learn and work on your Big Goal, you will need someone to provide you insight, accountability and direction to help you accomplish it. Yes, you could figure it out on your own, but rarely do people actually do that and the extra time it would take could derail you from ever finishing it. Get a Coach or Expert and simplify the process.

3. **Take Big Goal Action.**

   Every day you will have to take Big Goal Action. This means you can't just work on your Big Goal when you feel like it.

   Schedule a specific time and place to continually work on your Big Goal. When you condition yourself to do this, you will finish it in no time. Most of the time, we overthink the amount of time it takes to accomplish the goal, but when you commit to working on it consistently, you will be amazed how quickly it can go.

When you have a Big Goal, you win.

You feel better in life because you are using your energy for good.

You are moving forward towards fulfillment, and we fill up our internal happiness tank from fulfillment.

Don't waste another day without going after your Big Goals.

You deserve to make today and every day after, full of fulfillment and happiness!

Are you using your Big Goal to create the life you want to live tomorrow and every day after?

You're F-IN Powerful!

*"You are very powerful,
provided you know how powerful you are."*
~Yogi Bahaman

Understand this…You are POWERFUL!

You have a POWER in you that is massive and abundant.

It's something that you have only scratched the surface of.

It's like the iceberg in the Titanic…

You can only see the tip of it, but underneath it is massive and deep.

Nothing or no one can stop you.

When you truly understand this, everything will change.

You will take on bigger and better dreams in your life.

You will accomplish them faster and with ease.

Never think for a moment that you are powerless and weak.

You were not created to be weak.

You were created to be POWERFUL.

POWERFUL in order to make a massive impact on something or someone.

Don't roll your eyes and think I'm not talking to YOU!

I AM!

I'm not going to let you off the hook and think anything different.

You are POWERFUL and you are alive and reading this for a reason.

And…

If you truly take an honest moment and ask yourself why, the thing you have always been too scared of doing will pop in your head.

But…

You will most likely do what you always do.

Shoot it down and come up with a reason why you can't do it.

I'm here to tell you, you can do it and you must.

If you don't, you become less POWERFUL and develop something that won't hurt you too much right now but will in the last days of your life.

REGRET.

REGRET is a B#$@#.

It doesn't care about how it makes you feel.
It doesn't care if you had a fulfilled life.
It doesn't care if you are at peace with yourself.

REGRET wants to beat you up and rob you.

Rob you of the life you wish you would have had.

When you accept the fact that you are POWERFUL, REGRET doesn't have a chance.

You lop off the head of REGRET just by believing in yourself and the POWER you hold.

So…

Now that I have your ATTENTION…

Are you ready to let your POWER out into the world today?

Fully Commited Dreams

"Commitment is what transforms a promise into a reality." ~Abe Lincoln

Whether you like it or not, nothing meaningful will happen for you until you are willing to be FULLY COMMITTED.

FULLY COMMITTED to a better:

Life
Routine
Dream
Job
Focus
Goal
Happiness
Body
Health
Or You!

Being FULLY COMMITTED is massively important.

When you are not, many things happen…

You:

Procrastinate
Struggle
Feel Tired
Question Yourself
Become Depressed
Get Stuck
Are Indifferent
Become Negative

All of these are byproducts of not being FULLY COMMITTED.

One of the quickest ways to know where you stand in your current life is by looking at your daily actions and feelings toward the steps to achieve your goals.

If you feel or are doing any of the above byproducts, it's a result of not being FULLY COMMITTED!

When you aren't FULLY COMMITTED, you will continue your unhappy struggle for days, months, years or even decades to come.

Until you either become FULLY COMMITTED to your goals and dreams or change them, the same issues and feelings will continue to pop up day after day.

Sometimes you can think you are FULLY COMMITTED, but you really aren't.

You are half in and half out or less.

You are the person who has to dip their toe into the pool to feel it first, then you put one foot in, then the second, then knee deep, waist deep, then right up to your chest, then to your neck, all while grimacing due to the water temperature. Finally you have a 50% chance of getting your hair wet, because of course you might not want to deal with it getting messed up.

This is exactly why many people struggle with being FULLY COMMITTED and accomplishing their life dreams.

To accomplish something that is one of your big dreams you must jump right in.

When you do, the pain, discomfort or fear in your head will instantly go away.

The power of being FULLY COMMITTED is being able to speed up the process of accomplishing your dreams.

It's literally a short cut.

The easiest way to be FULLY COMMITTED is to believe when you jump in, you will be fine.

You will figure out what to do next because you are actually in the situation you need to be in to gather the information needed to accomplish the goals needed to achieve your dreams.

When you stop overthinking everything and get off the side of the pool, your perspective will change and everything won't seem as intimidating as you thought.

It might actually be way easier than you ever thought.

Almost all the time, people become FULLY COMMITTED, accomplish their dreams and wish they would have done it years before.

I see this almost all the time with knee replacement people.

They are so scared of having the surgery that they agonize over it for years until their knees hurt so bad that it has limited their life and they have no choice but to get the surgery.

Right after the surgery, every single one of them say the same thing, "I wish I would have done this years ago."

1. What do you need to become FULLY COMMITTED to so you can live your DREAMS?

2. What areas of your life are you just half in and half out?

3. In 5 years will there be something you wish you would have done that is currently causing you pain?

It's time for you to become **FULLY COMMITTED** and live a life you have only dreamt of.

**You are strong enough.
You are capable enough.
You are smart enough.
To become the best you!**

Go jump into today so that tomorrow is the day you say, "I wish I would have done this years ago!"

Fully Focused

"You get what you focus on, so focus on what you want." ~Tony Robbins

The enemy of Focus is distraction.

We are living in a world of distraction.

Not just simple distraction, but distraction that is calculated.

Calculated to keep you where you are.

Hey, if you are entertained, then you aren't a threat to what we have, better yet we can count on you doing X when we need you to.

Oh, and we can continue to condition you to think a certain way.

A way that will keep you stuck, frustrated and believing this is the best you can do.

Guess what?!

They are winning.

They are whooping your ass.

Not just a little bit, but a lot.

It slowly happened over the years, but now they have you full-blown controlled.

You are a victim of Distraction.

You didn't even know it until right now.

They have been going after you subconsciously and psychologically.

They understand you don't know you are in the game they are playing with you.

They know what you will do before you actually do it.

They have you conditioned.

Conditioned to act a certain way.

Conditioned to be and think the way they want.

It's time to wake up.

Wake up from the...

Distraction
Psychology
Tribalism
Consumerism
Marketing

It's time for you to recognize what's going on in the world today and how it's affecting you and your life.

You will have to wake up from all of the darkness of your comfortable slumber.

To do this, you need to be Fully Focused.

It's literally the only thing that will save you right now.

You are so deep in it right now, you are going to question what I just said.

You are going to be like, this guy is crazy.

Is he a conspiracy theorist?

The answer is no.

I'm just not that deep in.

I was where you are and got out.

I'm here to help you get out and create the life you really want.

No more settling.

No more this is good enough.

No more hopelessness.

No more weakness.

It's time for you to beat this and gain the clarity of being Fully Focused.

Here is how you become Fully Focused.

1. Plan

Plan a short amount of time at a specific time each day. I call it the 2-Minute Drill.

It can be as little as 2 minutes or as much as 15 minutes. Just start with 2 minutes.

Pick a task. Any task that will make you better. Make sure you have everything you need to work on the task (computer, exercise equipment, a book, a pen, clothes, etc.), and follow the below steps.

Set a timer for 2 minutes and then set a separate timer for the desired 2–15 minutes.

Before you start the task:

a. Close your eyes.
b. Breathe in deep.
c. Breathe out and count to 10.

Do this over and over again until your 2-minute timer goes off. When your timer goes off, start into your task and stay fully focused, with every fiber of your body, into the task.

Really focus on the details of what you are doing. Once your second timer goes off, you're done. Repeat this each day and adjust the timers as you get better at being Fully Focused.

2. Eliminate

Eliminate your distractions. In today's world that means technology. Turn it completely off and keep it out of sight during your Fully Focused time.

Also, look at how you can eliminate environmental distractions. What area of your home are you using? Is there a TV on nearby? Then find a quiet corner in another room. Do you need to go outdoors? Find a place that allows you to focus.

Figure out how you can set yourself up for success by eliminating controlled distractions in your environment like music, temperature, lighting, flooring, etc.

3. Lock In

Being in Full Focus is such a powerful gift, but you will have to work at it to be able to turn it on and off when you need to. This is what is called being Locked In.

This separates all of the super achievers from the average person. The fastest way to do this is to come up with a Fully Focused Routine. One that triggers your conditioned Fully Focused self to Turn On and Lock In. Here is how you do it.

1. Pick a trigger (place, sensation, phrase or thing).
2. Before you start your Fully Focused activity, use or speak or do the trigger.
3. Once you do this over and over again, you will condition yourself to be Locked In when you execute the trigger.

It typically takes 7–30 days to create and develop this automatic response. Once you do, it is an amazing, powerful tool for you to use at your disposal.

Once you understand what is holding you back (Distraction) from the life and dreams you want, you must constantly identify the distractions specifically and use Full

Focus to wake up from the subconscious psychological behavior.

You are 2 minutes away from being Fully Focused and living the life you want.

Don't let another day go by settling for this life.

Become Fully Focused on the things that will make today different from yesterday, and tomorrow Locked In on the life you want to live!

Mental Muscle

*"Strength doesn't come from what you can do.
It comes from overcoming things you once thought
you couldn't." ~Unknown*

Building anything can be hard, especially if you have spent years of your life doing so.

The sweat, stress, ups and downs that come along with building are not for the faint of heart.

When you build just about anything, you go through struggles and unforeseen problems.

One after another and when you least expect it.

Each problem comes out of nowhere and is more frustrating than the last.

Normally these unforeseen problems come in clusters.

Problem after problem after problem.

This is what makes building so challenging.

The problems during the process are literally trying to make you quit, make you throw in the towel and never try again.

Once you understand this is how it works, you can aim your focus where it needs to be.

When you take your negative focus off of all the consistent problems that keep tempting you to quit, you put all of your attention into solving the problem.

You turn a negative focus into a positive focus. You make the decision that no matter what happens, "I'm going forward!"

What you are using is called Mental Muscle.

Mental Muscle is one of your greatest gifts and abilities. It is a wonderful tool that you develop over time.

The great thing about Mental Muscle is it's automatic. Once you have it, it kicks in without you having to do too much.

When a problem pops up, your Mental Muscle says "No problem" to the problem.

It simply and logically says, "Let's do this. Let's try this!"

And so on.

Your Mental Muscle isn't worried, and knows it will win in the end.

It's strong enough to deal with anything that pops up in your life.

Mental Muscle is one of the highest abilities you have, because it works in the background. It is always there, guiding your building process and balancing any issues or roadblocks in your way.

When you understand and believe in your Mental Muscle, you will start seeing problems in a different light. They will become building blocks to your Dreams.

You will start to see solutions instead of problems.

You will start to see the bigger picture. The high rise view.

It's a totally different perspective when you are out of the weeds and looking down on everything from above.

You see things you couldn't see when stuck in the weeds.

That's what Mental Muscle gives you: a better perspective and better outlook.

The characteristics that Mental Muscle gives you are…

Hope
Strength
Decision
Confidence
Positive Outlook
Direction
Consistency
Focus
Fortitude

Just like a muscle in your body, you can strengthen, build and shape your Mental Muscle. Below are 3 steps on how to do so.

3 Steps to Increase Your Mental Muscle

Step #1: Assessment

You must start with a quick assessment of your Mental Muscle.

Let's look at how you think when a problem arises.

1. Do you get an adverse reaction in your body when a problem pops up?

2. Do you get a negative reaction with your thoughts when a problem pops up?

3. Do you get a drop in confidence that grows into doubt when a problem pops up?

Now that you have an idea of your reaction around problems, it's time to move onto Step #2.

Step #2: Creating a Base

You will have to create a base when starting to build your Mental Muscle.

This means starting with a low to moderate stressor.

The last thing you want to do is over-stress your Mental Muscle.

Start by reacting differently to your normal everyday problems.

When you feel yourself getting triggered from an unexpected problem, slow everything down and ask yourself:

1. "What's the best way to handle this problem in a positive manner?"

2. "What can I learn from this problem?"

3. "How can I avoid this problem in the future or at least make it not such a big deal?"

When you activate your conscious decision-making abilities as a problem arises, you automatically gain and build Mental Muscle.

Focus on slowing down and asking the above three questions.

Step #3: Set a PR

A PR is a Personal Record. You should choose one day a week or one day a month to really challenge your Mental Muscle.

Then do something that you aren't used to doing or have never done before. Something that scares you a little bit. Something that isn't guaranteed that you will accomplish.

A PR is needed to stretch your abilities and strength.

You will also get a massive amount of motivation from a PR.

1. What can you do to set a new PR?

2. What's the one PR that when you accomplish it, it will make the largest impact on your dreams?

3. What PR will make you shake your head in disbelief?

When you are constantly setting Personal Records, you tend to start to enjoy life just a little bit more.

There will be some struggle involved, but the success that comes with the struggle brings a completeness that few ever experience.

It's time for you to develop and strengthen your Mental Muscle.

You have the muscle inside of you to build the life you want.

Yes, problems will pop up out of nowhere and test your resolve, but lucky for you, God gave you the Mental Muscle needed.

Don't waste another day sitting on the sidelines of life taking what comes your way.

Stand up and build the life you want to live.

One brick.
One 2x4.
One nail.
One screw.
One shingle.
One step.

At a time.

Your life will not change if you don't.

It's time to build you.

It's time for you to work towards your dreams and build your life up.

Are you ready to use your Mental Muscle and set a new PR in your life today?

Get Moving!

"The first step towards getting somewhere is to decide that you are not going to stay where you are."
~Unknown

You might be experiencing a time in life you have never experienced before.

You might be completely lost and unsure what to do next.

You are stuck in a cycle of uncertainty.

It's hard to know what to do next when everything in your world has come to a screeching halt.

You will find it harder to get started each day.

To focus.

To perform.

To be the old you.

You will try to search and ask, "Why is this happening to me?!"

You might even have thought about just giving up. Something you never thought you would actually face in your life. It crossed your mind or it is crossing your mind right now.

You're not happy with your current life and you don't know how to fix it.

You definitely don't know this version of you. You are used to having yourself together and on top of everything. You feel guilty that you let things slip.

You know deep down it's time to get back to your old self.

What you are going through is hard as hell.

How you feel is not uncommon, but for you it is.

It's not easy, not pleasant, and will take some Mental Muscle to get yourself back.

You are experiencing this for a greater reason that will allow you to accomplish your specific purpose.

Identifying this hurts.

The reality hurts.

Starting over hurts.

But living like this another day doesn't just hurt, it kills.

It kills the best part of you.

It turns you into a hopeless zombie walking around cynically looking at the world lifeless.

The time to save you is now.

To bring you back to the other side.

The side that is you.

Where you are full of life.

A life filled with…

Positivity
Passion
Confidence
Hope
Fulfillment
Purpose
Strength
Empathy
Motivation

It's time you get yourself back to being your best.

It's time to stop sitting on your hands and stand up.

Stand up for you and your Dreams.

Yes, what you went through, are going through, and the scary choice to command something different sucks, but you deserve to be your best.

We deserve your best.

It's time to Get Moving.

Get Moving…

Forward…
In a New Direction…
To a New You…
Towards the Best You…

The you that everyone needs.

Your time is now. The more you wait for things to correct themselves, the deeper the whole you dig.

The closer you are to losing the best side of you. The side that makes you happy and a difference maker. The side that dreams big and uplifts everyone around you.

It's time to Get Moving.

It's time to build.

To build you, one simple step at a time.

To do this you must Get Moving in a new direction.

The one that you can honestly say you are scared of.

The one you don't know how to be successful at.

The direction that will challenge you.

The direction that will scare you.

The direction that will teach you.

The direction that is uncertain.

The direction deep down you know you need to go.

The direction that will get you back to who you are.

Now that you know which direction you must go, Get Moving!

Habit Stacking & How It Can Change Your Life

"If you cannot do great things, do small things in a great way." ~Napoleon Hill

The easiest way to stay focused and accomplish your goals is to use Habit Stacking.

Habit Stacking is when you pick two or more habits to do at once.

Habit Stacking also has something called a trigger.

A trigger is something specific you do that triggers your habit or series of habits to start.

This makes creating a habit so much easier!

The trigger can be anything from brushing your teeth, drinking a cup of coffee, listening to a specific playlist or even a phrase you say in your head.

An example is…

> As I lay my head down on my pillow to go to sleep (trigger), I take a moment to find something to be grateful for from today (habit #1) and then focus on some great things I want to have happen tomorrow (habit #2).

It's that simple and is a massively powerful tool for you to accomplish your goals and dreams.

The beauty of Habit Stacking is you are creating and using a powerful subconscious tool you might not even know you have.

It's your internal autopilot system.

This system allows you to do certain actions without thinking.

The trigger turns on the autopilot system and then the rest automatically happens without too much thinking.

If you haven't used your autopilot system before, you must take the time to prime and prepare it to kick in.

This happens by Habit Stacking.

Here is how you do it…

6 Steps to Creating a Habit Stack

1. Pick a habit or two to start. (Keep it simple.)
2. Set a predetermined duration of time to do the habit or habits. (Start out with shorter periods.)
3. Schedule a specific time to do it. (Time, days of the week, etc.)
4. Pick a trigger. (Going to a specific area, doing something specific, saying something specific, etc.)
5. Start the habit. (No matter how you feel, start the habit. The resistance is in the feeling, not the habit.)
6. Keep the streak going. (If you miss a day, no worries. Start the next day.)

Start Reading A Book Example: Start reading every Monday at 8 a.m. for 10 minutes (habit) while sitting in my living room on my comfortable chair sipping coffee (trigger).

You can insert any habit from physical to educational or even spiritual to financial.

The beauty of Habit Stacking is once you get it going, you don't have to really think about it at all.

It's simply something you do.

This allows you to:

1. Not get burned out.
2. Not get frustrated with having to remember to do the same task each day.

As you continually use Habit Stacking, you will get so good at it that you create more down time and less stress in your life.

You will become efficient and effective in all areas of life.

Once you are at this point, you will find a calming feeling.

This feeling is a result of your Habit Stacking and how much better you have personally gotten from it.

I will close with this—once you know there is a better way to do things in life, it is your duty to yourself to do it.

Many people want to complain about their situation while making excuses of why everything isn't going the way they want.

This is becoming extremely popular in our modern world.

It's gotten to the point of blaming others for their situation.

This is the harsh reality…

You know better and must do better today, tomorrow and into the future.

No one is coming to bail you out or hold your hand.

You have to take ownership of your situation and do something others won't.

You are here for a reason, and that reason will change you and everyone around you for the better.

Are you ready to own your situation and do better for yourself today?

Choose OUT-STANDING!

"If you want to stand out, don't be different, be outstanding." ~Meredith West

You are either with us or against us.

At least that's what it feels like in today's world.

The majority is now Average.

They have Average:

Beliefs
Expectations
Health
Bodies
Goals
Hopes
Dreams
Lives

But that's not all.

The Average is spreading the Average Way.

The Average Way is…

The safe and secure way.
The "do what the majority believe and we will accept you" way.
The "don't think for yourself" way.
The "trust us, we know what's best for you" way.

The majority want you to stay in your lane.

They want you to walk around accepting the life you have, not the one you want.

The pressure is only increasing by the day.

They use a tribal force to convert and grow more people to their Average Way.

This strong force puts a ton of pressure on you to fit in.

It's called Social Pressure, and it is created to make you feel like an outcast.

Social Pressure is designed to make you feel unsafe in some form or fashion so that you fall back into the mindless, think-and-look-like-everyone robotic line.

The Average Way uses Social Pressure as a tool.

One that is constantly being hammered into you.

Chipping away at you.

Chipping away at your hopes and Dreams.

Making you feel that trying is impossible.

The Average Way wants you to do what they are doing so you'll be safe.

Safe from Failure.
Safe from Disappointment.
Safe from Danger.
Safe from Fear.

But the problem with this Average Way of thinking is…

You will be safe from all the good in life too.

Safe from Hope.
Safe from Joy.
Safe from Passion.
Safe from Fulfillment.
Safe from your Confidence.
Safe from your Purpose.
Safe from your Goals.
Safe from your Dreams.

You will miss out on who you are truly supposed to be and the purpose of your life.

The Average Way might be in the majority right now, but it doesn't mean it's the right way for you.

The secret to beating the Average Way is actually pretty simplistic.

It's the opposite of the Average Way.

It's an antonym of average.

It's being OUT-STANDING.

This is when you are believing and doing things that are so far above the Average they are OUT-STANDING.

You are fighting the Average Way.

Fighting to get OUT.

OUT—of the Average Way thinking.

STANDING—to Fight for you.

Standing on your own. Believing and trusting in yourself, not the myth of the Average Way.

When you are fighting to be OUT-STANDING, you are fighting for yourself and for the people that need you, and you are fighting with the few that can save the average.

You are fighting for:

Your Hope
Your Joy
Your Passion
Your Fulfillment
Your Confidence
Your Purpose
Your Goals
Your Dreams

Each day you will have to make a decision to follow the Average Way or go for OUT-STANDING.

It will be a constant choice with consequences.

The more you choose OUT-STANDING, the faster you will become the best you.

The more you choose the Average Way, the more frustrated, lost and stuck you will feel.

Being OUT-STANDING isn't going to be easy, but it will be worth it.

Are you ready to OUT-STAND the Average?

Forget Fear

"Everything you want is on the other side of fear."
~Jack Canfield

Fear is all you know.

It's what keeps you up at night. It's what doesn't allow you to feel good about yourself. It's what makes you have more bad days than good days.

Fear F#$#s with you in many ways.

Bigger than that, Fear steals your joy.

It steals your happiness. Your fulfillment. Your passion. Your Life.

Fear sucks and makes you suck at life.

It sidelines you from what you were made for. What you were created to do in this world.

Fear makes you question every step you take. It makes you wish for a better future, but freezes you in place at the same time.

Everytime you take a step forward, Fear F#$@s with you.

It makes you soft and weak. It holds you and your abilities down.

Fear is the only thing holding your power back.

Everything in life that you want but are too scared to even recognize is stopped by fear.

Fear is a belief.
Fear is a thought.
Fear isn't real.

Fear is what you make it.

How you act when you feel fear will determine how successful you will be.

When you feel Fear you can respond in a few different ways.

You can let Fear freeze you.
You can let Fear push you.
You can let Fear teach you.

The trick to conquering Fear is to understand you are in control of it.

You can use it to make you better, or you can use it to break you down.

When you change your attitude on Fear, bigger things start to happen.

Like when you are so fearful you don't do something for a long time, and then one day you do it and say, "That wasn't actually scary at all!"

Right now there is something that you are thinking of which freezes you with Fear.

It's probably the one thing that will make you become better and upgrade your life.

It might even be the missing piece to accomplishing your Dream.

Do you know what it is?

Do you?

I know you do.

Because I've been there, done that and got the punch card.

The best way to beat Fear and become thawed out from Fear is to go knock on its door. When you look at Fear as a door and to conquer the feeling of it you just have to knock.

Some doors are easier to knock on than others.

The kind of door I'm talking about is the one that when you go to knock, your hand is shaking and every bone in your body wants to turn and run.

The best way to knock is as soon as possible, before you let doubt and worst case scenarios build up falsely in your head.

Once you knock, just see what happens.

Does the door open, stay closed, or do you hear a massive dog growling behind the door?

If the door opens even a little bit, walk through it and let yourself see what happens next.

If the door stays closed, knock again and see what happens.

If you hear a massive dog growling behind the door, knock again but be ready to run if things don't go well. Or go knock on a different door.

No matter what, you will have to face Fear one knock at a time.

But when you use this approach, it allows you to keep it simple. It allows you to experience different directions and make educated decisions based on the doors that are opening for you.

You might be so paralyzed by Fear that your current mentality won't get you to your goals or Dreams.

You will have to knock on a couple doors that might lead to other doors you never thought would possibly open.

Never waste another day living in Fear and growing your doubt.

You are meant to live the life you want.

Forget Fear one knock at a time.

See the good that comes from an open and closed door in your life, but never be scared to keep knocking.

The New Way

"It's hard to see the world in a new way when you are doing things the same old way."
~Dorie Clark

Man the Old Way is getting Old.

And…FAST!

The thing about the Old Way is it's great until it's no longer great anymore.

One day it's working the way you want it to, and the next day it's old and outdated.

This isn't a complete shock.

As the days have gone by you started to be okay with how the Old Way was going.

You knew it wasn't as good as it used to be but it was easier to go with what you knew.

The lesser evil right?!

The problem is, as you turned a blind eye to the Old Way, you became detached from the reality of the situation.

The Old Way died a long time ago…

You just kept holding onto it for comfort, nostalgia and hoping it would be revived like a bad Woody Allen film.

And now you are stuck in some comfortable, nostalgic Old Way that needs to be put out to pasture.

It's time to let go and move on.

Don't move on to just anything, and please don't grasp and try to add back another Old Way.

You need a New Way.

A way that is fresh and updated.

It's like getting a new haircut. Once you get a new haircut or ladies a new color, all of a sudden you feel:

Refreshed
Energetic
Recharged

And like a New Person.

Sometimes all you need to let go of the old is something new.

Maybe it's a New Passion.
Maybe it's a New Relationship.
Maybe it's a New Career.
Maybe it's a New Idea.

Whatever it is, it's New to you and that's a good thing.

When you decide to go in a New Way, you will feel a bunch of different emotions.

From…
Scared
To…Confident.

From…
Tired
To…Energized.

From…
Frustrated
To…Focused.

You will see an immediate difference in how you feel, look and think.

You will become different and updated.

You will be with the times, not behind the times.

When you constantly think about a New Way, everything starts to fall into place for you.

It's as if this happens because of some universal law.

A law that rewards you for evolving. For becoming a better New version of you.

Once you understand that your Old Way is standing in the way of the life you want, you will start to realize you are now in control.

Not just any control, but in control of what happens next.

You can dismiss that you are the problem, or you can acknowledge it and start on your New Way.

Yes, this might scare the shit out of you, and it will not feel good at first, but day by day it will not only get easier but it will become Your Way.

Your Way you help others.
Your Way you are passionate.
Your Way you are a better parent.
Your Way you are a great leader.
Your Way you are a better you.

Don't waste your days unhappy and stuck in Your Old Ways.

It's time to do something different.

Something New, Refreshing and Needed.

Your New Way can start today if you choose to acknowledge that the Old Way isn't working anymore.

Out with the OLD and in with the NEW will make you better, too!

Your Motivational Fire

"The most powerful weapon on earth is the human soul on fire." ~Ferdinand Foch

Are you Motivated?

Yes or No?

That's the question I have for you today.

There is no room for "I'm not sure" or "Sometimes."

You are either Motivated or Not.

It's a great question because it's pretty much a black or white question.

Yes or No and no in between.

So…

Are you Motivated?

Yes or No.

When you take the time to be extremely truthful when answering this question, it allows you to know where you stand and what you need to work on to change your answer or keep that Yes going.

The fastest way to get your Motivation back is what I like to call Spark.

I like to call it Spark because that's all you need.

Just like the way a fire starts with one tiny spark.

You need to hear something, see something or do something that will provide that Spark.

The Spark can come from anywhere.

It can be borrowed.

It can be paid for.

It can be earned.

Either way, to create this Spark inside of you will require you to take action.

Specific action that will create the Spark.

Just like starting a fire, your Spark will have to come from either another fire, a lighter or by rubbing two sticks together.

Whichever method you choose, you must take an action to Spark your Motivational Fire.

Once you do, your Motivational Fire will grow.

As you create your Motivational Fire based on actions, you will need to constantly feed your motivation different types of fuel to keep the fire burning strong.

Some fuels will keep your Motivational Fire exactly where it is. (Think Paper.)

Some fuels will slowly grow your Motivational Fire bigger and bigger. (Think Firewood.)

Some fuels will explode your Motivational Fire all at once. (Think Gasoline.)

The goal with Motivational Fire is to keep a steady baseline level and to grow it over time with the occasional explosion that helps you tackle those big moments in life.

The difficulty with most of us today is we are using only 2 of the 3 fuel sources to keep our Motivational Fire going.

We are mainly using Paper and Gas.

The problem with this is that when we use Gas, we are getting a huge short explosion of Motivation.

This Motivation is fast, creates a large amount of it, but is short lived.

After using this high, short-term explosive resource too much, you can risk depleting your fire's base to a very low level.

It could also be completely put out depending on the amount you use, how often you use it or for how long you use it.

The difficulty in creating a balanced fire is that once our Motivational Fire comes back down, it will return to a lower level than before or could completely go out.

Your fire will need additional time to build back up with more of the other, longer-sustainable resources before you can put the gas back on.

You can get addicted to using the "pour gas on it" type of Motivation, as it causes a euphoric high.

It can also lead to overuse and depletion of this Motivational resource.

The second resource that we tend to use is paper.

This fuel is small and you need a lot of it to keep your Motivational Fire going.

You are constantly tending to it and always focusing on it.

This can be flat out tiring.

As you get tired, you let your Motivational Fire dwindle down because it's simply too much work to continually feed the fire.

Once this happens, you grab the gas to pour on top so that you get a quick explosion of Motivation, which brings your fire back up quickly.

This creates a never ending loop of tiring lows to exciting highs.

Your Motivation becomes like a roller coaster of really high ups and really low downs.

You can deal with this for a little while, but after some time you get sick from all of the ups and downs.

You completely give up on your Motivational Fire and it goes out.

Until you fully recover, you will wonder what happened with your Motivational Fire, which will make it much more difficult to restart with yet another new Spark.

Sounds terrible, right?!

The amazing part about your Motivational Fire is there is a third resource option.

One that is lasting.

One that strengthens you.

One that prepares you.

Firewood.

Firewood is great because you can choose the amount, the size and the type needed for the situation your current Motivational Fire needs.

It's not just a one size fits all approach.

It's specific.

It's controlled.

It's structured.

You gain more control over your fire with firewood.

Yes, it will take some work at the beginning, but it will grow over time and is so much easier to maintain for longer periods of time.

You can actually plan with this type of resource.

You can choose what type, size and amount you need to throw into your Motivational Fire to have it build up to your needs.

You get to create a system that works for your Motivational Fire.

It doesn't have to be an all gas or nothing approach.

You have options and can use many different types based on your current motivation, your current life situation and what you want to accomplish in your future.

There is no need to keep the current cycle of a lifetime of ups and downs with sweating your ass off to create yet again another start over Spark.

When you choose firewood, you are strategically supporting your Motivational Fire.

You are Sparking your future and building your Motivational Fire one piece of firewood at a time.

You are only one Spark away, one piece of firewood and one Motivational Fire from your Dreams!

Go Spark today so that you are on Fire about tomorrow!

Forget Normal

"Be a fruitloop in a world of Cheerios."
~Unknown

Forget Normal. That isn't you.

But in a good way.

You don't actually want to be normal.

Normal is average, boring and lets life drive you. Normal makes you at the mercy of life. The mercy of some day, some time, some magical wish.

You are here to have an impact on life, the world and the people directly associated with you!

You are by no means Normal and you should start taking Normal as an insult.

When you are called Normal, you should be pissed off.

Normal is the status quo. Normal is what everyone is doing. Normal is okay. Normal is forgettable. Normal is a regrettable life.

You are way way way more than that.

You were made for more. For more...

Happiness
Fulfillment
Confidence
Impact
Change
Hope
Faith
Compassion

You are far from Normal and need to keep it that way.

Normal will never allow you to accomplish your dreams or create the life you never thought was possible.

Normal will kill your drive and passions.

You will trade them for other unfulfillments like alcohol, food, social media, Netflix and drama.

Normal makes you labeled as weird when you do something out of it.

Normal will constantly make you do things you really don't want to do.

Normal will lull you into a life you don't want.

Normal will keep you on that hamster wheel with fear. Fear of the unknown, Fear of the different, Fear of change.

The battle is real and you will need this one thing that Normal despises. This one thing is so powerful that Normal can't even touch it. It's a complete mismatch and guarantees a win for you everytime.

It's Yourself.

Be who you truly are.

Be your passions.
Be your dreams.
Be the person you have always wanted to be
Be who God created you to be.
Be the greatest _____.
Be the impossible.
Be the best of you.

Be Yourself.

When you do this, Normal doesn't even matter anymore.

It's not even on your radar.

Do what you know is right and be you.

Stop thinking about what the Normals will think.

Do you.

Be Yourself.

Be the difference to the people in your family, communities and world. Be the change that people say we need. Be the driver of your life and the influence that creates a new story that outlives you.

And Finally… Be the you that has no regrets in your last moment and your last breath.

The legendary are the few, not the many.

Are you one of them or just a Normal Joe?

YOKWYK

"The more you know, the more you know you don't know." ~Aristotle

Yes, I made up a word, but it's something that can change your life at the drop of a hat.

It's bigger than just about anything you can do.

It's an acronym for...

You
Only
Know
What
You
Know

I have no idea how you would say it, but I would guess it would be **Yok-Wyk**.

The deal with Yok-Wyk is you really are at the mercy of only knowing what you currently know.

We have an epidemic going on in our world today where the majority of people are making decisions without really knowing what's going on.

They don't take the time to slow down and ask themselves, "What do I know about this?"

They also aren't honest with themselves and don't admit they don't know anything about it.

Yet they still make a decision. It turns out to be a terrible one because they are stuck in a box or have a lens that isn't focused and sharp enough to know what's going on.

When you condition yourself to do this over and over again, you create a routine that works against you and limits your abilities.

The moment you wake up and realize that **You Only Know What You Know**, you start to do life differently.

You tap into a part of your brain that asks questions, tells you to slow down and finally makes an educated decision instead of an emotional decision.

In our modern world we run off of emotional decisions far more than we do educated decisions.

We tell ourselves we have researched it or slowed down to make an educated guess, but in reality all we have done is created an emotional opinion.

Now you know why we have become more opinionated than ever before.

Typically there is a stark anger or over-aggression behind this opinion, because deep down you know you didn't actually slow down, research it and let the logical part of your brain make a good decision.

You feel guilty and fearful you will be found out.

So, how do you use **Yok-Wyk**?

1. **Identify Your Wheelhouse**

    What areas do you really know a large amount about through research, experience or lifestyle?

    Not just any experience, but years of experience. Once you understand the specific areas, you will have to let your Ego know that anything outside of these areas you don't know enough about to make an educated decision.

    More importantly, you need to take time to learn more before making the decision. This allows you to break that emotional response routine that could be fighting against you.

2. Find a Credible Expert or Resource

Take the time to do your homework on this person or resource. Make sure they are good at what they do, have been doing it for a while and don't have an ulterior motive.

Most people fall for marketing today. Marketing is different from truth.

Understand the difference by how you feel. If you feel any emotions while reading the headline, you just got marketed.

Remember you want to take the emotional decision out, because that's the one that causes you all the trouble.

3. Personal Development

Sometimes when we use personal development, we stay in one lane and get comfortable.

We don't venture past our comfort zone, which only allows us to see things through one type of lens. The truth is, to develop yourself you will have to constantly sharpen and widen your lens to see things differently. When you do, you will realize that **You Only Know What You Know**.

So, say it with me: **Yok-Wyk**.

Use it, know it and decide that the best way to get to where you want to go is by understanding…

You
Only
Know
What
You
Know

And everything outside of Yok-Wyk is where your Dreams come true!

Why Are You Stuck?

"God provides the wind, but man must raise the sails." ~St. Augustine

One of the most frustrating things in life is when you feel completely Stuck.

I know when I feel Stuck, I'm..

Restless
Tired
Unhappy
Searching
Annoyed
Wishing for different

These are just some of the thoughts and emotions that go through you when you are feeling Stuck and beat up by life.

The moment you feel this way, you will have a choice to make.

You can keep asking…

Why?
Why Me?
Why Now?
Why, Why, Why?

...Or any other form of Why you can think of.

The other choice you can make is to start doing something about it.

You may think you need to know why something happens, but you really don't need to know.

When you get too caught up in the why, you become Stuck like a truck spinning its wheels in mud.

You keep asking and doing the same thing over and over again while the same result is happening, but now you are digging yourself into a deeper rut.

The only way out of Stuck and all the thoughts, feelings and emotions that come with it is to start doing something.

Something that creates Simple Action.

Simple Action in a direction that interests you or that you have always wanted to do.

To recap, the way you can get unstuck is to stop asking Why and start creating Simple Action in the direction you want your life to go.

If you want to lose weight or improve your health, start taking the most Simple Action in that direction.

If you want more energy to be a better parent or spouse, start taking the most Simple Action in that direction.

If you want a new career path or to follow a dream you have always had, start taking the most Simple Action in that direction.

When you stop asking why and start asking yourself, "What Simple Action can I take next?" your life will dramatically change and that feeling of being Stuck will go away.

When you feel Stuck, it's your internal guidance system telling you, it's time to do something different.

It's time to let go of whatever you are holding onto and start living in the present moment.

It's time to let the frustration and friction go.

It's time to stop fighting the actions you need to take to have the future of your dreams.

Each day is a gift for you to either take Simple Action and live the tomorrow of your dreams, or stay Stuck in the monotony of yesterday.

It's your choice.

Which choice are you going to make today?

The Hard Truth

"Before you can win, you have to believe you are worthy." ~Unknown

I wish I could tell you that everything will be easy in life and you will be happy all of the time, but the truth is there will be hard times that will test you.

You have most likely already gone through some of them, and there will be more to come.

One of the hardest ones you will have to deal with is your sense of self-worth.

Worthy is a feeling.

Many things in life will make you question if you are Worthy of what you want or want to happen.

When you don't feel Worthy, you tend to subconsciously make decisions that make you go backwards.

You can make simple decisions that erode your progress over time, or you can make those not-so-good terrible decisions that blow up everything when you are close to accomplishing your goals, dreams and ideal situation.

No matter what, you will have to become awakened to this.

If you are consistently stuck in the same position over and over again, you must look at your sense of self-worth.

If you go up and down over and over again, gaining and losing the same 10 pounds, having your relationships be great and then terrible, your income up and down but never breaking through to a life-changing amount, or you are stuck in an "I'll start this today, okay maybe tomorrow, or someday" mentality.... Then you likely don't feel Worthy.

When you don't feel Worthy, you will subconsciously make poor decision after poor decision until you are back to your comfortable Worthy situation you are used to.

You are always fighting *comfortable,* no matter if it is good or bad for you.

Some signs you are not feeling Worthy in a particular area or dream you have are:

Procrastination
Anger

Frustration
Lack of Passion
Growth of Ego
Depression
Becoming Negative
Making Yourself Unavailable to Others
Losing Interest in Your Passions

When you start to see yourself do any of these, you must recognize sh@# isn't headed in the right direction and somewhere in life you are not feeling worthy of the good that is about to happen or is happening.

As I write this, I started to take breaks and mindlessly check my phone. That right there is some procrastination.

Maybe because there is a part of me that is not feeling Worthy to coach you on self-worth.

I began to get thoughts like, "Who am I to give this type of advice? I still struggle with feeling worthy. I haven't completely overcome this struggle in my life yet, either."

But...

Deep down I know that I am the perfect person to coach you on self-worth because I have constantly dealt with it and I have beat it many times before, just like you can and will do.

As you focus your attention on where you want to go with your life, please understand that at times you will not feel Worthy and that is okay.

It's okay because that feeling is simply that.

Just a feeling.

It's not you.

You get to decide if you want to believe it or not.

I would choose not to!

You are Worthy of your goals, dreams and life you want to live. When you truly believe that, your life will see a massive increase.

As you go into tomorrow, please take the time to decide whether you will believe that not Worthy feeling.

Just like anything else in your life, when you make it a habit to believe you are Worthy, you will start to magically stop having those feelings of being Unworthy.

That will simply make your everyday life so much better.

You will be able to focus all of your attention and energy on doing the things that will make your goals and dreams come true.

Make your today Worthy so that tomorrow can be the day you get to live the life you never thought possible!

How to Fight Resistance?

"Out of resistance comes strength."
~Napoleon Hill

To be honest with you, the word Resistance makes me cringe and think, "Not again!"

Over the years it seems like the older you get, the harder things become.

You can feel as if you are always fighting against something.

Whether it's dealing with a setback or your 20th problem of the day.

It literally feels like life is fighting you.

This feeling and reality is Resistance.

Resistance comes in many forms, but always does one thing… it makes you choose either to stand and deal with it (fight) or run from it (flight).

The magical thing about Resistance, is when you stand against it, you come out better on the other side of it.

Resistance is there to develop, grow and strengthen you.

You literally become a better version of you!

Since there are two choices when it comes to Resistance, we will have to take a minute to talk about what happens when we run from it.

When you run from Resistance, you condition yourself to stop standing up to anything that isn't easy in your life and you condition yourself to stay seated and take what comes your way.

You become anxious, depressed and have feelings of hopelessness.

You become fearful, negative and pessimistic about what you are capable of in your life.

You create a self-contained box that limits your ability to be your best.

When you have been running from Resistance for a long time, you tend to only see things from your limited perspective.

That perspective is normally from an unrealistic vantage point that has a skewed point of view.

You can beat Resistance by using STOP!

S – Stand
T – Turn around
O – Observe
P – Push

When we Stand, it forces us to stop what we are doing and take in what is going on around us.

It allows us to regroup and gain a better perspective.

When we Turn around, it allows us to see where we have come from and if we are still on track.

It allows us to decide if we want to keep moving in the direction we are currently going.

When we Observe, we see what is around us that can help make things become easier for us.

It allows us to find support and guidance that helps us along the way.

When we Push, we do things that are out of our normal routine.

It allows us to go against what we are naturally conditioned to do.

When you choose STOP, you surprise Resistance and get a competitive advantage on it.

You must understand, Resistance knows how to play you.

It knows if you like to run or stand and fight.

It knows if you like to sleep in or eat ice cream at night.

It knows if you like to procrastinate or work from home.

It knows that when you have a long day, it will win every time.

Resistance knows you and wants to take you out.

It's time for you to recognize that you are in a fight, whether you like it or not.

Are you ready to STOP and start beating Resistance in your life again?

Tomorrow Is Going to Be Better!

*"None of us can change our yesterdays,
but all of us can change our tomorrows."*
~Colin Powell

This is something you need to hear today…

Tomorrow is going to be better for you.

We are not just talking about the future, we are talking about a valuable principle.

That principle is believing that tomorrow is going to be better.

No matter what happened today, always condition yourself to believe that tomorrow is going to be better.

No matter the odds that are for you or against you, make sure that you truly realize that everything resets after today and you get to decide what will happen from this moment forward as you go into tomorrow.

This is the single biggest difference between successful, happy people and people who are stuck and struggling through their lives.

I'm not going to sit here and lie to you and say I've only been on the successful side of things.

I've been on both sides, and I've had to fight my way back over once I lost my way.

And…

So will you!

Since life isn't created to be a perfect straight line to success, you will go through todays that make you want to give up.

Todays that shake you at your core.

Even todays where you make massive mistakes and have to mentally face the fact that you screwed up and can't fix it.

No matter what you think, there will be a moment during today where you will have to believe tomorrow will be better.

On the other hand, everything could be going the best it has ever gone for you today, and you will still be faced with a moment that whispers to you that says, "This is as good as it gets."

You must make a decision to either believe that whisper and create an artificial ceiling on your tomorrow, or go back to the principle and choose to know that tomorrow will be a better day.

The most dangerous time for you is not when you are having a bad day. It's when your today goes really well. When your day goes really well, you believe this is as good as it gets or you take your foot out of the pedal slightly as you create comfort.

There are a couple ways to combat this form of resistance.

1. **You are in control of tomorrow.**

   Understand that when each today is done, there is a start to tomorrow, and you dictate how that goes.

   If you believe that yesterday was as good as it gets, then your current today will not measure up.

2. **Condition your thinking.**

   When you condition yourself to believe the reality that tomorrow will be better, you are choosing to take control and not allow life to just happen to you.

   You are happening to life and must condition yourself to realize it, understand it and believe it.

As you close out today and think about tomorrow, believe that tomorrow will be better and watch how your dreams start to come true.

Are you ready for your tomorrow to be better than today?

Traveling Up, Up & Away!

*"You cannot change your destination overnight,
but you can change your direction overnight."*
~Jim Rohn

As humans, we are used to staying still. We are used to staying in one place and not venturing out past our comfort zone.

For instance, 79% of people will stay in the same town they were born in. Never really venturing out to live in a different place. They only know one environment. The one that they grew up in.

This can be great for some and not so great for others.

Sometimes, when you want to accomplish big things, your environment can stop you or hold you back.

Your environment is made up of all kinds of aspects that influence how you live and act. From geography, to the size of the town. From how many people, to how those people think and act. All of these aspects matter in your environment.

When you want to make a drastic or simple improvement towards a goal, you must go above your environment.

You must:

Think
Act
Be

Different!

Sometimes that's hard when you are stuck in a certain environmental situation.

If you want to go UP in your life, you will have to change your environment.

You will have to improve 1 of 3 aspects of your environment that will help you go UP.

1. **Smart People**

    You will need to get around people who think at a higher level and expect more from themselves.

2. **Supportive People**

You will need to get around people who will support you and challenge you to be better.

3. Positive People

You will have to have positive people in your life that will pick you up when you stumble or fall.

When you make the choice to go UP, it can come with some difficult decisions.

Decisions that make you uncomfortable short-term, but will accelerate your life in many ways long-term.

Changing your environment is one of them.

All of the challenge and fear is in the thought of changing your environment.

It's the unknown.

The ifs and buts.

It's in the "what if I fail"s.

All of this runs through your head and doesn't allow you to go UP.

You simply can't go UP with certain negative influences pulling you back down.

It's time for you to go UP UP And AWAY to the life you deserve to live.

What do you need to let go of in order to go UP?

Have a GREAT Day!

*"When we are no longer able to change a situation,
we are challenged to change ourselves."*
~Victor Frankl

In your life you will have days that are Good, GREAT, and Lousy.

There will be a mix of these days in your life depending on what you decide to do.

The mix could be more Good days, more GREAT days or more Lousy days.

Where would you rank the majority of your days currently?

Good?

Great?

Lousy?

Whichever you choose, you must understand that your thinking and actions have determined the number and kind of days you currently experience.

You will only increase or decrease the number of your current Good, Great or Lousy days going forward if and when you decide to think and act differently.

You must constantly decide to take action.

Action in how you think and act on the supporting things you do each day to create the outcome you are looking for.

Of course, you want more GREAT days.

Who doesn't?!

Days where everything goes perfectly and you feel on fire about your life.

The problem with creating more of these days is your thinking.

First off, you must realize that these days don't naturally occur. They are the results of all your day in and day out actions.

The other part to reflect on is your expectations. What you typically expect is what you typically get.

When you expect more GREAT days, you normally get more GREAT days.

When you expect more Lousy days, you normally get more Lousy days.

Now, you might be in a place right now where you are having way more Lousy days.

I've been there and done that multiple times.

I understand how you feel.

Down
Unmotivated
Uninspired
Frustrated
Hopeless
Wondering Why?
Unsure
And…Ready to Give Up!

If you have ever felt this way, it's not a good place to be.

But I will tell you right now, it is a good place for you and here are two reasons why.

1. **You have no choice but to go up.**

    You're down right now and stuck in the Lousy day cycle and it sucks, but you are also in the perfect place to rebuild your foundation.

Your foundation is the part of you that creates a strong base for you to grow yourself to higher heights than ever before.

When you get knocked down, you have three choices: stay down, keep getting beat down or stand up and fight back.

Choose to fight and magically you will find new inspiration and start having more good and GREAT days. The Lousy days cycle will become a thing of the past.

2. **Massive Advancement.**

   Almost always when you get knocked down there is a silver lining that comes of it. It comes in the form of a massive increase or life advancement.

   Sometimes you have to see things from another perspective to understand the direction you need to go. Sometimes it will be from the top, sometimes it will be from the bottom and sometimes it will be from somewhere in between.

   What you need to fully accept is that you needed that perspective to get to the next BIG thing. The next GREAT day. The next accomplished Dream. The next better version of yourself.

It's time for you to decide what you want to do next.

Are you ready to be the creator of your life and create the days you want to live?

GREAT days only happen when you decide you deserve them.

Think, act and be different today so that tomorrow can be one of the Greatest days of your life!

Stretching for Success

"A time comes when you need to stop waiting for the man you want to become and start being the man you want to be."
~Bruce Springsteen

Everyone knows Stretching is great for you. It leads to more flexibility, mobility and strength. It also brings help and relief to your aches and pains. One of the best daily routines should involve Stretching.

Aside from stretching physically, you can also stretch yourself mentally.

When you are Stretched mentally in life you become better.

The term Stretched in life has come and gone over the last 10 years.

You can sum it up as you are being pushed out of your comfort zone or moving further than you are used to.

Just like physical Stretching, you can only gain the benefits of Stretching by going just a little further than you are used to.

The problem all of us face in our modern lives is the growing pressure to be comfortable.

I could argue that most of society's problems are related to people being lulled into the belief that a life of comfort results in happiness.

In the end, though, the average person is depressed and unfulfilled with their lives.

Is this you?

Are you reading this and wishing you were truly happy and on fire about your life?

If you answered yes, it's time for you to start Stretching.

Not just the physical stretching (which is proven to help depression, by the way), but the mental kind of Stretching.

The beauty of Stretching is you don't have to go extremely out of your comfort zone or a large amount further than you are used to.

You just have to go a little bit more.

1% more

1 second more
1 degree more
1 inch more
1 rep more

Stretching yourself will change your situation faster than you could have ever imagined.

The hardest step in Stretching yourself is actually starting.

You have been conditioned to not feel. Society says that if you feel anything outside of your norm, it can't be good for you. They say come back to comfort.

Come back to what we are doing.

Come back to the 9–5.
Come back to the coffee.
Come back to the alcohol.
Come back to the food.
Come back to Netflix.
Come back to hours of social media scrolling.
Come back to the unhappiness.
Come back to the depression.
Come back to the comfort.
Come back to the normal.

Here is the deal: people will put pressure on you to stay the way you are currently. They want this because it's comfortable for them.

They know what to expect from you, which makes them comfortable.

You must break through this pressure and start Stretching yourself each day.

Life will not magically change for you. You will have to change your life.

A hope or a prayer without action will always leave you stuck in your comfort zone.

STRETCH yourself today and see how much further you get tomorrow!

"I Don't Feel Like It!"

"You can never expect to succeed if you only put in work on the days you feel like it."
~Unknown

Have you ever suffered from a case of "I don't feel like it"?

Your "I don't feel like it" could be anything. Maybe you don't feel like...

Eating Well
Exercising
Working
Reading
Cleaning
Going to Church
Going Shopping
Pushing Yourself
Doing the Right Thing

Giving in to this sense of "I don't feel like it" conditions you to create a habit of only doing the things you feel like doing in a particular moment.

When you do this, it weakens your resolve to improve in many areas of your life.

You only think emotional instead of logical.

Once you start down this road, it's very hard for you to turn around and go back in the right direction.

A good example of this is when you want to make a U-turn.

You can't just make one whenever and wherever you want.

You have to continue driving down the road, waiting for a place where you can complete the U-turn to go back in the right direction.

You are stuck going further than you want or need to, which means now you have to make up more ground to get back to where you started.

In order to stop yourself from giving into the "I don't feel like it" sensation, you must first recognize you are doing it.

Once you recognize it, ask yourself why? Why do I not feel like doing this?

Honestly answer.

Once you get your answer, ask yourself one more question.

When I do this particular thing that I don't feel like doing, will it help me go in the right direction?

If the answer is Yes, you must start doing it immediately. Don't wait another second.

You must take action and at least start.

When you start, you condition yourself to use action as your primary driver instead of inaction.

You trigger the part of your brain that makes logical decisions instead of staying in the emotional decision replay you are used to.

The more often you focus on this in all areas of your life, you will see everything fall into place.

Life will dramatically go smoother for you.

The other benefit is when you start the "I don't feel like it" task, you typically figure out new details that allow you to finish it faster and easier than you first thought.

There will be days where you feel like it and days where you don't.

The true attribute that separates successful people from struggling people is they take action no matter how they feel day in and day out.

They continually show up and complete the needed action regardless of the short-term result.

When you want a better you, you have to create the habit of showing up and taking action day in and day out, no matter if "I don't feel like it" pops up or not.

Are you ready to make your U-turn and go back in the right direction?

Do you want to see parts of your life magically take off?

Then today is the day to take action and show yourself how great you can be!

The Power of Resistance

*"Courage is resistance to fear,
mastery of fear, not absence of fear."
~Mark Twain*

There is great power in Resistance.

Throughout the world's history there have been plenty of resistance groups that popped up and changed the course of civilization.

For the US, it was in 1776 when a group of Americans decided to resist British rule.

They banded together with the idea for a better union and country developed on the idea of freedom.

Freedom was brought about by Resistance.

In your life right now, you are looking to grow your own freedom.

Freedom of:

Time
Health
Wealth
Happiness
Fulfillment
Living Life
YOU!

No matter what you currently think, you will always try to become free from something you don't currently like.

You will do whatever you can to get away or stop something that is causing you pain.

But sometimes the opposite happens. You start to get beaten down by the constant failures you have come to know.

Every time you try to get this pain out of your life, you run into another wall that stops you.

You become exhausted from the fight.

You start to think nothing will ever change, and start to condition yourself to not even try.

You sadly lose your fight and gain the perspective that this is just your modern life.

You see everything as impossible or a waste of time.

You slowly lose your Resistance and ultimately your freedom.

When all of this happens, everyday life gets dark, depressed and detached.

You let life dictate what happens, and even if you don't like what's going on or know deep down it's wrong, you still allow it to happen with little to no resistance.

Worse yet, you have become so cynical that you start bringing down others.

When you see that they are doing well or trying something you wish you would, you subconsciously have ill will towards them.

You judge, have a strong opinion or ridicule them because deep down you wish you had the nerve to take the steps they are.

You know something is missing inside of you, but you are too conditioned to not try anymore.

Something you used to have, but has slipped away from you...Resistance.

Resistance, which ultimately leads to Freedom, has something big behind it.

It's called PASSION.

Passion is what everyone is looking for.

Once you understand that Passion leads to Resistance and Resistance leads to Freedom, then you know that Passion is the ultimate answer to your Freedom.

How do *you* get passion?

First, you must look outside of yourself to fix and grow your situation. You will have to gain Passion through action for others. Whether it's your family, friends, a specific group of people, activity or a cause.

Second, once you have identified it, go all in on it. Do more of it. Spend more time doing it or thinking of who you are doing it for.

Once you understand the great power in Passion and Resistance, you can use these powers to get the Freedom and life you are looking for.

Don't let another day go by without standing up for yourself and creating the Freedom you want.

Grow your Resistance and get your fight back so that you can be passionate about your future Freedom!

It's Time to Fight Back

*"Whatever you fight, you strengthen,
and what you resist, persists."*
~Eckhart Tolle

It's your time to fight back.

You have been sitting on the sidelines way too long. It's time for you to fight for what you want out of life. Not just a little bit but with everything you have.

It's time to throw your first punch in the direction of your dreams.

No more "I'll start tomorrow" or "Maybe when I have time."

Stop NOW and fight. Throw that first punch with everything you have.

When you want to go after your Dreams, you will have to put everything behind your punches. Your goal is to knock out everything in the way of your Dream.

Right now you might feel down and washed up. You might think you have no power to even throw a punch.

Guess what?

You do. You have way more power inside of you than you realize.

When you start your fight and throw that first punch, many different things could happen.

You could knock out the obstacles to your goals and get your Dream. You could totally miss. You could land a punch and get a point.

No matter which one happens, you threw the punch and now you can throw another one.

Once you do this over and over again, you gain momentum and confidence.

When you fight for yourself, good things will happen. Not just something small but something massive and life-changing.

The other positive of fighting for you is who you become along the way. Regardless of what happens, you become better. You learn and you gain confidence and motivation.

When you learn how to throw multiple punches at the obstacles in the way of your dream, you develop something called a combo.

A combo is when you throw multiple different types of punches in a row.

This allows you to knock down those obstacles from different angles, which allows you to weaken them faster or even lead to a quicker knockout.

Are you ready to fight?

Are you ready to make you better?

Are you ready to see yourself win the fight?

Don't waste another day getting knocked out by life, stand up and throw a punch! You never know, it could be the knockout punch you needed to live the life you always wanted.

Rise UP

"The first step toward success is taken when you refuse to be a captive of the environment you first find yourself in." ~Mark Caine

There will be a time in your life when you will have no choice but to Rise UP.

It won't be easy. It will be unpopular. And you will be in the minority.

You will put it off and look the other way until you have no other choice but to Rise UP!

Your back will be against the wall, and you will have to risk everything.

When this time comes you will be scared and unsure. You will be tempted to go with the flow like everyone else. You will be tempted to sacrifice your morals to stay in good favor with the modern world. You must fight against these feelings and go deep.

Deep into your heart.

Deep into your spirit.

Deep into what you know is true.

Your time is coming. Your time to Rise UP!

You will have to Resist the wrong, the incorrect, the popular flawed opinion. It will be a fight that you don't have to go through, but when you do, it will change your world and our world for generations to come.

Don't be fearful, as once you Rise UP you will win. You will win the battles and the war of what is right and true.

True for you.

True for me.

True for others.

True for us.

Never waste your talent and calling because it won't be easy or popular. Do what you hold is true in your heart, and you will see a happiness and satisfaction that will last for a lifetime.

Your dreams will come true, but bigger than that, you will uplift others to such a high level that their dreams will come true, too.

So, my question for you is…

Are you going to Rise UP?

Are you going to fight the resistance and fear that stand in your way? Are you ready to fight for your true freedom? Not just basic freedom but the freedom to really live the life you want. The one that makes you a role model, a mentor and a legend.

You will have to Rise UP to get what you want in your life today.

The fear and resistance will always be there, no matter what you think. Life is only full of gumdrops and rainbows when you decide to be the creator of it. Your true freedom is only ever just one day away.

Are you ready to Rise UP and grab it?

Your Heart Is Gold

"Wherever you go, go with all your heart."
~Confucius

You will have many different situations happen to you in life.

These situations will be good. These situations will be bad. And these situations will be great.

Each one of the situations will pop up when you least expect it.

They will be tiny turning points in your life. They will also shape who you become. They will require you to make the right decision.

This decision is called a Golden Decision.

A Golden Decision is a decision that you will have to make from your heart. It's a decision that you will have to make in fear, uncertainty and without any support or direction. It's one of the rawest moments in your life.

There is no one around to ask advice. It's 100% on you.

If you make a fearful or morally compromised decision, there is no one to blame but you. But there also is no one around to know except you.

Your Golden Decision will strengthen your heart.

If you don't follow your heart, you will gain a heavy regret that will follow you through sleepless night after sleepless night.

You will try to run from it. You will use all sorts of distractions to mitigate the constant feeling of something being wrong.

These distractions can be one or more of the following:

Alcohol
Drugs
Food
Busyness
Anger
Bad Relationships
Money
Entertainment
Poor Health
Etc.

You can't run, because your heart will always chase you faster than you can run from it.

The sleepless nights, the unfulfilled days and the feeling of knowing you are going in the wrong direction will only strengthen.

The only thing that will save you is the Golden Decision. The decision to follow your heart.

No matter what you or others think, you must trust your heart's calling. It's there for a reason, and once you connect fully with it, you will have a massive amount of freedom.

The thing about creating a Heart of Gold is that it has to be forged.

Forged in fire.

The fires are the tiny turning point situations where you have to make a Golden Decision that will strengthen you.

The forge is hot and requires you to make Golden Decision after Golden Decision.

When you do this, you strengthen your Heart of Gold and knock off the slag that is holding you back.

The slag is the fears, compromises and distractions you have chosen in the past that have limited your ability to follow your heart.

Slag builds up over time and blocks your ability to listen to your heart.

The beauty of the forge is that it is a new opportunity to reset and reconnect you.

As you condition yourself to make Golden Decisions after Golden Decisions, you will find it dramatically easier to follow your heart.

Once you have conditioned yourself to follow your heart, you have knocked off all the slag to make it pure again.

You have a heart pure of gold.

Trust it.

Understand it.

Believe in it.

Are you ready to knock off the slag and follow your Dreams??

Double Down

"The two most important days in your life are the day you're born and the day you find out why."
~Mark Twain

There is going to be a time during the day where you will be on fire.

Everything will go better than planned and you will be full of confidence!

Not just any confidence, but BIG confidence. The kind that makes you feel invincible and like you could run through walls. It's one of the best feelings.

There will also be a time during the day where you have feelings of doubt and unworthiness.

Your energy will be zapped and you will feel like you are struggling just to start the simplest task. You will feel weak. It will be a weakness that makes you question everything you are doing.

There will be a moment where you think you should just give up on what you are doing.

It's one of the worst feelings.

This moment is vital. It's the moment that is integral to what's going to happen next in your life.

This moment is also the same moment after the feeling you get of being on fire and invincible.

What you will have to decide in both moments is, "What am I going to do next?"

The answer is Double Down.

Double Down on being on fire and invincible.

Double Down on that wonderful feeling.

Protect and nurture that feeling so that you can keep it going, and more importantly, replicate it.

The flip side of that moment is the "I wanna give up" feeling. It all starts when you feel like your energy is zapped, you're tired and it's easier to stop.

When that moment happens, you need to Double Down.

Not on the "I wanna give up" feeling, but on your commitment.

Your commitment to your goal or dreams.

Your commitment to your WHY.

Your commitment to the people that will be affected by you not giving up.

Whatever your goal is, Double the commitment.

Be over committed. Do something extra.

Go the extra mile.

Work longer, work harder and go for the death blow.

Double Down, Double Down!

Make sure you beat the hell out of that "I wanna give up" feeling so it does not pop up again.

The beauty of Doubling Down is that you stay locked in on the direction you want to go.

You are linking together the pieces and focus needed to accomplish your BIG Goals and Dreams.

Double Down today so that when tomorrow comes you are on fire about the direction you are going!

Don't waste a moment believing you should give up.

Double Down on YOU today, tomorrow and every day going forward.

You deserve to feel invincible and on fire about your future!

The Sun Will Come Out Tomorrow

"A winner is a dreamer who never gives up."
~Nelson Mandela

I don't know about you, but I love a sunny day.

It makes me feel great. There is something about the warmth and brightness of the sun that makes you feel good.

A sunny day always brings more opportunity to do things outside.

It opens the possibilities to the things you can do. You always feel so much better when you have options and the sun is out.

When you have a bunch of sunny days back to back, it affects you and the people around you.

You can see not only your mood but their moods improve.

It's gotta be all that extra vitamin D, or something bigger than that.

Take a moment and close your eyes. Picture in your head one of the best sunniest days you have ever had. It could be on a vacation, a certain celebration or just some random day. Take your time and picture it again. Enjoy the sounds, sights, memories and feelings.

Once you open your eyes, you will automatically feel better.

Understanding the power of vision is priceless.

You and every person on the planet have access to vision. However, most people don't know how to use it.

What I just took you through was how to lock in your vision and truly feel it.

When you feel your vision for the future, it will come true.

But…

Most of the time people have something they want in life and put zero feeling behind it.

When you can put feeling behind any vision, it will become a reality.

So, what's your sunny day?

What's the one thing you want to accomplish in your life that you have dreamt of? How will you feel when you accomplish it? Who will it impact and how will it change how you think of yourself?

Take a good 5–10 minutes (set a timer) and answer these questions while visualizing the answers actually happening in your life.

Ready, Set, Go!

Now that you are back…

You either actually took the time to do the vision exercise, or you are still skimming through this message.

Either way, you had an opportunity. An opportunity to get one step closer to what you ultimately want out of life.

These opportunities come in many forms and are not always there. But when you take advantage of an opportunity and do the work, everything changes for your good.

If you are the person who just took the opportunity, kudos to you! If you are the person who just skimmed through, start focusing on your opportunity muscle.

The opportunity muscle is there to act without hesitation. It is automatic.

The stronger your opportunity muscle is, the stronger your outcomes in life will be.

Now, it's not your fault if your opportunity muscle is weak. You probably didn't even know about it until you read this message. But now you do, so it's time for you to go back a couple of paragraphs and own the opportunity by doing the vision exercise.

Sunny days will happen no matter what you do.

What matters is that you take the opportunity to enjoy them and create a memory that will last a lifetime.

Are you ready to make the most of your sunny days?

People Need You

*"We make a living by what we get.
We make a life by what we give."*
~Winston Churchill

There is someone out there that needs you.

They need you to listen.

They need your opinion.

They need your direction.

They need your expertise.

They need your hope.

They need your friendship.

They need your support.

They need you.

Sometimes you can go through life and think—

"No one needs me."

"I have nothing to offer."

"I don't have the skills to help them."

This is wildly untrue.

Every single person who is breathing right now has something to give, but more importantly there is someone who needs you right now!

They need you to show up in their life. To make a difference and be a light in their dark place.

One of the major problems with fear is what it does to people. It makes them angry, depressed and hopeless. As days turn into weeks and months turn into years, they lose faith that anything will get better.

You are their shining light. You are the person that needs to step in and fill that gap for them.

Bring your light to their darkness.

You are the one person that can give them hope and belief that things will get better for them. A helping hand, no matter what kind it is, can save someone from a world of pain.

You might be going through one of the biggest struggles of your life, or you might be seeing yourself climbing to new heights.

It doesn't matter.

What matters is that no matter how small or how big you are, people need you and they need you now.

Your skills don't matter.
Your bank account doesn't matter.
Your time doesn't matter.
Your "feel like it" doesn't matter.

What matters is you answer the call for the people who need you.

When you do, the hope you give them will turn into faith.

In turn, they will use that faith to bring hope to others, and everyone rises.

What you decide to do next matters.

Deep down when you hear the phrase "People need you," people pop into your head right away.

Once they do, who are they? What do they look like? Are they your friends, your family, your co-workers, your clients, your kids, your community, someone hurting?

Who needs you?

The answer is clear as day and now it's your obligation to show up.

Not just once, not just twice, not just when you feel like it, but each and every day.

When someone needs you and counts on you, it's the biggest gift from God you will ever receive.

Never waste another need.
Never waste another moment.
Never waste another opportunity to be someone's light in their darkest moment.

Be the best you can be for the people who need you today, tomorrow and each day to come!

Trust yourself enough to know that you are everything they need!

Alone Syndrome

*"Sometimes life is too hard to be alone,
and sometimes life is too good to be alone."*
~Elizabeth Gilbert

You are not meant to be Alone. Life is meant to be lived with others.

Your internal fulfillment and happiness meter is filled by others. By truly meaningful relationships.

Different people, small groups and communities are needed to fill your tank.

When you do not get this, you will feel depressed, frustrated and unhappy.

The problem you are facing in today's world is a lack of true connection with others.

Technology and a change in social acceptance has created a vacuum-like vortex of what I call the Alone Syndrome.

The Alone Syndrome is when you are simply not around enough people to have or create the meaningful relationships needed to fill your fulfillment and happiness tank.

You know you're there when you feel:

Depressed
Unhappy
Tired
Overly Stressed
Not Connected
Life Is Passing You By

Our world is suffering from this big time right now.

People and maybe even you have traded in meeting up with others for a constant fake relationship of the social scroll.

The social scroll appears to build a relationship, but unfortunately it's just a surface one. One that brings no real deep down fulfillment. It just gives you a quick fix—a light high to keep you coming back for more—with the appearance that it's equal to being with the person in reality.

The social scroll is one of the creators of the Alone Syndrome, and has caused you to negate being around people for the instant and easy quick high.

Now, I just did one of two things to you right now. I either offended you or I woke you up to an unconscious habit. Either way, I am here to tell the truth and let you decide what you are going to do with it next.

I have noticed in this age, there is less time for family, friends and meeting new people. Our in-person world has tightened up and closed in on itself. This has created more skepticism, lack of empathy and loss of social skills needed for true connection.

Understanding that Alone Syndrome is a real thing and becoming conscious of it is the first step.

The great positive about being around people and creating true relationships is that your fulfillment and happiness tank gets filled up, but so does theirs.

You gain more energy, passion and a positive outlook when you are fulfilled.

Now is the time for you to become more intentional about how you spend your time.

The average person spends 2 hours and 35 minutes a day on social media.

That's 35.5 days a year on the social scroll.

That's more than a month of your life each year!

No wonder the average person doesn't have enough time not to be alone.

As you become more conscious of what you could improve in your overall life, understand it doesn't mean social media is evil or that you have to stop using it.

There is a place for it, but there must be some guardrails around it.

Ask yourself: Are you stuck in a habit that isn't serving you the best it can? Are you creating balance in your life with the social scroll? Do you find yourself looking around and realizing, "I haven't seen so and so in quite some time"?

Do you feel as if you don't have enough time in the day to do the things you want to do?

Once you have become aware of your situation and whether you are suffering from Alone Syndrome, it's time to take control of what you are going to do next.

First off, start by setting a social media timer on the social apps you use. This will allow you to snap out of the social scroll and switch your mind over to a conscious state again. Then you can choose the length of time you will allow yourself to spend on your phone, so that you can add in more significant, meaningful time with others. Since we don't want to be average, cut your time on social media in half and that should be a good amount of time that is put back in your day.

Second, start with your family. Start scheduling or creating routine times where you spend meaningful non-technology time together. Something where everyone is participating in the same thing. This will make everyone engaged in the present moment, which is how we create meaningful relationships. This also is how we create lasting memories.

Third, reconnect with your friends. Connect with them individually or in a small group. It doesn't have to be formal. You can simply have them be around you. You can go shopping together, exercise together, eat together, do any activity together. Really you just need to be around them and everything will take care of itself.

By doing just these 3 actions, you will start to break out of the Alone Syndrome and notice that you are happier and more satisfied with your relationships again.

Being aware of our situation will always be the first step in creating the truly satisfied life you want to live each day.

Never let a day go by without living and being around the people that fill your tank.

Each day is a blessing for you to experience and give to others.

Are you ready to do meaningful life with the people who fill your tank?

Redo?

*"Life never gives a chance to undo,
but it gives the chance to redo."*
~Akash Deep Bhagat

Do you need a Redo in an area of your life? Are you in a place where you thought your life would look different by now?

If you answered yes to either of these questions, you might need a Redo.

A Redo is a great thing. It allows for you to give yourself a do over.

Maybe you are in a place in your life where you don't recognize yourself, or maybe you have made a couple of mistakes that you have not given yourself permission to let go of.

No matter the situation, you feel that you would benefit from a Redo. You need to make some areas of your life right again.

You might need a Redo in your...

Career
Relationship
Health
Wealth
Spirituality
Sexuality
Body
Mind
Family

It doesn't matter what happened before. The beauty of the Redo is you get a fresh start.

You get to move on from that heartache, the hangup and the misstep.

What you must accept is that...

1. You are human.
2. You are not perfect.
3. This happened for a greater reason.

Once you accept these terms of conditions, you can start your Redo.

Your Redo is the moment you get to start new. Without any hangups from before.

It's the next steps you take. It's how you act going forward.

The past is void and you are only looking at the present moment.

Your Redo is not restrictive in any way or any form.

You get to decide who you are in this Redo. You get to dictate what happens next. You are in complete control of you.

No more excuses.

No more "I used to do this."

Now it's "I do this."

No questions.

Just raw truth.

A truth that will make you a better person, spouse, mom or dad, leader, world changer.

Once you embrace your Redo, you will be unstoppable. You will gain a sense of renewed passion and peacefulness. You will become the confident, happy, focused and fulfilled person you know you are meant to be.

The doors that will open for you will be massive, and bigger than you can comprehend.

The Redo is all positive and zero negative.

It's all gas and no brakes.

The Redo is jet fuel. It launches you at such an explosive rate you have to be buckled in.

Your Redo is just one step away.

It will push you upward at a fast rate.

It's ready to launch, but are you? Are you ready to let the past go? Are you ready to live in the present?

Are you ready to have your life go light years away from where you are right now?

It's time for your Redo.

You know it, I know it, and deep down there is no other option for you.

Let's go Redo Today so Tomorrow you can launch into your Dreams!

Why Your Energy Matters

*"Great things are done by a series
of small things brought together."
~Vincent Van Gogh*

Your Energy is one of the single most important aspects of yourself.

Once you realize this and understand how to tap into it, bigger things will happen in your life.

Energy is a stored resource in your body and is also renewable.

It can grow and become larger.

It can charge others.

It can become contagious.

It can become more powerful.

It can bring you back to life.

Your Energy is vital. Every single one of us underestimates our energy and how useful it can be.

You don't really know the power you have inside yourself and it's true capabilities. You take it for granted and abuse your energy on a daily basis until you and it are depleted.

As our world evolves, we treat our energy as a magical force that we have no control over.

You beat the hell out of it without even thinking twice.

You get mad or sad when it's not there.

You expect more and more from it.

You demand more and completely exhaust it.

You…

Caffeinate it.
Under Sleep it.
Under Exercise it.
Over Alcohol it.
Over Eat it.
Over Entertain it.
Over Stimulate it.
Over Stress it.
Over Consume it.

You beat the crap out of it and wonder why you have none or wish you had more.

We have an epidemic of great proportions in our world. It's an Energy problem. It's Your Energy that is the problem.

You don't know how to use it, or how to recharge it or even how to make it grow to an abundant, self-sustaining level.

You are stuck in a fog of low energy days and wonder why you don't have the energy for your Dreams.

It's time for you to harness Your Energy, make it work for you and support your Dreams.

The fastest and easiest way to get Your Energy back is addition.

You want to add back 3 vital rechargers.

1. Movement
2. Motivation
3. Mindset

I don't care what you do or how long you do it for, but you must start doing something in each one of these realms to recharge Your Energy.

Think back to a time when your energy was at its highest. What were you doing each day? Who were you around? What did you do that brought you joy during those days?

Answering these three questions will help you understand what you need to add back.

The three questions identify the positive parts of your day and you want to add those back in as quickly as possible.

If you are in a terrible place and are energy depleted to the level of depression, I'm going to give you 3 rechargers to start today that will get you going in the right direction.

1. Start walking outside.

Don't overthink it. Just go do it for any amount of time. You will feel better after and more importantly, you will feel better tomorrow when you do it again.

If you are limited and can't walk, do 3 stretches first thing in the morning. You can even do them in your bed.

(Get the 3 easy energy-recharging stretches plan by messaging me on my Social Media!)

2. **Read each day.**

   Each day, read something motivating and inspiring. It can be the same book or a different one. Just read 5–10 pages today and do it again tomorrow.

   If you need an even easier approach to get started, listen to a motivating audiobook while you are driving, walking, washing dishes or just during the first 10 minutes of your day.

   (Get 3 great book and audio book ideas by messaging me on Social Media!)

3. **Go get some support.**

   Join a group, find someone to guide you or just hire a mentor that can help you build Your Energy back up.

   The biggest mistake I see is when you try to do everything yourself. You feel like it's you that has to move the mountain, but this is simply not true. You need to be around people who can pour into you. They will automatically recharge you by being around them.

   It's as easy as getting a neighbor or coworker to walk with you, join a church, play on a recreational sports team, go to a convention that has passionate people at it, reach out to your friends and start a weekly group meetup, etc.

The more you are around people, the more Your Energy tank gets filled back up and expanded.

Now you have some concrete ideas on how to recharge Your Energy.

That's great, but Guess What?!

That doesn't mean anything unless you take action.

Consistent action.

Start Today by picking 1, 2 or all 3 of the Energy Rechargers.

When you do, you will start to notice yourself becoming less tired, depressed and worn down.

Get Your Energy back today so that tomorrow you will have enough of it to live your Dreams.

Just BREATHE

*"Give yourself permission to take time
to breathe, to live life, to give, to love, to reflect,
to be present, and to just be."*
~Unknown

Have you ever heard the expression Breath of Life?

It has some biblical connotations, but also was a commonly-used phrase way back.

The phrase means to BREATHE New Life into someone. To Uplift their spirit. To bring them back to life.

When you BREATHE into someone, you stimulate their spirit.

You decide that they are worth Breathing into. Worth your time, energy and ability.

You might be able to think of someone right now that needs you to BREATHE life back into them.

Maybe they are going through a tough time.

A Health Problem
A Divorce
A Death
A Job Loss
A Hurt
A Hangup
A Fearful Time

You have the ability to brighten their day with just one Breath.

Maybe it's a smile.

Or maybe it's comforting them as they cry in your arms.

It could be that one motivating message you sent them.

Or that simple "I love you."

No matter which one it is, you can BREATHE life into the people around you.

When you do, you will Uplift their Spirit. You will Uplift their hopes, dreams and outlook on tomorrow.

The moment you take for someone else is the moment you are truly living the life you were meant for.

As our world gets busier and busier, we tend to overlook this aspect.

We overlook how we are breathing.

Not just within ourselves but within others.

We rush our Breaths.
We forget about our Breaths.
We take for granted our Breaths.

The fact is you are designed to BREATHE New Life into others. To be the one that supports their Spirit. The person that does the right thing at the right time that makes all the difference.

Don't miss your opportunity.

All it takes is one Breath. One Breath can trigger an amazing turn of events for you or someone who needs it. This Breath can be small or large. Long or short. Exhausting or energizing. Life changing or life saving.

All that matters is that you BREATHE New Life constantly.

When you do, you will build up not only yourself but all the people around you.

On the other hand, you might be in a place in your life where you need someone to come along and give you a Breath. Or two or three.

You might be in a place where you need full-on CPR.

Either way, to give a Breath of Life you need a new breath.

You need to get filled. Filled with a new concentrated Breath that will revive your Spirit. A Breath that makes your lungs expand and your nostrils open back up.

You need to take deep Breaths that move you again.

Your Spirit needs to come alive and push you to go after your dreams. The dreams that you hold inside, which are designed to give you the life you want.

When you go after your dreams, it fills your spirit, which fills your lungs, which allows you to BREATHE New Life into the world.

Are you ready to BREATHE New Life today to live a New Life tomorrow?

Turn On Your Light

"Most of the important things in the world have been accomplished by people who have kept on trying when there seemed to be no hope at all."
~Dale Carnegie

You might be in a dark place.

It might be pitch black with absolutely no light.

You might be questioning yourself why you are here.

You might also be getting used to this dark place.

You have come to expect it, learning how to live in it, and are starting to give up any hope that it will ever change.

You are starting to embrace this dark place and build a life in it.

An unhappy, unmotivated and uninspired life.

The one you never saw for yourself.

It's definitely not the life you dreamt of.

Each day is passing so much faster than the last.

You never thought it was possible for your life to go by so quickly and with the growing fear that your time is running out.

Your life and chance for something much better eludes you.

You are trying to grasp anything around you to pull yourself up and out.

But...

You can't see a better future in the darkness.

You can only see darkness, and you are losing the past shimmers of light that used to motivate you.

Each day that goes by, you become more comfortable with this darkness.

You start to see everything through it.

The darkness changes what you believe about you and your ability.

It stops you from moving forward.

You're too scared to move without knowing what's in front of you.

All you see is a hopeless darkness and danger.

You need to make a change ASAP.

Not tomorrow but today.

You need some light. A bright light that takes away the darkness instantaneously.

You need to "turn on your light" right now.

You don't need a flash of light, you need a light so bright it will open your eyes. Open your eyes to the massive possibilities of your future. Open your eyes to your value and purpose.

When you "turn on your light," the darkness fades and your eyes get used to seeing the good all around you.

Once you understand that "turning on your light" is as easy as flipping a switch, you will start to see all the possibilities you possess.

You will also start to see the people around you that need you.

When your eyes are truly opened up, you will start to notice commonalities in the type of people you were designed to help.

They are a specific person that no one else can truly help and serve.

They really need just you.

You are literally the only one that can impact and uplift them the way they specifically need.

You might be thinking to yourself, "Someone else will show up and take care of them."

No.

Nope.

No one else is coming for them.

It's you.

And…You are their only and maybe even last option.

They need you and they need you now.

When you see them, serve them.

Don't wait another minute, day or month to see what happens.

Show up now.

Not just for them but for yourself.

When you serve your purpose, everyone wins.

The secret to "turning your light on" and making it brighter is practicing your purpose.

When you practice your purpose, you are constantly improving yourself and how you are serving the people who need it.

This results in you gaining confidence and passion in your people.

This allows you to meet them where they are and Uplift them to a higher level.

This allows you to "turn on your light."

The work you do with your people will brighten your light each day so that you can be the light in someone else's darkness.

I don't know if you need to hear this or not, but I'm going to say it: "It's okay to have been lost in darkness."

What matters is what you do next with your new light…

Who will you become?

Who will you help?

Who will you save?

Each day you have a massive opportunity to choose light over darkness.

Brightness over Brokenness.

People over Problems.

Possibility over Predictability.

You have the opportunity to be the light in someone's darkest moment.

You have the switch that will save them.

You are the brightness that will take their darkness away.

Are you ready to "turn your light on" for your people to be Uplifted out of their darkest place?

Replace the Lies

"If you get the inside right, the outside will fall into place. ~Eckhart Tolle

You are lying to yourself each day.

I guarantee it.

We all are.

You might be doing it more or less, but you are 100% doing it.

I'm not calling you a liar *per se*.

But I am telling you that some of the thoughts that go through your brain are lies.

And...Not just any lies, but lies that are holding you back.

These lies are sneaky.

They are there for so-called protection.

The lies are incorrect stories from your past experiences that keep you stuck, unhappy and really really frustrated with where you are in one area or multiple areas of your life.

These terrible lies are like a soundtrack that are being played over and over again on a loop.

Yes, sometimes they are shuffled around to limit you in a little different way each time, but it's the same lies.

This soundtrack is always playing in the background of everything you do.

You are completely used to it, but you can't identify it yet.

Until now…

These looping lies are making you believe things about yourself that are simply untrue.

You're not smart enough.
You're not good looking.
You're not going to get that promotion.
You're going to fail if you try.
You're just not that well liked.
You're going to be poor forever.
You're going to be overweight forever.
You're going to be depressed forever.
You're going to get divorced if you get married.
You're not ready to start that company.

You're going to die if you do that.
You're never going to accomplish your dreams.

There are many more "You're's" that are popping up in your head right now.

The problem with these lies is that they are what you believe.

So, every time you have a great idea or an opportunity pops up, you tend to allow that soundtrack full of lies to pop up and put you back in your place.

This is why when you say, "I'm going to change _____ starting on January 1st, you start, see some success, and the lies pop up harsher and harsher until finally it derails your opportunity to change and improve your life.

In your mind, there is something powering the constant individual songs that create the soundtrack of your looping lies to yourself.

This powersource in your head powers your soundtrack and needs to be rewired or rebooted to your newest software update.

The only way to rewire or reboot you is to replace the lies with the truth.

You must go after the powersource, not the soundtrack.

The powersource is the issue.

Once you solve the powersource problem, you will be rebooted and start with a new soundtrack that will create and match up to the life you want.

There are 3 ways to do this.

Each requires you to Replace the Lies with the Truth.

Way #1 – Reverse Engineer the Result

When you don't like a result you are getting in life, reverse engineer it backwards.

1. Go from the current result to the action that created the result.
2. Go from the action to the thought before the action.
3. Go from the thought to the feeling before the thought.
4. Go from the feeling to the past experiences you have had with that feeling.

Once you do this, you must either deal with, forgive or make peace with the situations that caused the specific feeling that led to the thought, that led to the action, that led to your unwanted result.

See how it works?

While doing this, always understand that everything that has ever happened to you can be used as a benefit in your future, but it is ultimately up to you to accept that truth and use it in your new soundtrack going forward.

Way #2 – Replace the Lie with the Truth You Know

When you have a thought that is leading you to take an action you know is not helping you, identify it as a lie and replace it with the truth.

Thought: "I want to look good in my swimsuit at the beach"

Your Reply Lie Thought: "You haven't looked good in a swimsuit in 5 years, so don't even try."

Your Truth Replacement: "I remember when I looked good in a swimsuit and I can make it happen this summer."

The goal is to find the truth and debunk the lie.

Way #3 – Replace the Lie with a Borrowed Truth

When you have a thought that is leading you to take an action you know is not the best option for you, identify it as a lie and insert the borrowed truth.

The borrowed truth can come from a successful person, a group of expert people or it can come from a spiritual nature (e.g. God).

No matter when the thought pops into your head, replace it with the borrowed truth.

These borrowed truths could be anything from quotes, bible verses or mantras that give you an emotional charge.

Thought: *"I want to become a better person and help and teach others with my experiences."*

Your Reply Lie Thought: *"You're not strong enough to change now, you've already messed up too many times and no one will listen to you!"*

Your Borrowed Truth Replacement: *"I will instruct you and teach you in the way you should go; I will counsel you with my loving eye on you" (Psalm 32:8).*

You replace the lie with a truth that gives you faith. Faith in a better you. Faith that completely wipes out and replaces the Lie Reply Thought looping through your head.

Faith gives you massive strength and consistent confidence to move forward into the unknown. It allows you to be comfortable with being uncomfortable. You can use that to overcome these lies in your mind.

No matter what is currently playing on a loop in your head right now, you can change it.

If you aren't 100% satisfied with your situation, it's time for you to reboot the loop and replace it with an amazing soundtrack.

A soundtrack that you create. One that you get to choose.

You've wasted too much of your time worrying about tomorrow and not living today.

It's time for you to be your best again.

It's time for you to delete your current soundtrack. It's time to rewire, reboot and rewrite the songs in your life.

Don't spend another day stuck listening to someone else's soundtrack for you, or the lies you tell yourself.

Replace the lies with the truth today and make your soundtrack of tomorrow the one you can't wait to turn up!

How to Be Driven in Your Destiny

"Destiny is no matter of chance. It is a matter of choice. It is not a thing to be waited for, it is something to be achieved." ~William Jenning Bryan

Did you know that you were made for a Destiny? A real purpose?

You were literally put on this earth to play a major role. A role that only you can fulfill.

However, your Destiny is not guaranteed.

It's not just going to happen. You aren't going to just stumble upon it.

What you choose to do each day will determine your Destiny.

There will be massive roadblocks. There will be little roadblocks.

There will be uncertain situations where you will have to take a blind leap of faith.

But… Everything will be worth it in the end.

For you to live and accomplish your Destiny, you will have to be Driven.

Not just when you feel like it, when it's convenient or when it's easy.

Every day you will have to show up to your Driven Destiny.

Your Driven Destiny is the one thing that you love doing. You enjoy it and want to do it each day. Your passion grows when you are around it.

You also have this ability that makes you good at your Driven Destiny.

This ability is unique to you. It's your special talent or maybe even a hidden talent.

You can refer to this ability as your Unique Ability.

You use your Unique Ability to live and accomplish your Driven Destiny.

Sometimes it's hard to find your Unique Ability.

But when you take the time to review your life and yourself, you will notice that what you truly love doing and what comes natural to you encompasses your Unique Ability.

Once you understand your Unique Ability and Driven Destiny, you will be able to fasttrack your goals and dreams.

When it comes to your Driven Destiny, you want to ask yourself some questions.

1. Who do I help and serve in my Driven Destiny?
2. What problem do they have that I can fix?
3. How do I show up, help and serve them in their problem?
4. What is their definition of success for their problem?
5. What's my constant promise to them?

Now that you have a clear, detailed idea of the who, the what and the how in your Driven Destiny, it's time for you to start.

Start by working on you and your Unique Ability.

Define your Unique Ability in one Statement.

> I help _____
> (people in your Driven Destiny)

that are _____
(their specific problem)

by _____
(your unique ability process specifically used to help them)

so that they can _____
(their definition of success)

in or by _____
(your consistent promise to them)

(People in your Driven Destiny) + (Their specific problem) + (your unique ability process specifically used to help them) + (Their definition of success) + (Your consistent promise to them) = Your Unique Ability Statement

Example: "I help Peak Performers that are stuck in a rut by coaching and uplifting them so that they can change the world around them in 90 days or less."

Once you create, grasp and understand this Unique Ability Statement, you will know exactly what you need to work on next.

This one sentence allows you to be locked into your vision.

When you are locked into your vision, you are all in on your Driven Destiny.

Life is too short for you to be unsure of what you are meant to do and are alive for.

You deserve to be Driven. Driven to a Destiny that makes you feel alive.

Alive for the first time.
Alive for the second time.
Or…Alive again.

Your Driven Destiny is always greater than you think.

It's simpler than you think. It's more impactful than you think.

You won't have to move mountains for you to accomplish your Driven Destiny. When you use your Unique Ability, the mountains will move themselves.

Sometimes you can get stuck motionless thinking, "Who are you to move these mountains? Who are you to even try? Who are you?"

You are the person who has been given this Unique Ability to help create a better world for a specific part of it.

You have been given everything you need to accomplish your current Driven Destiny and future Driven Destiny. One step, one situation, one person at a time, you have been chosen to change your world.

Never waste another step, situation or interaction with a person to share your Unique Ability.

You were Created for this.

You were Developed for this.

You were Driven for this.

Let yourself use your Unique Ability to be Driven to the Destiny you were designed for.

Screwed Over

"Getting over a painful experience is much like crossing the monkey bars. You have to let go at some point in order to move forward."
~C.S. Lewis

No matter who you are, someone has done something wrong to you.

They have intentionally tried to screw you over.

Sometimes you can feel this is going to happen and sometimes you can't.

The problem with expecting to get screwed over all the time is it narrows your lens of the world.

You think everyone is out to get you.

You miss opportunities to become a better you because of your skepticism.

When this happens, you start to become standoffish to people, situations and opportunities.

Yes, that person was totally in the wrong and you got screwed, but now you are choosing to get screwed over again each day.

You will need to completely let it go to see the benefit.

It sucked, but that's all you need to take from it.

If there was a lesson learned in it, too, great.

If not, let it go and move on to the benefit.

You might not see the benefit now, but it will come later on in the future and you will say, "Oh, that's why that happened."

"That's why that relationship ended."
"That's why that job ended."
"That's why the partnership ended."
"That's why they needed to move on."

All of this will happen for a reason and in a certain season of your life.

When you are growing into the person you need to be to accomplish your Dreams, you will have to go through tough situations.

These tough situations make you and prepare you for larger, abundant seasons in life.

This cannot happen when you are hanging on to a hurt, or carrying the hangup with you into the next day.

Too often, you can hold on to the wrongs done to you.

You hold grudges or create false statements around that person, or label an entire type of person because one specific person did something that screwed you over.

As you go after your dreams and purpose, someone will screw you over.

It's a guarantee.

It won't feel good.

You won't like it.

But it's part of being human.

The best way to absorb the wrongdoing is to allow yourself to get your emotional reaction out and then move on.

Make sure that emotional reaction doesn't cause chaos or worsen the situation, but get it out!

Obviously, two wrongs don't make a right, so take the higher ground and simply forgive and forget.

Maybe not forget 100%, but don't let it phase you or your view of the world.

Remember only the lesson you learned, not the emotion or feeling associated with it.

If you decide anything else besides this, you will be creating a bad root that will limit you from growing towards your goals and dreams.

Every day you will have an opportunity to be a victim of someone.

You will get what you are looking for, or worse, waste the space in your mind that could be used for something so much bigger....Your Dreams!

As you close out today, are there any heavy wrongs you have been carrying with you each day that you need to leave behind for tomorrow?

What do you need to let go of today to make tomorrow just a little bit lighter and brighter for you?

Your Big JUMP!

"You cannot always wait for the perfect time, sometimes you must dare to jump."
~Unknown

Very soon you will have a Big JUMP in your life.

Once you choose to beat the fear and start toward your Dream, you will see a massive increase in your life.

It will be the biggest JUMP you have ever seen.

You will feel as though you have the magical touch.

You will feel a great relief and new excitement.

You will feel a ton of gratitude and confidence.

All of this is great!

It's a highlight in your life.

Something you should be very proud of and hold as a great memory.

The one thing you must learn and understand about this BIG JUMP is that it will command you to do bigger things.

Bigger Impact
Bigger Leadership
Bigger Problem Solving
Bigger Choices
Bigger Distractions
Bigger Highs
Bigger Lows

This comes with the massive increase.

Any BIG JUMP is followed by the feeling to slow down or enjoy the moment just a little too long.

This can derail you and cause you to backslide in the future.

When your BIG JUMP happens, you must learn to work harder and become a better, bigger version of yourself.

You will have to evolve in many areas to continue forward.

As a result of this, you must expect all of these things on the way to your next BIG JUMP:

Bigger Problems
Bigger Emotions

Bigger Distractions
Bigger Decisions
Bigger Demand
Bigger Challenges

As you go for your next BIG JUMP you will need to have a bigger mindset.

You will need to be laser focused and continue to become better, but also spend a majority of your time replicating yourself.

You will need a large amount of support behind you.

You will be creating a great Team.

You must pour into them with everything you have to create the next BIG JUMP on the way to your Dreams.

Support is key in this next phase in your life.

You might have gotten your first BIG JUMP without a lot of support, but to get to your next one you will need a Team of people around you.

There has never been a single person who has ever done anything truly world changing on their own.

You must understand this and accept the fact that for you to get your next BIG JUMP, you will need a good deal of support.

The tough part about receiving support is being okay to ask for it.

A lot of the time as you have one BIG JUMP after another, your ego starts to bubble up and create some lies in your thoughts.

You will hear thoughts that are completely incorrect but make your ego feel good.

When you start catching yourself using a lot of I's and Me's instead of We's, your ego is starting to take over.

Most of the time your ego is powered by a deep-rooted insecurity.

This bad root is typically from a past childhood experience.

Your ego is designed to protect you, so it's finding new ways to grow.

The bigger the ego, the bigger the appearance of protection from that painful root.

As you go for your next BIG JUMP, you will have to deal with the bubbling up of your ego but also the root cause of it.

This is the single most differentiating factor between someone becoming successful in their dreams and not.

I know that last sentence was a punch in the gut but it is the truth.

You will have to develop bravery to go after that painful root.

This bravery needed to pull out the root will bring a new light and new life into you.

It's simply the missing piece to the success you want. The fulfillment, happiness and acceptance that comes with it is unreal.

Now, you are probably scared as hell and asking, "But How?!"

The answer is:

Acknowledgment
Acceptance
Advancement

Acknowledge the situation happened or is happening, and it's not a benefit to you.

Accept the situation and that it doesn't have to define you or your next move.

Advance to the next step in your life; stop looking back and lock in on the present moment.

Once you deal with that tough root, allow yourself some grace and let yourself start with a clean slate.

It's not pretty... Pulling deep roots is hard and takes effort. Your hands will get dirty and you will have to dig down deeper than you think, but once you do, you won't have to deal with your personal weeds popping up each and every new season. You will be able to take multiple steps forward to your future without taking a step back.

It's hard work but it's worth it.

Once you pull that root, you have a recurring, magnificent peace and speed up the time to your next BIG JUMP!

Now that you have a gameplan to uproot your old fears...

Are you ready to JUMP?

2.5 Seconds

"The bad news is, time flies. The good news is, you're the pilot." ~Unknown

Your life is short. Shorter than you think.

In the big schemes of the history of the world, you're about 2.5 seconds.

That's it.

You are equivalent to a 2.5-second vapor in the history of the world.

My question for you is...

What are you doing with your 2.5 seconds?

Are you going to be remembered?

No one likes to acknowledge that their time in this world is short. You might think you have more time to start tomorrow, but the simple fact is your tomorrow is not guaranteed and your tomorrows are running out.

Right now is the time for you to get laser focused on your 2.5 seconds.

You can choose to do the things that will impact massive amounts of people, or you can choose to massively impact one person.

The choice is yours and will determine your future and theirs.

The deal with your 2.5 seconds is it is all controlled by you. You get to decide what you do with it. You get to decide if it's memorable, impactful or forgetful.

Each day you have a new opportunity with your 2.5.

You can take advantage of that opportunity or not. You can push back against the resistance of life or succumb to it. You can decide to make life about you or about others. You can choose to Dream or have nightmares. You can choose today or tomorrow.

Each choice will decide the fate of you and your 2.5 seconds.

The great thing about you is that you were born with value.

You are simply valuable.

Valuable to us. But more importantly, valuable to the people around you.

You could be struggling with the who.

Who should you help?
Who should you serve?
Who could you save?

You could have no idea and that's okay.

This is the best way to discover your "who" and make the most of your 2.5 seconds.

INSIDE OUT

Think of a circle.

There are 3 circles of people in your life.

1. The Inside Circle

The Inside Circle is the one that includes yourself and the people you interact with each day. They are the closest relationships you have. They need you the most and require the greatest amount of your time. You must put them first and prioritize them. This circle is the most important, as it's what recharges you and creates higher levels of fulfillment for you and them.

Start with you and everyone inside your circle.

2. The Middle Circle

The Middle Circle would be your friends, co-workers and acquaintances. You must show up with them constantly for mutual beneficial growth and relational development. They can be a mixed bag of different types of people interested in different things, but the constant needs to be you. The beauty of the Middle Circle is that it's normally the people you see more frequently but the pressure to fulfill an everyday need of theirs is not there as it is in The Inside Circle.

Once you grow your impact in the first two circles, go onto the third.

3. The Outer Circle

The Outer Circle is actually very important. This is the circle that allows your overall impact to grow. The Outer Circle that needs you is your local community and/or a specific group of people. They need you to serve them and meet them where they are. You were designed to help and show up for them in a specific way.

They need a helping hand and someone that cares specifically for them.

When you were born, you were commissioned to help a certain person, group or community of people.

You have a job to complete in your 2.5 seconds.

Once you understand that all of the tools you need to complete your job are in your current possession, you will find it much easier to lend a helping hand.

Very often you can think, "I'm no one special" or "I don't really have what it takes to help them."

These thoughts are simply untrue and suppress your willingness to start.

Remember, you only have 2.5 seconds, it's time to start moving...

During your 2.5 seconds you will want to...

Give up
Take for granted your time
Wish it was easier
Get too comfortable

All of these things will be feelings along the way that can get in the way of your 2.5 seconds.

These are just feelings and equate to the Positive Resistance Reassurance that you are on the right track and headed in the right direction.

It's also a good sign that you are making the most of your 2.5 seconds.

As you continue through this resistance, you will start to see improvements in yourself, your feelings and the impact of the INSIDE OUT choices you are making.

You will start to want to…

Become better
Share your impact
Grow your impact
Build your impact

As you see the successes build up and the people in your life grow, your 2.5 seconds starts to seem much longer.

Much more real.
Much more motivating.
Much more fulfilling.
Much more like a dream than just 2.5 seconds.

You have a chance today to make the most out of your time.

So…Who are you going to help with your 2.5 seconds?

Please Unsubscribe!

*"If you don't design your own life plan,
chances are you'll fall into someone else's plan.
And guess what they may have planned for you?
Not much."* ~ Jim Rohn

Seriously, Unsubscribe to this idea.

Please Please Please Unsubscribe from the ideas of the modern world.

You are stuck because you are trying to configure to this world.

This world and what it tells you to do is completely broken.

The "Many" are the loudest and the "Few" are the quietest.

But the "Few" know the secret to success and living the life they want.

The "Few" are:

Healthy
Confident
Humble
Helpful
Gracious
Faithful
Motivating
Uplifting
Focused
Strong
Logical
Positive
Happy
Fulfilled

The "Few" unsubscribe to the loud voices of the "Many."

They unsubscribe to the idea that you must follow the way it's always been done.

The "Few" want to create a new world, not just live in the current one.

You are part of the "Few" because you are reading this.

Being part of the "Few" is impactful.

The "Few" are the largest impactors and balancers of our world.

You have the unique abilities to not only impact the "Many" and "Few" alike, but you help bring hope to the hopeless. Bring help to the helpless.

You are the Up to someone's Down.

Each day you will be faced with many modern world ideas that you will have to Unsubscribe from to continue your success.

It won't be just one or two ideas or once or twice.

You will be inundated with them, multiple times, over and over again, with the goal of getting you to come back over to the "Many."

Remember, the "Many" want you to fall back in line, get back on your hamster wheel, and just do what the "Many" say.

The "Many" want you to subscribe to their way.

Their way of average.
Their way of limit.
Their way of non-freedom.
Their way of fear.

The "Many" use this tricky tool on you each day to weaken your resolve.

It's Repetition Manipulation.

They use Repetition Manipulation to sneak into your subconscious and slowly get you to subscribe to untruths. Simple ones first, then more complex ones later on.

They want you to just give up on thinking and believe their ways.

$2 + 2 = 5$

Trust us, that's right.

No, $2 + 2 = 4$.

Stop thinking and Trust Us, it's 5.

No, it's 4.

Trust Us, when you look at it this way, it's 5.

Etc.

This happens over and over again until you either subconsciously subscribe or consciously choose to Unsubscribe to this strategy.

Either way you are being targeted with large amounts of Repetition Manipulation in the modern world.

Even more alarming is the multiple channels that are being used to target you to either stay in the "Many" or come back from the "Few."

Social Media, TV and something called Influencer Solicitation.

I'll explain Influencer Solicitation, as this is the next big, powerful channel that can erode your thinking.

Influencer Solicitation is someone on social media that has a large following that you found enjoyable, start to like, start to follow, then trust.

This Social Solicitation Influencer pushes their predetermined and most of the time paid ideas on you subconciously through multiple prescripted posts, videos and pictures.

They are a master at using Repetition Manipulation to lull you into thinking a certain way that gives them the goal of their hidden motive.

Influencer Solicitation is dangerous because you stop conditioning yourself to thinking logically and don't realize you are just watching a bunch of someone's commercials without even knowing it.

They are Influencing your subconscious and either keeping you in the "Many" or pulling you away from the "Few."

This is the newest way the "Many" are keeping you stuck and unhappy.

The "Many" grasp at you with…"But wait, if you watch us and buy X, you will be happy…Trust Us."

As you choose what you subscribe to, make sure that you are never losing what makes you part of the "Few": thinking logically and thinking differently than the "Many."

Never waste another day stuck, unhappy and hopeless in the Repetition of the "Many."

Either come over to the "Few" or continue unsubscribing from the "Many."

There are very "Few" people like you.

We need you and the people around you need you.

Unsubscribe today so that tomorrow you will have the power, impact and happiness of the "Few"!

Mission Impossible

"The only place where your dream becomes impossible is in your own thinking."
~Robert Schuller

You have a dream in your heart that is special.

This Dream is something that is needed by someone.

It's not just your Dream, it's your Mission.

The reason why you are here is to accomplish this Mission.

Let's be real…

You think your Mission is Mission Impossible.

You have been sitting on your hands suppressing the feeling to start.

Start your Mission.

Start your Impossible.

Start to think it's Possible.

Your Mission Impossible is actually your Mission Possible.

Let's keep being real…

The only thing holding you back is you.

First, you will catch yourself saying, "But"….

Where do I start?

How do I start?

When do I start?

Second, you will catch yourself saying, "I'm"…

I'm too old.

I'm too young.

I'm not experienced enough.

I'm too busy.

I'm not sure.

Third, you will catch yourself saying, "Scared"…

Scared to start.

Scared to lose.

Scared of what others will say.

Scared of winning.

Scared of failing.

You will catch yourself all the time stuck in the "But I'm Scared" Cycle.

This Cycle is what makes you believe in Mission Impossible.

It is what continues to block you from starting your Mission Possible.

"But I'm Scared" has to be put to death for you to move forward.

To move forward, you must rewire and replace these lies.

Once you do, all of a sudden you will see the possibilities.

This is the moment you go from Mission Impossible to Mission Possible.

Mission Possible…

Changes you.
Improves you.

Motivates you.

Saves…

Your Positivity.
Your Passion.
Your Purpose.

You…

From Unhappiness.
From Heartache.
From Regret.

Mission Possible Saves You!

But…Also saves the people around you.

The day you realize that all along you have had what it takes to fulfill your specific Mission Possible, is the day you really live your life.

Your growth in life has always been linked to your Mission Possible.

Without it you will shrink, become unhappy, depressed and ultimately lost… Resulting in the limited loop of the "But I'm Scared" Cycle.

It's time for you to close out this Cycle and replace it with a new possibility.

Your Mission Possible.

Are you ready to accept your Mission Possible?

What's Right?

*"Stop being afraid of what could go wrong,
and start being excited about what could go right."*
~Tony Robbins

Sometimes in life your perspective matters more than anything else. How you look at yourself and others matters. How you see situations matters.

How you react to the good and bad in your world matters.

A lot of the time life can become difficult and put a ton of pressure on your Positive Perspective. You can feel as if you are getting punched or kicked in the face at every turn. You can be mentally beat down by a series of negative events that completely wear you out. The series of struggles can leave you feeling hopeless and stuck in a negative perspective.

When this happens, your perspective has shifted to one that only sees problems. More than that, your Positive Perspective has been eroded to only look for problems.

Your brain is stuck only looking for and seeing problems. This makes you subconsciously create more problems in your day to day life.

If this is you, it's time to not feel guilty or feel like it's too late for you.

It's time to start looking for what's right.

The cool thing about looking for what's right in your life or the world is now you are reconditioning your brain's perspective.

On top of that, you are solving any Negative Perspective issues and turning them into the Positive Perspective needed to be your best.

You might find it hard at first to start identifying what's right in your life, so here is a little exercise for you to do.

Get a blank sheet of paper. Get a pen. Start to write everything down that is going right in your life. Make a list. You can start by writing whatever comes to mind.

Having enough food
Having clothing
A home
Your family
Friends
A job
Etc.

Once you complete the list, you will start to change or improve your Positive Perspective.

Anytime you feel like your Positive Perspective is slipping, go back and complete the exercise.

Each time you get punched in the face by life, make your Positive Perspective list.

Remember, no matter what happens to you, you get to control your perspective and what you decide to do next.

There is massive power in catching yourself doing the right things. You just have to take some time to slow down and notice how well you are doing.

Your Positive Perspective is only one list away.

Your best self is only one Positive Perspective away.

Your uplifting impact is only one shared Positive Perspective given to someone in need.

You never know how much your words or actions impact the story of someone's life. You will never see the massive impact you make behind the scenes in someone's life.

All it takes is…

One positive perspective
One positive action

One positive word

…from you!

Are you ready to turn a punch in the face into a Positive Perspective that changes the world?

Rebuild

*"The secret of change is to focus all your energy,
not on fighting the old, but on building the new."*
~Socrates

You might have just gotten rocked.

You might have just had something happen that forever changed your life. Something totally out of your control that has altered your life for the future.

It might have been awful. It might have been disastrous.

It might be something you can't seem to get over.

It might just be a hard time in your life full of uncertainty, unawareness and unwanted situations.

You might be in a place where nothing seems comfortable or right.

As the days turn into months and even years, you are hoping for it to just go away.

It doesn't and won't.

It's time to REBUILD.

REBUILD your new way.

REBUILD your new normal.

REBUILD your foundation.

When you can identify and come to the realization that everything will not magically go back to normal, you will understand that it's time for you to do something different.

It's time for you to move on.

It's time for you to walk into your new life.

The life that is waiting for you and is pretty awesome.

You can't see it yet but it's there…

Waiting for you!

Wishing you would step into it. Live it. Enjoy it.

This awesome life wants you to discover the joy and fulfillment that comes with it.

All it takes is one step, one realization, one message that shakes you awake.

Once you accept the situation and the necessity for you to REBUILD, you must start with focused action.

When you start to REBUILD you get to…

Regroup
Recover
Refocus
Start Fresh
Start Over
Start New
Build Better
Build Stronger
Build Smarter

As you REBUILD, you gain a *New* opportunity that you didn't have before.

The opportunity to build from new.

A new place
A new situation
A new perspective
A new confidence
A new you

New is exciting.

New is necessary.

New is needed.

When you REBUILD you get all of the advantages and perks of *New*.

As you continue each day, you will have to decide if you will continue to be stuck by the tired past and current events of your life.

Once you make the decision to do something different, then it's time for you to choose to REBUILD.

As you shift your focus from fighting the current backwards momentum to starting the *New* exciting process of rebuilding, let go of the tired past and allow yourself to REBUILD the *New* future.

Once you REBUILD, you will be stronger than ever.
Once you REBUILD, you will be better than ever.
Once you REBUILD, you will be changed forever.

Choose to REBUILD your *New* tomorrow today!

Where Does My Story Go from Here?

"You can't go back and change the beginning, but you can start where you are and change the ending." ~C.S. Lewis

So what are you going to do next?

You are the writer.

The writer who is in control of your story.

Your story could be one of the following:

A Comeback Story
A Perseverance Story
A Strength Story
A Survival Story
A Life-Changing Story

You get to write your story.

You get to write it right now.

You get to choose what happens next.

It might be the hardest thing you ever do, or it might be the most freeing thing you ever do.

The truth in your story is that it matters.

It matters if you waste your story or use it.

It matters to a certain...

Person who is lost in the dark.
Person who wants to give up.
Person who might not want to take their next breath.

You will never truly know how powerful your story is, but I'm telling you it's powerful and life-changing to that person.

Every day you can get derailed and distracted by the world around you. You can get sidetracked from writing your story.

The simple fact is no one is going to write your story for you. Only you can be the writer.

Only you can be that person's light in their darkness. Only you can be that person's uplifter when they want to give up. Only you can be that person's breath of fresh air that makes them want to take their next breath.

You must write your story and share it with that person.

They need to hear the hope in you and your story.

One of the most powerful things in the human world is the story.

Stories have been told for thousands of years. From caves to campfires. From books to radio. From tv to social media. Stories are powerful and can change a life in an instant.

Your story can change that person's life in an instant.

You can change in an instant.

Are you ready to be the writer of your next chapter?

Are you ready to let your story change the world around you?

30 Thousand

"It is not uncommon for people to spend their whole life waiting to start living."
~Eckhart Tolle

So, we have come towards the end of the messages.

This last message makes it 30 thousand words.

30 thousand words that will mean nothing to you unless you take action.

Not just a little comfortable action, but pull-up-your-pants-and-lift-something-heavy action.

You will not improve or change anything by sitting still and waiting.

You must take Heavy Action.

Heavy Action requires you to do something you are not sure you can do.

Heavy Action has 90% failure and 10% success.

Heavy Action takes that 10% success and multiples it by 1,000% so the payoff is life changing.

Heavy Action will make you sweat, struggle and earn every inch.

Heavy Action will pay off and set you light years ahead of what you could have ever expected.

The problem with just reading the 30 thousand words is it's just Light Action.

Light Action keeps you where you are.

You don't go forward but at least you don't go backwards.

Heavy Action is turning to the last page and having a real moment with you.

Not a pep talk or pat on the back for finishing another book, but a real moment of reflection on where you are in life. Not just your normal life but compared to the one you want.

What hurtful things are you dodging that derail you from taking Heavy Action?

Who's the person you need to forgive? What do you need to accept happened and move forward from? What do you need to add to your new life? What do you need to subtract?

Heavy Action will bring tears to your eyes. It will test your ability to own your mistakes and move on from them.

Heavy Action is your life saver.

The question is, "Do you know you're drowning?"

After these 30 thousand words is when you get to decide how your story goes from here.

Who do you become?

Who do you help?

Who do you guide?

Who do you save?

Who will be around you as you take your last breath?

It's F-in real.

Real life out there that's going to be moving with you or against you.

Real People
Real Situations
Real Problems
Real Failures
Real Pain
Real Reality

What's your choice?

Are you going to take Heavy Action or turn the last page and pat yourself on the back?

30 thousand isn't sh#$ unless you get back to being real and choose Heavy Action again and again.

Don't waste these 30 thousand words.
Don't waste your Heavy Action opportunity.
Don't waste your today.
Don't waste your tomorrow.
Don't waste your dreams.
Don't waste your 2.5 seconds.
Don't waste your people.
Don't waste your purpose.
Don't waste your power.
Don't waste your light.
Don't waste your life.

Turn the page of this life and take heavy, life-changing action.

Lift heavy, Lift often and UpLift others.

There are 30 thousand reasons not to waste another moment of your life, and you just read them all!

Let's go UpLift!

So, Who Do You Think You Are?

Have you ever gotten a thought to do something that excites you or you are super passionate about?

Did you ever get an inspirational thought and then say to yourself, "Who do you think you are?"

"Who do you think you are that you could actually do that?"

Or

"Why should you even try?"

Who are you to…

Give advice to them?
Write that book?
Try to lose weight yet again?
Break that addiction?
Expect things to change?
Go after your dreams?
Live the life you want?

This happens to me every time I get an idea. It feels awful and I don't like it.

It kills my confidence and makes me think, "Why even try?"

I think this happens to you, too.

I don't like that, either, and I'm going to help you beat it.

Not just once, but every time, until it completely goes away.

Until you get that thought and say, "I can do this!"

"I have what it takes."

"I'm enough!"

I'm…

Strong enough!
Smart enough!
Confident enough!
Talented enough!

When you believe that you have what it takes to accomplish anything that you choose to do, you uncover a wonderful peace.

This peace is created by you acknowledging that you are enough. That you have everything you need to be the successful you.

You don't need to go searching or wandering around looking for it. It's right inside of you.

All along, you have had enough.

You were created with it.

You were designed to have enough.

So, who are you?

I might not know you personally, but I have a good idea who you are since you are reading this message.

You are a special person. Someone who is on this earth for a reason. A reason so big you can't comprehend it.

You're alive right now at this specific time for a massive purpose. Something that will change the world and the people around you.

You have this wonderful power inside of you that is linked to you and your purpose.

You're not only an Uplifter, but you are part of the 1%.

The 1% of people who take that scary step in creating the life they want.

These same 1% of people and you WIN. You WIN each time you are completely committed.

Each time you constantly choose to make the decision to become the true you.

Each time you fight through the darkness and turn on your light.

Each time you choose your new way.

Every time you make a decision to fight, you make the people around you better.

You might not realize it, but they are watching and learning what to do next from you.

You are:

Their **Motivation.**
Their **Breath of Life.**
Their **What's Next?**
Their **Tomorrow Is Going to Be Better.**
Their **Faith over Fear.**
Their **Fighting Resistance.**
Their **Fully Committed Dreams.**
Their **Up, Up & Away.**
Their **It's Time to Fight Back.**

Their **U-Turn.**
Their **Passion.**
Their **Mission Possible.**
Their **Stretching for Success!**
Their **Great Day.**
Their **Sunny Day.**
Their **Worthy Enough.**
Their **Forgetting Normal.**
Their **Double Down.**
Their **Heart of Gold.**
Their **Way to Rise Up.**
Their **Yok-Wyk (You Only Know What You Know).**
Their **People That Need You.**
Their **Scary Solution.**
Their **Full Focus.**
Their **Energy.**
Their **Forgetting Fear.**
Their **Redo.**
Their **Rebuild.**
Their **Alone Syndrome Fix.**
Their **Motivational Fire.**
Their **Call That Will Change Their Life Forever!**
Their **Get Moving.**
Their **Mental Muscle.**
Their **OUT-STANDING.**
Their **New Way.**

When you realize that your purpose and job in life is to be an Uplifter to the people around you, massive mountains will move for you.

The grind, the pain and the stuck-in-the-weeds perspective will stop.

The wounds will heal and the darkness will diminish.

You will become the Uplifter needed for:

Your People.
Your Children.
Your Spouse.
Your Neighbors.
Your Community.
Your World.

One step at a time you will Uplift each moment, situation, and today. Each heartache, hurt and hangup.

You will be the light in someone's darkness. The Inspiration in their depression. The positive in their negative. The comfort in their sorrow. And...The courage in their fear.

You will be there for them when they need you most.

You are their Uplifter.

The person that coaches, mentors or just shows up for someone in need.

As an Uplifter, you create the biggest impact in our world.

You create a domino-effect impact that becomes life-changing for your people.

Your actions create a contagious community of people who need you to lead them.

Lead them to their best life.
Lead them to their best self.
Lead them to their dreams.

This is the thing you are meant to be.

Your One-Thing.

Your Purpose.

It's the missing piece you need to accomplish your dreams.

It's who you are supposed to be and to continually become.

You were made for this.

You are meant for this moment.

You are meant for this next question.

So, who do you think you are?

You're an F-IN UPLIFTER.

Who Are You Going to Uplift Next?

1. _____

2. _____

3. _____

Pay It Forward

Most likely you got this book for FREE!

Congrats!

What you don't know is that it was because of our Pay It Forward Initiative.

Someone just like you got this book for FREE, read it, got Uplifted and decided you were someone that has what it takes to change the world.

This is your opportunity to pay it forward and Uplift someone you know.

It's likely that the person has already popped into your head at this very moment.

They could be a family member, friend, co-worker or colleague.

The fact is they need you and need to be Uplifted.

Follow the link below or scan the QR code to Pay It Forward to them.

I will personally send them a copy of UpLift for FREE!

marcusbrugger.com/Uplift

Thank you for Uplifting the world one person at a time!

Marcus Brugger

About the Author

Marcus Brugger is the founder and CEO of Movement Fitness, Inc.; Daring Weight Loss, Inc.; and National Stretching Institute, Inc. He carries 16 years of experience in the fitness industry with owning multiple personal training studios, and is a Certified Personal Trainer, Certified Weight Loss Expert, Nutrition Certified and Stretching Certified. He is passionate about improving the health and wellness of his community and helping coaches develop highly successful careers and health/wellness studios!

Marcus enjoys holding fundraising events for local charities, and has raised tens of thousands of dollars for non-profits such as Carried to Full Term, Sunshine Kids, and SERVE.

Marcus is passionate about business development and engages in continuing education opportunities with other leading fitness and business experts throughout the nation. Marcus teaches business development classes and also certifies Health & Fitness Coaches to become Stretch Certified. He also partners with George Mason University to help train aspiring fitness professionals through their Kinesiology Internship Program.

In 2017, he was published in an Amazon #1 Bestseller, *Fuel Your Soul, Transform Your Body*. In 2019, he was published in *Look & Feel Great Over 40!* He lives to inspire and motivate others to take action day in and day out to create the lives they never thought were possible.

Marcus is a Virginia native, where he lived the majority of his life. He recently relocated to Florida with his wife, Tara, and their children, Hannah, Jacob, Clark, Marcus Jr, as well as their loving dog, Moses.

You can contact him directly to share your story or if you need help taking the next step in your coaching career on Social Media or at marcusbrugger.com.

WHO?
DO YOU UPLIFT...

Become the leader of your life and UpLift
the people around you!

Made in USA - North Chelmsford, MA
1306887_9798787845389
02.28.2022 1550